SUBJECT TEACHING
in PRIMARY EDUCATION

SUBJECT TEACHING
in PRIMARY EDUCATION

Edited by
PATRICK SMITH and LYN DAWES

Los Angeles | London | New Delhi
Singapore | Washington DC

Los Angeles | London | New Delhi
Singapore | Washington DC

SAGE Publications Ltd
1 Oliver's Yard
55 City Road
London EC1Y 1SP

SAGE Publications Inc.
2455 Teller Road
Thousand Oaks, California 91320

SAGE Publications India Pvt Ltd
B 1/I 1 Mohan Cooperative Industrial Area
Mathura Road
New Delhi 110 044

SAGE Publications Asia-Pacific Pte Ltd
3 Church Street
#10-04 Samsung Hub
Singapore 049483

Editor: James Clark
Editorial assistant: Rachael Plant
Production editor: Thea Watson
Copyeditor: Michelle Clark
Proofreader: Derek Morkham
Indexer: Avril Ehrlich
Marketing manager: Catherine Slinn
Cover design: Naomi Robinson
Typeset by: C&M Digitals (P) Ltd, Chennai, India
Printed and bound in Great Britain by Ashford
Colour Press Ltd

Editorial arrangement, Editors' preface and Introduction © Patrick
Smith and Lyn Dawes 2014
Chapter 1 © Sue Fawson 2014
Chapter 2 © Christine Hickman 2014
Chapter 3 © Helen Caldwell and Gareth Honeyford 2014
Chapter 4 © Jo Barter-Boulton and Jo Palmer 2014
Chapter 5 © Gill Chambers, Kate Coleman and Gareth Davies 2014
Chapter 6 © Ken Bland 2014
Chapter 7 © Mary Bracey, Paul Bracey and Sandra Kirkland 2014
Chapter 8 © Paul Gurton 2014
Chapter 9 © Alice Hansen and Balbir Ahir 2014
Chapter 10 © Carol Wetton 2014
Chapter 11 © Emma Whewell, Karen Woolley and
Robert Kellam 2014
Chapter 12 © Ellie Hill 2014
Chapter 13 © Babs Dore and Lyn Dawes 2014

First published 2014

Library of Congress Control Number: 2013948470

British Library Cataloguing in Publication data

A catalogue record for this book is available from
the British Library

MIX
Paper from
responsible sources
FSC® C011748

ISBN 978-1446-2-6788-2
ISBN 978-1446-2-6789-9 (pbk)

TABLE OF CONTENTS

EDITORS' PREFACE

The authors of the chapters in this book are teachers with a shared commitment to enabling children reach their potential. Many of the children you will teach will not have had the best start in life, but school should provide the necessary environment for *all* children to flourish. This book will support you as a teacher in providing rich learning experiences across the curriculum so that each and every child has the very best opportunities and an excellent start in his or her education.

This is not a book we expect you to read from cover to cover. We think you will be more likely to thumb through to the relevant subject chapter that is of interest to you. Wherever you land, however, we are confident that you will find a shared philosophy and love of learning as all the chapters have been written by subject specialists who are also experienced teachers. You will also find stimulating ideas, food for thought and suggestions for planning, and we hope that you will adapt our 'In the classroom' activities to suit your children's needs.

We have always enjoyed teaching our subjects, but, more importantly, we have enjoyed teaching children. We hope you will, too.

Patrick Smith and Lyn Dawes
August 2013

ABOUT THE EDITORS AND CONTRIBUTORS

About the editors

Patrick Smith is Associate Dean in the Faculty of Education, Health and Wellbeing at the University of Wolverhampton. He has many years' experience of teaching children in schools and working with trainee teachers in higher education. He is a Fellow of the Higher Education Academy. His specialist subject area is physical education and he has led numerous staff development events for teachers in the UK and overseas. He believes that children who experience high-quality physical education can reap huge benefits and are more likely to enjoy lifelong physical activity.

Lyn Dawes taught secondary science before retraining to become a primary teacher. Now an education consultant, Lyn has taught science and education at the University of Bedford, University of Northampton and University of Cambridge. She has a special interest in 'Talk for Learning' and regularly provides workshops for education professionals in schools around the UK.

About the contributors

Balbir Ahir is a senior lecturer in primary mathematics in the Faculty of Education, Health and Wellbeing, University of Wolverhampton. She joined Wolverhampton after being a primary school teacher and a leading maths teacher for a number of years and has supported continued professional development in mathematics of teachers in local authorities. She was involved in a number of primary National Strategies projects and initiatives and has research interests in fit for purpose pedagogy in maths lessons, as well as supporting learners with English as an additional language needs in mathematics.

Jo Barter-Boulton is Programme Leader for the PGCE (5–11) at the University of Northampton, where she teaches English on the BA (QTS) and PGCE programmes. Prior to working in higher education, she taught in primary schools in Northamptonshire and also worked for the local advisory service as an advisory teacher for English and drama, delivering CPD to teachers across the county. Jo is co-author of *Drama Lessons for Five to Eleven Year Olds* (Routledge, 2013), *Drama Lessons: Ages 4–7* (Routledge, 2012) and *Drama Lessons: Ages 7–11* (Routledge, 2012) and the three book series, *Role Play in The Early Years* (David Fulton, 2004).

Ken Bland has experience of teaching in primary and secondary schools and has worked in two universities, training teachers how to teach geography in primary schools. His research interests include the use and deployment of higher-level teaching assistants and the impact of forest schools. He has recently developed a forest school on a university campus and engages in consultancy on work outside the classroom for schools and field centres.

Mary Bracey has a BEd (Hons) from Wolverhampton Polytechnic. She trained as a history specialist. She has wide teaching experience in a range of urban and rural schools and has taught across the primary age group. She currently teaches at Yelvertoft Primary School and is coordinator for mathematics and history, with experience in coordinating science and RE. She is responsible for Key Stage 2 assessment and the lead teacher for promoting road safety and charities. Her school is in partnership with the University of Northampton and she undertakes the role of mentor and ITT Coordinator. She is engaged in providing a microteaching experience for primary education history specialists in the school.

Paul Bracey is Senior Lecturer in History Education in the School of Education at the University of Northampton. He coordinates and teaches history within both BA (Hons) and PGCE primary education courses and contributes to school placements and PhD supervision. He has a BA (Hons) degree in economic history from Leeds University, an MA in history, PGCE and a PhD in education from Birmingham University. Paul is secretary of Midlands History Forum and a committee member for the History Teacher Educator Network.

Helen Caldwell is a senior lecturer in initial teacher education at the University of Northampton, where she is curriculum leader for computing. Prior to this, she was the adviser on assistive technology to Milton Keynes Council, providing guidance on the use of technology across a range of age groups and for children with special educational needs. She is a member of the Primary National Curriculum for Computing in ITT Expert Group, supporting tutors and trainees in teacher training in preparing for the new curriculum. Her earlier roles included the post of South East Regional Manager for the Vital programme, which was managed by the Open University and funded by the Department of Education. Helen has over 15 years' teaching experience across the 5 to 16 age range and held an ICT coordinator role for nine years, working across a number of schools to develop their capability with ICT. Her research interests include ICT and special educational needs, eLearning and social networking in higher education and digital literacy in primary education.

Gill Chambers is a senior lecturer in primary English education at the University of Northampton, where she has taught for the last two years. Gill has 25 years' experience in primary education, working as a class teacher across the primary age range and holding leadership roles, including in English. Prior to joining the university, Gill worked as a local authority adviser for primary English, leading teacher continuing professional development and the Every Child a Writer initiative for Northamptonshire. Gill currently teaches on undergraduate and postgraduate courses and leads the coordination of systematic synthetic phonics across all programmes. Her other research interests include philosophy for children and developing trainee teachers as readers.

Kate Coleman is a senior lecturer in primary initial teacher education at the University of Northampton. She has 23 years' experience in primary education, working in a diverse range of primary schools in Surrey, the Home Counties and East Midlands with subject and senior leadership responsibility. More recently, Kate has worked as a local authority adviser, supporting schools regarding literacy and school improvement. She is currently teaching on the BA Qualified Teacher Status primary English, specialism English and primary professional studies courses and supports students in school. Kate has a particular interest in developing children's writing, particularly the impact and teaching of grammar.

Gareth Davies is a senior lecturer in primary and secondary initial teacher education at the University of Northampton where he has taught for the last four years. He has 35 years' experience in secondary education and 14 years' experience working with primary schools on transition and leading on cooperative working between secondary and primary schools. He has worked as a subject teacher, subject leader in English and drama, year head and, for 14 years, a secondary deputy headteacher. Gareth currently teaches on undergraduate and postgraduate courses and leads on English specialism and secondary postgraduate training. Gareth has a particular interest in primary to secondary transition, developing reading and the use of drama.

Babs Dore has many years' experience teaching in primary schools and higher education, working with undergraduate and postgraduate trainee teachers. Babs has published key texts in primary science and has a national profile in science education.

Sue Fawson is a senior lecturer in early primary education at the University of Wolverhampton, where she has taught and developed a range of Early Years courses, including the BA in early childhood studies, foundation degree in early childhood studies and BEd in early primary teacher education. Sue is currently developing a PGCE in Early Years education. Earlier in her career she managed Foundation Stage and Key Stage 1 settings and taught on a range of childcare and education and teaching assistant courses in colleges of further education. Her research interests are focused on early drawing development and education.

Paul Gurton is a senior lecturer in primary initial teacher education at the University of Wolverhampton, where he has taught for the last seven years. He has 20 years' experience in primary education, working as a class teacher in London and the West Midlands and latterly as headteacher of a Warwickshire primary school. Paul also has four years in international education spent in Rome. He is course leader for the BEd in primary education with European language placement and cluster leader for primary professional studies, BEd and PGCE courses. Paul has research interests in primary language teaching, reflective practice in trainee and beginner teachers and Philosophy for Children.

Alice Hansen is the Director of Children Count, an education consultancy company. She worked in England and abroad as a primary school teacher before becoming a senior lecturer in initial teacher education. After 13 years in ITE Alice became an education consultant. She publishes widely on primary mathematics education and develops mobile applications for teachers. Alice's research interests lay in technology enhanced learning in mathematics.

Christine Hickman has taught in secondary, primary and special schools in Leicestershire. She moved into the role of Learning and Support Advisor for

Leicester City LEA, having autism as her specialism. She has worked in higher education since 2000, having been at the University of Northampton before moving to Liverpool John Moore's University. Her academic background is in art and special educational needs. At Northampton, Christine was School of Education art coordinator and taught on all teacher training courses. Christine has an interest in creative and therapeutic approaches, especially in the fields of art and music. She is involved in various international link programmes, especially in Sweden. She is Programme Leader for the PGCE Early Years programme at Liverpool John Moore's University. In addition, Christine teaches across several programmes, including the MA and both postgraduate and undergraduate teacher training courses.

Ellie Hill has many years' experience of teaching in schools and higher education. Previously a primary school headteacher, she moved a school from special measures to good before joining the University of Northampton as a senior lecturer, specialising in ICT, RE and professional studies. She has recently relocated with her family to be at the heart of the Malvern Hills, and is senior lecturer in RE at the University of Worchester. Her role spans Initial Teacher Education (Primary) and Education Studies.

Gareth Honeyford is the Strategic Lead for Initial Teacher Training (Primary) for Essex County Council, running teacher training courses that encompass both School Direct and school-centred initial teacher training (SCITT). Prior to this he was the Programme Leader of the Primary PGCE and Northampton and ICT subject leader. A long-time advocate of the use of new technologies in the classroom, he has also worked in City Learning Centres, education action zones and for the British Educational Communications and Technology Agency (Becta). When he is not working with trainees in the classroom or staring at a screen, he enjoys spending time with his family in the great outdoors, cycling, camping 1970s style and narrowboating.

Bob Kellam is a teacher at a lovely primary school in Bicester. He has been teaching for five years, after qualifying at Northampton University. He is currently head of Years 3 and 4, school sports coordinator and has twice supported his class to win the school's film competition. He is passionate about teaching by combining excitement, experiences and creativity.

Sandra Kirkland has a BEd (Hons) and MA from the University of Leicester. She is an Associate Tutor at the University of Northampton and the University of Derby. Until July 2013 she was the Early Years Foundation Stage and Key Stage 1 Manager and teacher at Naseby CE Primary School. She was responsible for leading a number of subjects including history, science and personal, social and health education (PSHE).

Jo Palmer is curriculum leader for English in primary education at the University of Northampton. She teaches English and professional studies on both the undergraduate and PGCE courses. Prior to her move to Northamptonshire, Jo was on secondment at Canterbury Christ Church University, where she taught on the undergraduate primary education course alongside teaching in primary schools in the Medway area. Jo is currently engaged in developing international research opportunities among members of the initial teacher education team at the University of Northampton.

Carol Wetton is a passionate advocate of music for everyone. She believes that music has the power to transform and enrich the lives of everyone and it can transcend all barriers to help create a better society for all. For 30 years, Carol has been involved with music education as a teacher, lecturer, workshop leader, performer, composer and conductor. At present, she runs her own music school and choir, is a senior lecturer at the University of Wolverhampton and works as a primary school music leader.

Emma Whewell is a senior lecturer at the University of Northampton and Curriculum Leader for Physical Education. Emma leads on the postgraduate, undergraduate and school direct programmes. She has been teaching for 13 years as a physical education teacher, head of department and head of year. She is passionate about physical education and initial teacher training. Emma's research interests are the learning and teaching of vulnerable children and development of professional identity in physical education.

Karen Woolley is a senior lecturer at the University of Northampton and Pastoral Team Leader for Initial Teacher Training. She has taught for 14 years in middle schools and secondary schools as a physical education specialist and head of department. The move to initial teacher training has allowed her to follow her passion for working with children and adults with dyslexia, particularly in relation to physical education.

ACKNOWLEDGEMENTS

The editors would like to thank Moira Williams and Neil Mercer for their invaluable support and guidance. Thanks to James Clark, Monira Begum and Rachael Plant at SAGE. Finally, thanks to colleagues at the University of Northampton and the University of Wolverhampton who made a significant contribution to the publication of this text.

The image of Weymouth sea front (Figure 7.3, p. 143) was sourced from English Heritage (www.heritage-explorer.co.uk). Teachers can pick and mix from a database of over 9,000 images and find curriculum related resources, for all key stages, to use or adapt for their pupils.

Figure 6.1 (p. 113) and Figure 6.2 (pp. 114–115) are reproduced with the permission of the Geographical Association and Routledge respectively.

SAGE and the editors would also like to thank the following reviewers whose comments on the proposal helped shape this book.

Paul Frecknall – University of Bedfordshire

Justin Gray – Newman University

Tim Lucas – York St John University

Tim Roberts – University of Hertfordshire

WALKTHROUGH TOUR

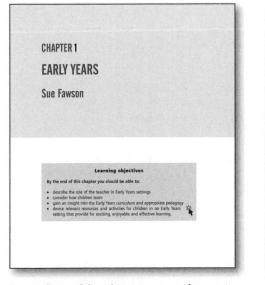

Learning objectives set out the main topics covered and what you will learn by reading the chapter.

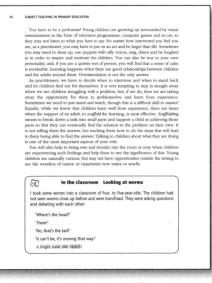

In the classroom real-life examples from schools demonstrate intelligent and engaging ways to teach different subjects.

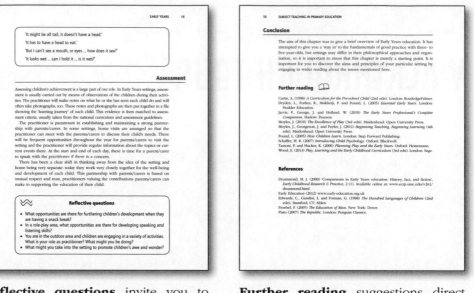

Reflective questions invite you to critically engage with what you have read and apply it to your own teaching.

Further reading suggestions direct you to more specialist literature.

INTRODUCTION

Patrick Smith and Lyn Dawes

As adults, we may have interacted with a lawyer, a plumber, a judge, an airline steward, or a hospital cleaner. We can admire them and find their jobs intriguing but we never really understand what it is that they actually do. Most of us have interacted with a teacher in our school days – and because of this, we all have an opinion about what it is that teachers do.

As children, we are marshalled, ordered, entertained, judged, instructed and disciplined by teachers. Such interaction, over days, months and years, colours our understanding of both what it is that teachers do, and why. We end up with an opinion of teachers as people and as professionals and as members of society. Some of you may think of teachers as friendly, approachable and supportive; for others teachers may seem to be frosty, bossy and harsh in their judgements. Teachers for some are part-timers with long holidays; for others, drudges who never leave the school building. The problem we as adults have with understanding what teachers actually *do*, is that we were children when we were at school; and so the rationales behind the endless rules, the strange mark schemes, the rewards and punishments, the interaction between ourselves and the teacher, were obscure to us and remain so in our memories. We did not know why we had to learn to read, look at an atlas or understand fractions. Even if we were told, it may still have been incomprehensible. In addition we live in a society where teachers are literally given a bad press; where parents who did not like school themselves pass their anxiety on to their children; and where teachers don't socialise with the children they teach, and so rarely appear human and ordinary.

All this colours our adult judgement. To be in the position that children find themselves in during their school days – which may be benign and encouraging at best, or grim at worst – is always to be a learner, someone who does not know things, and is part of a large group of other small anarchic creatures who must always be marshalled, organised and controlled. It can be difficult to see why anyone ends up liking their teachers, and yet it is common for people to be able to identify teachers that they admire. There seems to be often an awakening, however, when we realise what it is that a teacher is offering us, or trying to lead us to learn. A teacher may stand out as really caring of our progress, understanding of our needs, or really good at ordering thoughts or explaining things in ways that we find truly interesting.

So why would you choose to be a teacher? As adults it becomes obvious to us that a teacher holds a hugely responsible role and is much to be admired. Teachers are among the brightest and best educated members of our society. They are less concerned with getting and spending money than some, and more concerned with ideas, understanding, thinking, listening, and finding out. Primary teachers have the opportunity to work with others who are really good company – that is, children, who are charming, funny, clever and curious. They can create an harmonious environment, and spend time on any given day taking part in language activities, drama, music, art, science, physical exercise, learning about the world, the past, the future, and not only that, helping others to learn. They can change the world by influencing the plastic minds of children, and concentrate on using this influence for the better.

But this is an idealised vision of a teacher's world. Alternatively, on any given day, a teacher may find themselves dealing with distressed or fearful children and aggressive or angry parents. They may have to complete a daunting amount of paperwork, try to organise groups of children whose intention is to scupper all attempts at imposing order; they may have to deal with an irate, irrational child, or talk to other professionals, all of whom only ever see one or two children at a time, and yet make recommendations about what the teacher should do even though they will rarely work with classes of fewer than thirty. A teacher might on one day have to find out about the workings of the solar system, the correct grammatical use of subordinate clauses, how to use a particular bit of software to compile pie charts, and all about the Sahara desert. And, once lessons on these things are over, the teacher must be ready to evaluate learning and prepare new lessons for the next day.

But still, we find ourselves drawn to being a teacher. Every teacher will have different reasons for their choice, but for most, one key reason will be that teaching offers the opportunity to help develop young minds. This desire to teach is a powerful force. People like to inform one another; the contents of the internet are testimony to that. But to inform is not to educate, and this is the distinctive thing that teachers do. We teach; we match the starting point of the child with the desired outcome for their development, and create ways to help them have access to and begin to understand what it is they need next. And so it is that despite the school system we found ourselves in when we were children, despite our classmates, our youthful exuberance and our own natural attempts to avoid putting our minds to work too often, we were educated, and we have to acknowledge that it was teachers who were responsible for that. Being a teacher is the most important job there is.

What is it, though, that teachers actually do? This book is intended to help new teachers to get to grips with what it is to be a teacher in primary education. Teachers do enjoy teaching. They like sharing their love of their subject. They do have those ideal days, and they do find themselves in contexts where they can have a direct influence on a child's thinking, which will last that child's lifetime. Teaching can be complex, demanding and tiring. But it is also simple, interesting and inspiring, and it is never ever dull. What teachers actually do is to find out what children think and know, and organise things so that they can move on to developing their thinking, and knowing a bit more. It is as simple as that.

We have divided the book into subject chapters. This is because we found that each of our authors was in the grip of a passionate conviction that 'their' subject was the most important thing children could ever learn; and we wanted to give them chance to say why. Each chapter offers a rationale for teaching the subject which clearly indicates what it is about the subject that is distinctive, important, and necessary to ensure the development of the whole child. As primary teachers we can all teach any subject, but we are allowed of course to have our favourites, often gained from a teacher during our school days.

Children, schools and education have all been subjects of careful academic research. Researchers have used their data and insight to develop theories of how children learn, and how teachers can help them to learn. Theories are used to suggest how teachers might teach. There is no getting out of it by imagining that theory is unnecessary; everyone has a theory of education, that is, an idea of how they think children learn which might be different from how we think we learn ourselves. You can test your own theory of education quite readily. Imagine that tomorrow morning, you must teach thirty seven-year-olds how to…. what shall we say? It is not often your choice, what to teach. How to write a haiku poem; how to count to ten and say hello and goodbye in another language; or to know the order of the colours of the rainbow, and how they relate to the rest of the electromagnetic spectrum. The question is, how would you do it? Your answer to that question is an indicator of how you think people learn – your theory of education. You could sit them down and tell them. You could use an interactive whiteboard or provide access to laptops. You could organise a drama or a painting session, or get out the percussion instruments. You could have the children working as a class, in small groups, or as individuals. You could insist on silence while you talk for half an hour. You could check that they had learnt something by giving them a test at the end. You could even begin by giving them a test. You could ask a lot of questions. You could organise a discussion, or help them to generate some questions of their own. You could take them outside or to a museum.

You could get an expert in and then see what their theory of education is by looking at how they teach. People teach in ways that they think will enable learning; so how you teach reflects how you think children learn. This book offers the opportunity to think about theories of learning, and see what different ideas look like in practice.

Each author has worked with primary teachers to identify some 'In the classroom' examples. These are activities that have actually happened in classrooms, with their context and a brief analysis of their impact. These sections are not what are disparagingly known as 'tips for teachers'. It's actually fair enough to be disparaging about such things. They are only useful in the short term. It is no good providing a list of things to do, because once you get to the end of it, you would still not know what it is that teachers do, and how and why they do it. Instead we offer the theory, with some examples of practice. Making sense of what happens and why, and making your own decisions about what you think is important, is part of your building professional expertise.

We have also asked our authors to provide some key texts for further reading. No one book can do justice to the wealth of knowledge and understanding about education that is available to teachers; we are aware that each reader will want to pursue different aspects of understanding, so suggestions are offered for each of the curriculum areas.

A key focus for each chapter is on the importance of talk for learning. Talk is often suppressed in classrooms, and for some of the time, this is essential. You could not get through every school day with 30 children talking at will in a confined space. However the chance for children to articulate ideas, share information, discuss problems, and provide feedback are just some of the reasons why it is crucial that they are encouraged to talk to one another about their classroom activities. Another reason is that unless children talk to one another in class, there is little chance that they will develop into collaborative, fluent adults who understand that knowledge shared is knowledge more than doubled; who can engage with one another in rational, exploratory discussion. Talk for learning teaches children to be able to offer and accept challenges and gives them the strategies they need to question others, and to be able to change their minds when faced with a different point of view. That is, to be able to learn, and keep learning. Talk for learning is not difficult to organise; we just have to teach children what is meant by 'a good discussion', and teach them the skills to take part. Every child is entitled to such tuition. Every child may be more or less able to talk when they arrive in your classroom, but it will be your focus on dialogue, and your modelling of such talk skills as attentive listening, asking for and giving reasons, elaboration and explanation, and negotiating an agreement, that teach the child how to join in effective discussions with others.

Every child is only going to achieve their potential in your classroom if both you and their classmates have that as the aim. To be a teacher is to be in the powerful and important position of orchestrator of the classroom, manager of learning, and evaluator of progress. To be a teacher is to influence many different futures. We trust that this book with its collection of theory, practice and ideas will inspire and support you as you step in to this difficult and profoundly satisfying role.

CHAPTER 1

EARLY YEARS

Sue Fawson

Learning objectives

By the end of this chapter you should be able to:

- describe the role of the teacher in Early Years settings
- consider how children learn
- gain an insight into the Early Years curriculum and appropriate pedagogy
- devise relevant resources and activities for children in an Early Years setting that provide for exciting, enjoyable and effective learning.

Introduction

It is important to define the terms we use in this chapter. 'Early Years' has been the term used in different contexts for denoting children of specific age groups, such as pre-birth to three years, birth to five years, two to five years, three to five years, three to seven years and so on. In this chapter we will be using the term to mean children aged between three and five years.

The educational settings for this age group are sometimes part of a primary or elementary school or else a separate institution. They can be State-funded – the State having control or partial control of the curriculum and educational principles – or privately owned, so free to decide on their own ideals and practices. This type of setting may be called a preschool, children's centre, Foundation Stage unit, nursery, or nursery and Reception class, kindergarten or given other titles, depending on the country, the specific age range, the organisation, the controlling body and the philosophical context.

The term 'Early Years practitioner' in this chapter is used to mean a teacher or other professional (nursery nurse or teaching assistant) who is a confident and competent Early Years specialist, delivering the curriculum within a setting catering for three- to five-year-olds.

Teaching and learning in the Early Years

When non-Early Years practitioners (for example, student teachers or experienced teachers of 7- to 11-year-olds) are tasked with teaching 3- to 4-year-olds, they may have these contrasting preconceptions or feelings:

- 'This will be easy because the children only play; there's no "real" teaching or planning involved, no marking of work, no behaviour management problems, no need for detailed subject knowledge. It's much easier than teaching older children.'
- 'I'm very anxious because this is a "different world", one I don't feel comfortable with. I'm scared of making them cry or tripping over them. How can I teach them if they won't sit still and can't concentrate? If they can't do things for themselves, they will be reliant on me all the time – it will be difficult to meet the needs of all individuals in my class because each one will be so dependent and needy.'

Both views indicate a lack of knowledge of Early Years education.

Regarding the first view, being an Early Years practitioner is not an easy option: it is demanding intellectually and physically, and is time-consuming outside of the daily contact time with the children (time is needed for planning, creating resources, physically organising the environment, recording and evaluating assessments, discussing children's progress and achievement with colleagues and liaising with parents). It requires a range of specialist knowledge and skills and it is necessary to be well organised, creative and flexible.

The suggestion behind the 'only playing' comment is that playing is not important to children's learning. The reverse is, in fact, true, as playing is 'never trivial; it is serious and deeply significant' (Froebel, 2005: 55); it is at the heart of most learning and development for young children and should not be underestimated. There is, thus, a great deal of 'teaching' going on every moment of the day, but, because it is not always didactic or overtly imparting subject knowledge (a traditional view of teaching), it can go unrecognised to the untrained eye. There can be a great deal of planning and preparation undertaken by Early Years practitioners, too, and, while there is less marking and written feedback involved than when teaching older children, there is an enormous amount of assessment, recording assessments and giving verbal feedback in Early Years settings.

The 'fear' of this age phase expressed in the second view above is probably an easier one to deal with because it acknowledges the need for a different pedagogy and shows an awareness of the demands of the job. It does, however, reflect the traditional ideas of teaching furthering the development of the child's knowledge as such fear grows from not understanding how young children develop and learn. Once practitioners holding this view become aware that education for young children involves other areas of development as well as cognitive development, then they will be less anxious about the pressure of directly imparting knowledge to them.

The early stages of development in three- to five-year-olds does mean that teachers need to be well organised in order to meet the needs of all of the children, but it is a false belief that children of this age are totally dependent: it is surprising how much they can learn without direct input from a teacher, enjoying challenges and finding things out for themselves. As Malaguzzi, the main founder of the Reggio Emilia preschool approach (1998, in Edwards et al., 67), tells us, 'What children learn does not follow as an automatic result from what is taught. Rather, it is in large part due to the children's own doing as a consequence of their activities and our resources.'

It is good practice, then, for Early Years practitioners to begin to understand how young children develop and learn; only then will they begin to understand the pedagogical knowledge and understanding needed to be effective professionals in an Early Years setting. The next part of this chapter will discuss children's development and learning, and will suggest ways in which an effective pedagogy can be developed.

Child development

Young children develop in the following different areas.

- *Physical development* This comprises fine motor development (small body movements, such as use of hands and fingers) and gross motor development (large body movements, such as running, kicking a ball, throwing, climbing).
- *Sensory development* The development of the five well-known senses: sight, hearing, smell, taste, touch/feel. Also the development of two lesser-known senses.

  o *Vestibular sense* The sense in the inner ear that tells us if the head is upright and if it is moving. It affects our balance and sense of speed. This can be seen when children go round and round, either standing or while sitting, which results in dizziness and loss of balance. This gives some children a sense of pleasure – unless it results in sickness! It can also be seen when children run very fast, gaining pleasure from speed.

  o *Proprioception* This is muscle and joint memory, which is developed as a result of repetitive pressure on the muscles and joints of the body. This is sometimes why children like jumping down from a height – they are enjoying the sensation of the pressure put on their joints when they land. It is also a useful sense when developing fine motor skills, such as pencil control, as the repetitive action and pressure that is put on the muscles and joints of the fingers during handwriting practice helps the hand to remember the action. For example, it is easy for us to sign our name with our eyes closed because our fingers are used to the pressures and actions remembered as a result of writing our signature many times. This sense also tells us the position of the body. It is interesting to ask a young child to lie down on the floor so that his or her body is straight. Before the proprioception sense is well-developed, it is difficult for children to know where their body is and they may *think* that they are lying straight when, in fact, they are leaning to the side.

- *Intellectual, or cognitive, development* This area deals with the functions of the brain. There are six main components of intellectual development, which are:

  o concepts (knowledge)
  o problem solving
  o memory
  o concentration
  o imagination
  o creativity.

- Early Years practitioners see intellectual development as only one of several areas for development and do not treat it as more important than any of the other areas.

- *Language development* This is, in fact, part of intellectual/cognitive development, but, because it is such a large and important area of a child's development, it is usually seen as a developmental area in its own right. It comprises:

  o receptive language (comprehension) – hearing and reading, processing meaning and understanding
  o expressive language (communication) – verbal (speaking and writing) and non-verbal (body language, facial expression, gesture, mime).

- *Emotional development* This area involves developing an understanding of feelings. Children need to learn to name and understand different emotions in themselves and in others. Young children begin by understanding basic emotions, such as happy and sad, then continue to develop until they have an awareness of more complex emotions, such as fear, envy, jealousy, pride, guilt, empathy and so on.
- *Social development* The development of awareness of the self – of 'I' and 'me', of self-confidence, self-esteem, gender identity – and of social skills and interaction – the ability to share, take turns, work collaboratively, empathise, sympathise, help, have an awareness of others' needs.
- *Spiritual development* The development of the sense of awe and wonder (for example, at seeing a rainbow in a deep grey sky or a spider's web glistening when outlined by droplets of dew) and of calm and inner peace.
- *Moral and behavioural development* This is the understanding of right and wrong and what is acceptable and unacceptable behaviour; also, the development of the understanding of rules and boundaries. Young children initially see things in extremes – everything is 'black or white'. It is only as they develop that they begin to see the 'grey areas' and understand the complexities and effects of context on the concept of right and wrong.

There is much literature on 'milestones of development' – these are the stages children generally reach by a certain age. While these stages are useful, to give us an idea of what we may expect of a child at a particular age, it is crucial to remember that all children develop at different rates, according to their genetics, environment and state of their well-being. Not all children develop at a steady rate – they can suddenly have a surge of learning or can plateau for a while or can even regress.

It is also worth noting that, while we use such discrete areas of development for planning and assessment purposes, children never learn in only one of these areas, but, rather, they do so in all areas, to some degree, in every activity they undertake.

How young children learn

Young children learn in an integrated and whole way, with all areas developing at the same time to a greater or lesser degree depending on the experience and activity. We call this way of learning *holistic*.

Young children develop holistically in a variety of ways, such as via:

- movement
- the senses
- copying, imitating, role models
- exploration and discovery
- trial and error, experience
- repetition and memory
- enquiry and natural curiosity
- receiving praise, encouragement and rewards
- direct teaching
- stories, songs and rhymes
- real-life situations relating to their own lives
- success and a sense of achievement
- personal interests
- play.

What is play and learning from experience?

'Children learn through play', this is irrefutable and yet this ubiquitous phrase is often used without any *real* understanding of what is meant by 'play'.

Play is an activity that gives pleasure. Does all early learning derive from play? No. Research has shown that children learn very effectively via play, but it is not the only way – a child can learn from being told facts, experiences that are not pleasurable (for example, touching something hot or falling from a tricycle as a result of taking a bend too quickly) or doing a task that he or she has been directed to do. While, of course, no one is suggesting that we *plan* for children to have unpleasurable experiences in order to learn, it is important to be aware of these other ways in order to really understand what we mean by 'learning through play' and prevent the phrase being used glibly.

Interestingly, not all early education pioneers in the past would dismiss the idea of learning from unpleasant experiences. Susan Isaacs believed that children learned best from *any* experience and was content to allow children to dig up a previously buried dead rabbit to learn what happened to the body or pull a worm in half to discover what happens (Drummond, 2000).

We can accept that children learn from all experience, but it is useful to consider where you personally would 'draw the line' and examine the reasoning behind your decision. It is probably based on your ethical, moral and sociocultural beliefs and government guidelines and legislation, which may change from country to country (for example, health and safety laws).

Principles and approaches

The direction in which education starts a man will determine his future life. (Plato: 425b)

These words from Plato, a Greek author and philosopher writing nearly 2500 years ago, highlights the importance of early education in a person's life. These same beliefs have been shared over the centuries by philosophers, educationalists, learning theorists, psychologists and researchers. Basic principles, approaches, pedagogy, and practice have changed, however, under the influence of fashion, culture, society, research and government intervention.

Over time, the 'nursery' has taken on different roles. In the mid-twentieth century, nurseries were cosy places where children were simply cared for physically. Then, as more widespread research identified the importance of early education and the potential for nurseries to enhance children's learning, Early Years settings developed a new set of principles, a curriculum and pedagogical approaches. Today, Early Years settings see their role as developing the 'whole child', furthering all areas of development rather than teaching to develop each area separately.

There are different sets of principles for ensuring effective early education, originating from different cultures, philosophies and research studies. From these we can identify the following main themes:

- each child is unique, will have different needs and may learn at a different rate and in a different way from other children
- there should be a relevant curriculum based on the children's needs and practitioners' knowledge of child development, which should build on children's prior knowledge and experiences, taking into account their interests and culture
- all areas of development are linked and equally important – practitioners should know that children learn holistically and should be active in their learning
- each child should feel valued and have opportunities to develop into a strong, confident and responsible individual
- a safe, secure and stimulating environment is paramount in children's learning and they should have access to indoor and outdoor environments
- practitioners and parents/carers should foster a mutually respectful relationship and maintain effective methods of communication.

(The above principles are informed by a variety of sources, including Early Education, 2012.)

Different approaches to Early Years education

Different methods of early education can be seen in settings in different parts of the world, but also in neighbouring nurseries. Some settings have remained fundamental to the philosophy and principles of a particular approach, while many nurseries have taken on various aspects from internationally recognised approaches and integrated these to develop their own approaches.

The main philosophical tenets of each approach are too complex to explain in the space available in this chapter and it would be misleading to try to simplify their ideas and not give the full context. Therefore, we will simply list some of the major influential approaches and would urge you to investigate further:

- Reggio Emilia
- Steiner
- Montessori
- HighScope
- Te Whāriki.

One of the main reasons for needing to know about these influences is that some ideas that have been adopted can result in unexpected practices, such as in settings that follow the Reggio Emilia approach, where preplanning of the curriculum is minimal because the practitioners base the activities on the children's interests each day and flexibly change activities to follow their thoughts and attentions.

What can you expect to see in an Early Years setting?

✐ **In the classroom   An example of good practice in an Early Years environment**

Arriving at an Early Years setting, there is a covered area to park buggies, push-chairs and strollers, which can be a safety hazard indoors. The front door is security coded to prevent strangers from entering. The indoor entrance area is welcoming for parents and visitors. It shows what happens at the setting and reflects the ethos and principles to be found inside. There are also displays of photographs of the children engaged in a variety of activities, with labels explaining each one, and there is a parents' noticeboard to communicate important dates and events, as well as any messages from staff to parents. This is important, fostering a partnership with parents and allowing them to feel involved in their children's early education.

Beyond the entrance, the interior is light and airy, having large windows to let in natural light and fresh air, with blinds fitted for very hot, sunny days. The walls are a mix of vibrant or pastel shades – there is no evidence to suggest children prefer bright colours and some Early Years approaches prefer more natural hues for walls. There are display boards with a combination of photographs of the children taking part in activities and examples of the children's work.

There are several distinct areas that have different characteristics. There is a carpeted area for children to sit or play on the floor and non-carpeted areas for messy activities, such as painting, water and sand play. The carpeted area of floor is a good size to allow the children space to move around, sit in groups or to work on floor activities. The non-carpeted areas have tables and chairs for writing and tabletop activities; all the furniture is child-size.

There are other areas created for specific purposes. For example, there is a book corner, with a variety of books and comfortable child-size sofas and bean-bags, and a role-play area, dressed to provide a setting usually linked to the topic the children are focusing on at that time. A separate room is set up as a sensory room, with a variety of lighting effects, music and sounds, and tactile resources.

Around the main indoor setting are storage cupboards, shelves, trays and containers for resources. They are clearly labelled and safely accessible to the children, which encourages them to make choices regarding resources and gives them the freedom to retrieve resources and sort and put them away at the end of an activity, promoting independence and responsibility.

Outdoor space is particularly important and, here, there is easy access to the outside – the children have the freedom to move between the two. The outdoor area has a secure boundary fence and comprises a playground area for gross motor activities (for example, running, riding tricycles, climbing the climbing frame, and may be painted with number ladders, roads and pedestrian crossings, islands and sea and so on); a grassed area, including a wild nature area as a minibeast habitat, and a sensory garden (where there are plants that have different perfumes, textural qualities, and make different sounds as the wind blows through the leaves); and a sheltered area for children if the weather is hot or wet.

There is also a kitchen where food can be prepared, a staff room and children's toilets and basins. Child-height sinks are positioned in the wet/art area. Coat pegs are labelled with the children's names and each has an image, too, for easy recognition, to help them become independent. There is also a supply of water-proof clothing and wellington boots situated by the external door so that the children can go outside in all weathers.

The curriculum

Many countries have a specified national curriculum for their Early Years education. Some are statutory requirements with additional guidance. Although these may vary and have differing titles, there are key areas of the curriculum that are accepted as being good practice in Western cultures. We need to be mindful, however, that a 'good' curriculum has to be relevant, so what might be deemed as effective in a nursery in London, for example, may be inappropriate for a nursery in rural Nigeria. Please consult the requirements and guidance for the country in which you are practising. Below are general key areas for an Early Years curriculum in a developed country.

- *Language* speaking, listening, reading, writing, drama.
- *Mathematics* numbers, counting, simple calculations, sorting, matching, sequences and patterns, shapes, measurement, comparisons.
- *Personal, social and emotional development* self-awareness, self-confidence, relationships, social skills, understanding of own and others' feelings.
- *Physical development* gross and fine motor skills.
- *Knowledge and understanding of the world around them* science, history, geography, religion, culture, technology.
- *The arts* art, design, music, dance, drama.

In practice, the curriculum is usually split into adult-led activities and child-led and free choice activities. It is common for the day to start with a welcome session, where the children sit in small groups with an adult and discuss what will happen during the day and there may be some direct teaching or introduction to a topic. There will then follow a range of activities that the children can choose from. It is usual for there to also be an adult-led activity where a small group of children at a time will sit at a table with an adult and have support and help to complete a task. With older children in Early Years settings it is common for this time to be used for specific language and mathematics activities.

There will be breaks in the day for a drink and snack (usually water or milk and a piece of fruit). These times are very important as they are opportunities for developing children's social skills (sharing, offering, saying 'thank you', being kind and fair), maths skills (counting, one-to-one correspondence, sharing equally, as a banana is cut into pieces, for example), knowledge of hygiene routines (toileting and the importance of washing hands before eating), general discussion about the food and drink (colours, smells, tastes, what it looks like inside and out, where it comes from, how it is grown).

The activities after the break are usually child-initiated and a free choice. The children have the freedom to move from activity to activity when they wish and can

Table 1.1 Ideas for resources and activities

Area	Examples of activities and resources				
Water tray	Coloured water	Bubbles	A range of containers, funnels, tubes, water wheel	Fishing games	Sequins and glitter, shells, plastic toys, floating and sinking objects
Sand tray	Dry sand	Wet sand	A range of containers, funnels, wheels	Shells, plastic toys, spoons, small spades, lollipop sticks, twigs	Dry sand with water in a watering can for children to add as they wish
Art area	A range of paint, crayons, chalks, felt-tipped pens and other mark-making tools	A range of paper and card – different colours, textures, sizes, shapes; tracing paper, coloured acetate	Glue sticks, scissors, sticky tape, water pots, a range of different-sized paintbrushes	A range of fabric, wool, cotton wool, feathers, sequins, pasta shapes, shells and other collage materials	Reclaimed materials – plastic bottles, card packaging, card tubes, used greetings cards
Clay and malleable materials	Wet clay in a tray for moulding	Modelling dough – salt dough and manufactured modelling materials (ensure it is warm enough to be malleable). Gloop and flubber (see Internet for recipes to make these interestingly textured materials)	Plastic knives, plates, rolling pins, shape cutters, lollipop sticks, matchsticks, twigs, shells, pasta shapes	Picture cue cards, such as 'Make a fat cat and a thin cat', showing pictures of both. This will help with knowledge of opposites	Letter or number cards – the child can roll out a long 'worm' and shape it on the drawn letter or number
Role-play area	Themed, for example a real-life setting (a hospital or café) or a setting in a story or relating to a topic being studied	Child-sized equipment and resources, made for purpose (such as teapot and cups) and general objects (such as wooden blocks) so that children can pretend the objects are something else	Dressing-up clothes and mirror to see themselves Dolls + cuddly toys (to be patients or customers)	Opportunities for speaking and listening development, such as telephones, audio recorders and players, puppets	Opportunities for writing and drawing, such as notebooks and pens for taking a restaurant order or making a shopping list or writing paper and envelopes and a postbox
Gross motor activity	Climbing frames, slides, swings	Tricycles, scooters, pedal cars, pushchairs	Large building blocks	Large plastic tunnels to climb through	Dancing, rolling, running, jumping areas

(Continued)

Table 1.1 *(Continued)*

Area	Examples of activities and resources			
Fine motor activity	Any pencil grip activity – writing, drawing, painting	Threading beads, buttons, simple sewing or weaving	Computer, calculator	Sorting small objects	Construction kits
Book area	A range of books – picture books and text (it helps for children to see printed words even if they cannot read them yet)	Comfortable seating, space so they are not cramped, sufficient light, opportunities to sit together and share books	Easily accessible bookshelves or storage – makes it easy for children to return books to the shelves, too	Story sacks – that is, fabric drawstring bags filled with items relating to a particular book	Puppets
Floor area	Wooden blocks	Road mat for use with toy vehicles	Construction kits	Large dominoes and dice	Large pieces of paper and markmaking tools
Tabletops	Dolls' house	Jigsaw puzzles and other games	Construction kits	'Play people' – small plastic people and animals, such as farm or wild animals	Laptops, tablets, paper and pencils

go indoors or outdoors as they please. This type of structure is called *freeflow play* – each child is free to make decisions and can really get immersed and involved with what he or she is doing. The resources should be easily accessible to all the children so that they can choose what they need and so are not constrained by what the adult has provided for them. The activities during freeflow time should comprise resources and tasks to provide opportunities to further all areas of the children's development and involve the key areas of the curriculum. It is good practice to change the activities regularly so that the children have new experiences and are curious and excited. For example, the water tray may be available every day, but the colour of the water or the play objects in it may change daily to inspire the children.

Table 1.1 suggests some basic ideas that you can take and develop to create your own resources and activities.

What is your role as an Early Years practitioner?

The practitioner's role follows the usual professional framework and abides by the same legislation as that of any other teacher, but there are additional aspects of the role specific to Early Years settings.

Often an adult is assigned as a *key worker* for a small group of children. This means the adult is responsible for that particular group at the beginning and end of the day and usually snack times and perhaps story times, too. The groups are sometimes called *family groups* and they enable the children to get to know the others in their group and attach to one adult in particular. A nursery can have a large number of children and adults, which can be daunting for a young child; a key worker can offer security and sense of belonging to the child.

It is important for the practitioner to get down to the level of the children, either by sitting on child-size chairs or on the carpet with them. When talking with children, you need to be a good listener:

- be patient – don't rush them or finish their sentences for them
- show that you value what they have to say
- take every opportunity to promote further thinking and language development.

If a child makes a grammatical error while speaking to you, don't tell them it's wrong or make a fuss, just repeat the sentence, correcting the grammar, and the child will learn from this without any negative feelings.

We must never force a child to do something. If we see that a child never visits a particular activity, we can encourage him or her to give it a try, but it may just be that it doesn't interest him or her. Like adults, children are all different, with different likes and dislikes. We need to respect their feelings and wishes.

You have to be a performer! Young children are growing up surrounded by visual entertainment in the form of television programmes, computer games and so on, so they may not listen to what you have to say. No matter how introverted you feel you are, as a practitioner, you may have to put on an act and be larger than life. Sometimes you may need to dress up, use puppets with silly voices, sing, dance and be laughed at in order to inspire and motivate the children. You can also be true to your own personality, and, if you are a quieter sort of person, you will find that a sense of calm is invaluable. Learning happens when there are good relationships between children and the adults around them. Overstimulation is not the only answer.

As practitioners, we have to decide when to intervene and when to stand back and let children find out for themselves. It is very tempting to step in straight away when we see children struggling with a problem, but, if we do, then we are taking away the opportunity for them to problemsolve and learn from experience. Sometimes we need to just stand and watch, though this is a difficult skill to master! Equally, while we know that children learn well from experience, there are times when the support of an adult, to *scaffold* the learning, is most effective. *Scaffolding* means to break down a task into small parts and support a child in achieving those parts so that they can eventually find the solution to the problem on their own. It is not telling them the answer, but teaching them how to do the steps that will lead to them being able to find the answer. Talking to children about what they are doing is one of the most important aspects of your role.

You will also help to bring awe and wonder into the room or note when children are experiencing such feelings and help them to see the significance of this. Young children are naturally curious, but may not have opportunities outside the setting to see the wonders of nature or experience new tastes or smells.

✍ In the classroom   Looking at worms

I took some worms into a classroom of four- to five-year-olds. The children had not seen worms close up before and were transfixed. They were asking questions and debating with each other:

'Where's the head?'

'There!'

'No, that's the tail!'

'It can't be, it's moving that way!'

'It might have two heads!'

'It might be all tail, it doesn't have a head.'

'It has to have a head to eat.'

'But I can't see a mouth, or eyes ... how does it see?'

'It looks wet ... can I hold it ... is it wet?'

Assessment

Assessing children's achievement is a large part of our role. In Early Years settings, assessment is usually carried out by means of observations of the children during their activities. The practitioner will make notes on what he or she has seen each child do and will often take photographs, too. These notes and photographs are then put together in a file showing the 'learning journey' of each child. This evidence is then matched to assessment criteria, usually taken from the national curriculum and assessment guidelines.

The practitioner is paramount in establishing and maintaining a strong partnership with parents/carers. In some settings, home visits are arranged so that the practitioner can meet with the parents/carers to discuss their child's needs. There will be frequent opportunities throughout the year for parents/carers to visit the setting and the practitioner will provide regular information about the topics or current events there. At the start and end of each day, there is time for a parent/carer to speak with the practitioner if there is a concern.

There has been a clear shift in thinking away from the idea of the setting and home being very separate: today they work very closely together for the well-being and development of each child. This partnership with parents/carers is based on mutual respect and trust, practitioners valuing the contributions parents/carers can make to supporting the education of their child.

Reflective questions

- What opportunities are there for furthering children's development when they are having a snack break?
- In a role-play area, what opportunities are there for developing speaking and listening skills?
- You are in the outdoor area and children are engaging in a variety of activities. What is your role as practitioner? What might you be doing?
- What might you take into the setting to promote children's awe and wonder?

Conclusion

The aim of this chapter was to give a brief overview of Early Years education. It has attempted to give you a 'way in' to the fundamentals of good practice with three- to five-year-olds, but settings may differ in their philosophical approaches and organisation, so it is important to stress that this chapter is merely a starting point. It is important for you to discover the aims and principles of your particular setting by engaging in wider reading about the issues mentioned here.

Further reading

Curtis, A. (1998) *A Curriculum for the Pre-school Child* (2nd edn). London: RoutledgeFalmer.
Dryden, L., Forbes, R., Mukherji, P. and Pound, L. (2005) *Essential Early Years*. London: Hodder Education.
Jarvis, P., George, J. and Holland, W. (2010) *The Early Years Professional's Complete Companion*. Harlow: Pearson.
Moyles, J. (2010) *The Excellence of Play* (3rd edn). Maidenhead: Open University Press.
Moyles, J., Georgeson, J. and Payler, J. (2011) *Beginning Teaching, Beginning Learning* (4th edn). Maidenhead: Open University Press.
Pound, L. (2005) *How Children Learn*. London: Step Forward Publishing.
Schaffer, H. R. (2007) *Introducing Child Psychology*. Oxford: Blackwell.
Tassoni, P. and Hucker, K. (2000) *Planning Play and the Early Years*. Oxford: Heinemann.
Wood, E. (2013) *Play, Learning and the Early Childhood Curriculum* (3rd edn). London: Sage.

References

Drummond, M. J. (2000) 'Comparisons in Early Years education: History, fact, and fiction', *Early Childhood Research & Practice*, 2 (1). Available online at: www.ecrp.uiuc.edu/v2n1/drummond.html
Early Education (2012) www.early-education.org.uk
Edwards, C., Gandini, L. and Forman, G. (1998) *The Hundred Languages of Children* (2nd edn). Stamford, CT: Ablex.
Froebel, F. (2005) *The Education of Man*. New York: Dover.
Plato (2007) *The Republic*. London: Penguin Classics.

CHAPTER 2

ART AND DESIGN

Christine Hickman

Learning objectives

By the end of this chapter you should be able to:

- consider the place and value of art in both the curriculum and a child's development
- consider the opportunities available for children in art in the primary phase
- develop a deeper understanding of the potential of art in the primary phase
- have the confidence, despite your current perception of your artistic ability, to become an effective teacher of art.

Introduction

The aim of this chapter is to demonstrate that art in primary schools needs to be taken beyond the role of a 'service subject' for other curriculum areas, to stand far more securely in its own right. Children's experiences of art and design in the primary years should have creativity at their heart. This is stressed in the National Curriculum, which comments that, 'Art, craft and design embody some of the highest forms of human creativity' (DfE, 2013a: 182).

So, this chapter will challenge common practice in our schools, arguing that art in the curriculum too often lacks both a fostering of skills and a root in creativity. Art is frequently taught by teachers with too little training and little confidence in delivering the subject. In primary schools, art as a subject has also been threatened, 'largely as a misguided drive to get back to basics' (Hickman, 2010: 10). One might maintain that art is itself the most fundamental of 'basics', being an act that is at the foundation of human expression.

In the classroom   Inspiring drawing through movement

A teacher of four- and five-year-olds, during the topic of 'Myself', wanted to encourage the children to think about their bodies and how they could use them.

The teacher began the drawing lesson with a session in the hall. The children did a variety of movement exercises, the teacher emphasising the labelling of body parts and giving descriptions of the children's actions – 'Stretching out with arms and stretching fingers'.

The children then returned to the classroom and set about drawing themselves. The teacher was delighted by the additional details in their drawings, such as hands, fingers, toes, hair. The drawings were dynamic, too, showing movement. The children's self-perceptions had been heightened, enabling them to focus on their bodies when representing them.

The progression in art education can be viewed as fractured. There exists a significant division between primary art, secondary art and the practice in art colleges. The belief held by many secondary school teachers is that the art in primary schools can be discounted, students really beginning their art education at the age of 11. Just two-fifths of primary schools in Ofsted's 'Making a mark' report (2012) provided good or outstanding art, craft and design education lessons. After positive work in the Early

Years, practice dips, with a greater percentage of 'satisfactory' grades. This is clearly of concern for practitioners involved in the primary sector (Penny et al., 2002: 20):

> Schools often have a paradoxical attitude towards the subject. On the one hand they will display work and care enormously about the visual landscape of the school, but, at the same time, not invest in appropriate resources, or release teachers to undertake training.

Time devoted to the teaching of art on initial teacher training courses in primary education tends to replicate its status within the curriculum, with taught sessions sometimes totalling fewer than ten hours. Many teachers assume that they have no useful art knowledge, based on a belief that, unless you can *draw* realistically, you are without artistic ability. This erroneous opinion overlooks the fact that we are all able to observe and we can all make judgements (seen in our choice of clothes and home furnishings) based on colour, line, tone, pattern, texture, shape and form. These are the elements of art.

It is heartening that the curriculum (DfE, 2013a) highlights the need for both individuality and originality, something that this chapter will make reference to. Also, the notion of thought being linked crucially to creativity and art is a thread that will be explored. Again, this concept is included in the new curriculum: 'As pupils progress, they should be able to think critically and develop a more rigorous understanding of art and design' (DfE, 2013a: 182).

The aim here is to provide practical yet theoretically sound ideas to enhance understanding and the delivery of art, keeping imagination, creativity and the nurturing of specific art skills at its heart. Unless the practitioner has a clear vision as to *why* art should be taught and some understanding of the specific skills inherent within it that are not developed by continual synthesis with other subject areas, art will indeed be a service subject with little value or progression.

Art in the primary curriculum

Overview

The National Curriculum for art provides a framework that can be used flexibly for planning art activities. It is a minimum framework, allowing schools to decide how to teach and balance the curriculum (Herne, Cox and Watts, 2010: 8). It recommends no particular artists or cultural traditions that must be taught and does not have a statutory list of practices, but gives the following examples: painting, collage, printmaking, digital media, textiles and sculpture (Cox and Watts, 2007: 2). However, many students and, indeed, teachers assume that there is a great deal more prescription in the delivery of primary art.

The QCA (DCSF/QCA, 2000) schemes of work were born out of the post-1992 attention that the teaching of art was given (Cox and Watts, 2007: 17) – in itself a very positive move for the subject. However, these schemes of work are sometimes considered to be 'the curriculum'. It needs to be stressed that they are not compulsory, schools can follow their own plans, and the schemes can be adapted to suit the profile of the class, school or community. The schemes have a great role to play in supporting the inexperienced or unconfident teacher of art, but they should be amended, adapted and developed as opposed to becoming a standard and static 'recipe' for the art experience within a school.

The importance of art and design

When asked whether or not art has value as a subject in primary schools, teachers will reply, 'Yes, of course'. Yet, if we take this questioning further, there is often some lack of clarity as to exactly *why* it is.

At times, it is felt, and articulated, that art enables the children to have a 'break' from the more rigorously academic subjects, that children enjoy the freedom and 'mess' of art or it is 'good for children to be able to express themselves'. The danger is that, if a subject is labelled as simply 'expressive', it may then be regarded as having no intellectual function (Southworth, 1982, cited in Herne, Cox and Watts, 2010). Such statements can therefore have the effect of trivialising art as a subject and are often the reason so much art teaching is based on a recipe model of activities and skills that are used to complete a predictable and acceptable outcome.

Eglinton (2003) makes a strong and articulate case for art having a fundamental role to play in children's development. Art plays a vital role in social utility (the contribution to and role within society), personal growth (self-expression, intuition and imagination) and visual literacy (promoting knowledge and understanding of visual form, culture and heritage, plus developing aesthetic perception) (Hickman, 2010: 57).

Eisner (1972) raises three areas that should be given attention in art education and these serve as useful points to consider in primary teaching:

- the visual aspect
- individuality
- human consciousness.

The notion of art as a visual language has links with the Reggio Emilia approach, in which children are considered active communicators from birth, their expressions not confined to any one form: 'They move naturally and easily between, for example, drawing, speaking, singing and moving' (Fawcett and Hay, 2004: 234).

> Children see before they speak, make marks before they write, build before they walk. But their ability to appreciate and interpret what they observe, communicate what they think and feel, or make what they imagine and invent, is influenced by the quality of their art, craft and design education.

This quotation, from Ofsted (2012), underlines the notion of a visual language having validity. Visual perception plays a significant part in the learning process. Thinking and observing are crucial skills and yet are all too frequently underdeveloped aspects of art. In primary schools, there are often demands on time, space, resources and purpose, which leads to the main requirement being an achievable, relatively mess-free, storable, 40-minute activity that can be displayed with ease.

No two children are alike and the need for a child to be him- or herself in art should speak for the uniqueness of the subject. Individuality in primary schools could be seen as being catered for by processes of differentiation. However, it could also be said that this is concerned with the rate of progress as opposed to identity. It is the fostering of a sense of self that art can address. It links in to children's experience and understanding of the world around them. Sadly, the production of individual work is not always encouraged. All too often a class group's work is done en masse, following a prescribed format, with children barely able to pick out their own work at the end.

Interestingly, Ofsted's 2012 training resource in art, craft and design does stress that good practice needs to include a focus on the individual. This is especially important in order to raise boys' attainment. Provision was felt to be weak when teachers made the choices as opposed to the children, and learners were expected to use writing as the only mechanism to demonstrate their understanding. Learners' own experiences and imagination had little influence on their work.

Creativity is at the heart of art, yet many would argue it is a misunderstood concept. According to Odena (2001) the term 'creativity' is frequently overused and within education is used with little understanding of what is meant by the word. Fisher and Williams (2004) give a useful definition of what is required for creativity:

- motivation
- inspiration
- gestation
- collaboration.

These four points serve well as an aide memoire when planning any activity. Question what *stimulus* you provide for the children, how you are going to *inspire* their work, how much *time* you need to provide so that ideas can take shape and be reworked. This last point is crucial. If children's work has to be started and finished within 40 minutes to an hour, there is no room for making mistakes, learning from them and redrafting. It is therefore little wonder that children fail to progress and become disaffected with their work. Finally, ask what opportunities there are for teamwork so that the children can spark ideas off each other and learn from each other.

In the classroom   Creativity – the classroom environment

A newly qualified teacher was very keen to facilitate a creative environment for her eight- and nine-year-old pupils. She wanted the children to have a sense of awe and be stimulated by the unexpected and change.

During the half-term break, she emptied the classroom of chairs and tables and filled it with artificial Christmas trees of differing sizes, sprayed with fake snow. Tissue paper was put over the windows to give a different type of filtered light. She made a lamppost from cardboard and had that near the door.

When the children came in for their first day back, they were clearly amazed and delighted, immediately saying, 'Narnia!' She then stood up at the back of the class, dressed as the White Witch and welcomed them to her 'country'. The children were spellbound.

Work done over the next four weeks was completed mainly by sitting on the carpet. The focus was on literacy, drama, art, geography and science. The children talked about this month all year.

As noted above, the National Curriculum for art and design (DfE, 2013a) states that art and design embody the highest form of human creativity. It therefore aims to ensure that all pupils:

- produce creative work, exploring their ideas and recording their experiences
- become proficient in using drawing, painting, sculpture and other creative expressions
- evaluate and analyse artistic works using the language of art, craft and design
- know about the great artists, craftsmen and designers, and understand the historical development of their art forms.

Ofsted found that, where provision was outstanding, the subject made its mark deeply on the individual children and more widely across the school and community.

In those schools, the subject was clearly valued by senior leaders, leaders of other subjects and parents and carers. The best practice was promoted by energetic subject leaders who ensured that the exciting and ever-changing world of art, craft and design was reflected in and beyond the classroom. Their impact was reflected, too, in working environments that were visually stimulating and embraced work in art galleries; self-motivated pupils and students who showed great commitment to the subject in and outside lessons; strong teamwork between staff and with creative practitioners; vibrant displays and challenging exhibitions of work that revealed equally high levels of thinking and making (Ofsted, 2012: 5).

The DfE (2013b) states that, during early primary education, children need to:

> develop their creativity and imagination by exploring the visual, tactile and sensory qualities of materials and processes. They learn about the role of art, craft and design in their environment. They begin to understand colour, shape and space, pattern and texture and use them to represent their ideas and feelings.

Progressing to upper primary education, the intention is that the children (DfE, 2013b):

> develop their creativity and imagination through more complex activities. These help to build on their skills and improve their control of materials, tools and techniques. They increase their critical awareness of the roles and purposes of art, craft and design in different times and cultures. They become more confident in using visual and tactile elements and materials and processes to communicate what they see, feel and think.

It is specified, for the whole primary phase, that teaching should ensure 'investigating and making' includes 'exploring and developing ideas' and 'evaluating and developing work'; 'knowledge and understanding' should inform this process (DfE, 2013b). It is also pointed out that there are cross-curricular opportunities with, for example, literacy, with regard to speaking and listening, mainly in terms of discussion of their own work and the work of others. I will take this notion further below, especially in the section on drawing.

Approaches to primary art

Our own ideas about what exactly constitutes art, craft and design are shaped partly by our own experiences. How much do you know about artists, craftspeople and designers? When was the last time you visited an art gallery? What art do you remember from your schooldays?

Trainee teachers were asked to write the name of a famous artist on a piece of paper. Out of a group of 30, 29 named artists who were dead, all were white, 28 were

European and 29 were men. The majority cited were Van Gogh, Picasso, Monet, Matisse and Leonardo da Vinci. The one female was Tracey Emin. Non-Europeans were Warhol and Lichtenstein. Impressionists were the most popular.

This underlines the assertion that to be an artist you need to be dead, white (preferably European) and a man. This is the model of art appreciation and knowledge many adults work from. This is why, as we walk around many primary schools, we see Van Gogh's sunflowers by 8- and 9-year-olds and Monet's garden by 10- and 11-year-olds. While this has some merit (discussed later in the chapter) it perpetuates a notion of art that does little to increase children's and teachers' ability to create art which is diverse, culturally aware, original and relevant to today's society.

If we consider the range of processes children are able to engage with at school, we might think first of drawing and painting, then three-dimensional work such as clay, modelling, sculpture and multimedia collage. Possibly less likely are printmaking, textiles, digital photography and animation. The DfE (2013a) specifies that, in lower primary, children should be taught creativity in art, craft and design by:

- using a range of materials to design and make products
- using drawing, painting and sculpture to share their ideas, experiences and imagination
- developing techniques in using colour, pattern, texture, line, shape, form and space using clay and printing to a large scale and in 3D
- being taught about the work of a range of artists, craftsmen and designers, describing the differences and similarities between different practices and disciplines, and making links to their own work.

In upper primary, children should be taught to develop their techniques, including their control and their use of materials, with experimentation and an increasing awareness of different kinds of art, craft and design. Children should be taught:

- to create sketchbooks to record their observations and use them to review and revisit ideas, plus collect visual material to help them develop their ideas
- to improve their mastery of techniques, such as drawing, painting and sculpture, with materials (such as pencil, charcoal, paint, clay)
- about the greatest artists, architects and designers in history.

There is no specification of which artists and designers should be chosen. There is arguably less emphasis on cultural perspectives in the 2013 curriculum. The elements of art – that is, colour, pattern, texture, line, shape, form and space – can be viewed as the art 'vocabulary' from which we draw in order to create art. Sometimes one or two elements will be present, while in other activities more will be combined (Cox and Watts, 2007: 3), but they need not be taken in isolation for teaching.

Indeed, some of the most effective and engaging work comes from almost incidental inclusion.

Using the descriptors above as a guide, a variety of processes within art will be discussed in more depth. It is by no means an exhaustive list – there are many more processes, such as printmaking, textiles, collage and using ICT in art. The following have been focused on for their immediacy and ready availability.

Drawing

Drawing, or markmaking, is something that in early childhood is natural and done without undue consideration. This mindset alters radically with age. 'When my daughter was about seven years old she asked me one day what I did at work, I told her I worked at the college – that my job was to teach people how to draw. She stared at me incredulous, and said "You mean they forget?"' (Ikemoto, cited in Aimone, 2009: 8).

Drawing is possibly the aspect that we judge artistic ability by – 'I'm no good at art, I can't draw' is a common statement. Interestingly, children have a shift to this kind of self-perception in art at a very young age. By the age of eight to ten years old, many children will have stopped taking innate pleasure in their own work and experimenting. They will say that they are 'rubbish' and they can't, or won't, draw. This may be because, in trying to draw realistically, children often fall short of their expectations, become disappointed and so increasingly reluctant to draw (Roland, 2006).

A number of theoretical models have been offered over the years to explain children's drawing development and it is generally accepted that, without adult support or instruction, children will not reach the latter stages of development. The question for many teachers is how to facilitate this progression.

Teachers will frequently question their ability to teach drawing effectively if they do not possess the skills themselves. I have heard adults saying to children, 'Don't worry, I can't draw either!' This would be unthinkable if the word 'draw' was replaced by the word 'read'. It is seen as acceptable to be 'rubbish' at drawing, but why is this?

I would argue that it is because people's notion of drawing is incredibly limited. Drawing is seen as needing to be unequivocally realistic, as in beautiful portraits and bowls of fruit. Anning (2002, cited in Burkitt et al., 2010) observed that primary school teachers encouraged even very young children to produce more life-like representations, which soon discourages them in their school-based drawing activities. It is not seen as markmaking in its broadest sense. Everyone has the ability to make marks. Everyone (with the exception of those with severe visual impairment) has the ability to observe, which is the second strand of drawing. Teachers should think of drawing as a verb, not a noun, and see drawing as part of the process of learning, not as a product (Cox and Watts, 2007).

It has been argued that drawing can foster development in observation, communication, creativity and the expression of children's fascinations, fantasies and fears (Power Drawing, 2002). Sometimes a child's drawing can be a reflection of his or her inner worlds, depicting various feelings and relating information concerning psychological status (Malchiodi, 1998: 1). It has value, too, for children with communication and behavioural difficulties and those for whom English is not their first language. Drawing is, therefore, a powerful form of expression and merits time and commitment being given to nurturing it in children.

Matthews (2003) makes the explicit link between drawing and literacy: 'Drawing especially helps the child's understanding of symbols, and signs and representation, understanding that will become crucial in her encounters with sign and symbol systems at home and school'.

In the classroom   Drawing exercises

Just as we warm up in PE, we can 'warm up' in drawing. Provide the children with a line 'vocabulary' to use. Asking children to depict a line that is, for example, 'angry' or very wispy and light encourages them to master the range of tones a pencil is capable of producing and it provides a resource bank of lines that they can then use within a drawing.

A good exercise to introduce drawing and looking with children in upper primary classes is to ask them to draw a portrait of their partner, *but* not look at their paper while they do so. This necessitates drawing very, very slowly and not taking your pen off the paper. You can say to the children that the end results are *not* going to be realistic, like photographs, but they *are* about looking and making your own individual response to what you see.

The big reveal will generate much amusement as eyes are outside faces and mouths below chins, but children can then begin to realise that drawing can be 'imperfect'.

Providing children with a range of drawing materials is essential. This does not have to be costly – children respond well to using felt-tips and ballpoint pens. Indeed, these are particularly useful in that you cannot undo mistakes. It is important to teach that mistakes can be rectified, they can exist and they can be worked around – they are not the end of the world! Good-quality pencils are essential. Children can be taught the difference between a 6H and a 6B pencil from a young age.

Drawing for different purposes and looking at widely differing subject matter helps develop knowledge and skills. Some children are better at one type of drawing than another. Give them the opportunity to do detailed small-scale work with pen as well as larger-scale work using charcoal, for instance. Vary paper sizes. Give the opportunity for tiny work and the super-large. Encourage drawing from different perspectives and angles using viewfinders.

Encourage children to draw at home and ask parents to talk to their children as they draw (see Talk in art, below). Use free drawing as an activity at times other than wet playtimes. Having their free drawing valued and being provided with time to do it can be an important aspect of the school day for a child with emotional and/or behavioural difficulties. It is a mode of expression and release.

Drawing from first-hand observation has huge potential, yet can be a concern for teachers. It can also be difficult if begun in upper primary classes without the children having been used to doing this from their earlier years. If children do draw from observation, they need to appreciate the *observation* part of the process. Take time to look, ask them to describe the object. Look at it with one eye closed. Smell the object. Close your eyes and feel the object, narrating what you can feel. Engage the senses. The children are trying to translate a three-dimensional form into two dimensions, so give them opportunities to problemsolve by means of exploration.

Painting

Painting is not coloured drawing. Painting is, however, synonymous with colour (Cox et al., 2009). Children need to become familiar with colour, be able to name them, to see each colour's qualities and be able to mix colours themselves. It is important to balance building skills in colour with time for freedom to experiment.

Painting can help children concentrate for prolonged periods of time and provide a depth of visual experience that aids memory, prompts questioning, discussion, language and conceptual development and forms the basis for personal expression (Cox et al., 2009: 39).

Painting is also dependent on the materials provided. There is a world of difference between oil paints, ready mixed paints, watercolours and acrylics. There is no reason for even young children not to have experience of all of these. Too many classrooms and art stock cupboards are full of just ready mixed paint in every conceivable colour. When buying ready mixed paint, it is far better to buy the three primary colours (red, blue and yellow) with white and black.

Watercolour paints and palette sets are very useful, especially if painting outdoors. The water element of watercolours needs to be appreciated. If children are left to their own devices, the wet and fluid quality of this medium will not be appreciated. If watercolour paints are to be used, then teachers should invest in good-quality watercolour paper. This is a typical point in art where teachers' knowledge can affect the effectiveness of the teaching and learning. If watercolours are used on ordinary cartridge paper, it will 'bubble' and distort as it dries. This will detract from the paintings themselves. If watercolour paper is used, however, the tool fits the medium perfectly.

If you want to use acrylic or oil paints, rather than canvas, a cheap way of doing this can be to paint on thick cardboard that has been primed with white emulsion.

Children also need to be able to use brushes of differing sizes and qualities. Just because children are young does not mean that they cannot be taught to use fine brushes. Sponges, rags and sticks can be alternatives to brushes, too. Think about ways to add a different texture to the paint, too. Sand, glitter, sawdust, dried pasta can all be used.

Being aware of good preparation within a painting lesson can make a huge difference to its management and success. Such preparation needs to be explicitly taught to the children. Talk to them about keeping brushes clean and cleaning between each change of colour. Have plentiful small water jars (baby food jars are ideal). Instil the idea of keeping the water as clean as possible. Have rags on each table for the children to use to wipe excess water off their clean brushes. Having individual palettes will help children with their mixing skills.

The painting done in primary schools is frequently related to the work of a famous artist (see Using the work of other artists, below). The children's painting experience is therefore one of pastiche. While there are definite positives to and reasons for looking at the ways in which famous artists applied and used paint and colour, it could be argued that it is an easy option in terms of providing a painting activity. All too often the paintings done by children when taking part in activities presented in this way are addressing the *subject matter* or the named artist for its relevance to their own particular theme or topic. They are not necessarily using the artist's work to explore ways of applying paint or understanding colour. Pastiche therefore has far less value than original work done after analysis of the famous work, using it as a stimulus for their own subject matter rather than copying it, for example.

Paint can be explored and used once there is some understanding of colour and colour mixing. Colour is the key. Familiarise children with primary and secondary colours. Put a colour wheel up for reference. Talk to the children about shadows – they are not pitch black. Experiment with painting a shadow from an object, mixing colours to do so, and banning black.

Three-dimensional work was highlighted by Ofsted (2009) as being an area that schools do not address. There are several reasons for this. Space is often at a premium in primary school classrooms. Mess is difficult to deal with or accommodate. Storage space can be a problem, too.

It is worth overcoming these difficulties, however, as there is evidence that working in three dimensions connects more powerfully with children than two-dimensional work, particularly boys (Ofsted, 2009). We also need to realise that young children learn about the world by means of exploration in movement and play. Giving children access to malleable materials, such as clay, and construction materials is not only a tactile experience but it also provides the opportunity for another form of representation, in three dimensions. It is a superb way to problemsolve and encourage collaboration, too.

Clay can be used in primary schools with ease. Clay has vast potential. It is immediate and intensely pleasurable to use. It can be worked on over a number of weeks, if kept moist. It can be an individual or group activity. The possibilities are endless – from pressing leaves into a slab to make prints to the construction of figures, natural forms and containers.

Clay provides great opportunities to work through problems in construction. Children who find translating three dimensions into two (in drawing or painting, for example) difficult, will often surprise you with their clay work. For some children with special educational needs, too, it facilitates their understanding of form and perception.

It is as true of clay as it is of all media – if children are to become accomplished at using it, they need to practise and refine their skills. Therefore, a one-off clay lesson will, ultimately, be of little value.

Papier mâché is another cheap and easy method to use to construct all kinds of things. This can be done in two ways. Newspaper, kitchen or toilet roll can be soaked and mashed to make a pulp. With the addition of wallpaper paste (not containing fungicide), this results in a malleable material that can be used to model objects. Adding watered-down PVA glue will also make the model stronger.

Another way of using paper is to layer it to form a laminate. Strips of paper are soaked in wallpaper paste or watered-down PVA glue and then laid over a frame, building up layers to create a surface. A wide range of objects can be used as or made into a frame, such as wire, withies (lengths of willow), boxes and cardboard. The strips form a layer that hardens and then can be painted.

Large-scale papier mâché projects are perfect for teamwork, with a variety of tasks available to the group. Such work fits in very well with thematic learning and enthuses the children when they see a large creation take shape. Also beneficial is that less confident children are able to find a role within the group and learn from the work and thoughts of their peers.

Sketchbooks

The curriculum specifies that sketchbooks are to be used with upper primary classes. However, the reality is that the vast majority of schools do not use them or, if they do, they are unsure how to use them effectively. Sometimes they are used as you would an art exercise book – that is, to do complete drawings in instead of using single sheets of paper.

The problem possibly lies in the name. A sketchbook is a book for ideas, for thoughts, and should be intensely personal to its owner. Ownership is very important in this context. Teachers should not write in them. Children should become independent using them (Robinson, 1995). I would also encourage teachers to start using sketchbooks themselves. Extend the use of a notebook to incorporate a book for reminders, lists, thoughts and plans as well as incorporating some visual 'notes'.

Another issue with the use of sketchbooks for teachers is determining when and how to use them. AccessArt (2013) provides some practical guidance:

- use sketchbooks throughout the day when children would benefit from thinking around subjects
- start the day with a sketchbook exercise that focuses children's ideas or challenges them to think creatively
- end the day with a sketchbook session that aids the reflection and absorption of learning
- encourage the children to enjoy more personal sketchbook space at home.

The work the sketchbooks contain should reflect each child – his or her interests and abilities. It is the perfect place to write down thoughts, doodle, write out plans or work things out, as well as practise visual and graphic 'notes'. Their use can go far beyond art activities. Earlier in this section there was mention of creating a visual 'vocabulary' and of doing an art 'warm up'. These are perfect activities to record in a sketchbook.

Teachers need to stress that to make mistakes and rework a picture is not a bad thing, it is not something to be avoided. Sketchbooks are a useful vehicle for this. Photographs, pictures cut out from magazines and any visual material that appeals can be put in the book. This will ultimately mean that it fulfils its remit of being a resource.

Photography

In making and using images for different purposes, children will become visually literate in the same way that they acquire literacy by practising using descriptive, transactional and expressive language. Children need to be visually literate to function effectively in a society where visual images enter our lives all the time and everywhere via the mass media, and because so much information is presented to us by visual means in our everyday environment (Clement and Page, 1993).

We live in a digital age and taking photographs with a mobile phone or digital camera is accessible to virtually everyone. This has made photography commonplace, yet it is still not seen a great deal in most primary schools. If it *is* used, it is often to record as opposed to being a standalone art form. Photography is a superb medium for children who have weak fine motor skills and it can also be used to embrace more abstract concepts, so is a useful extension for gifted and talented pupils.

Projects that use photography as part of the work should be encouraged. If the children are going on a trip or a walk, then the camera can be used to record what is underfoot every ten minutes, for example. It is important for teachers to realise that images taken from a child's height are in themselves important as they show the children's perspective on their surroundings.

Rob Fairley, first artist in residence for Room 13 (Room 13, 2012), discovered that the children, aged between 9 and 11, lacked confidence with drawing, so he gave them some disposable cameras.

The students roamed the school in pairs and each was allowed to use half the film in the camera. After a couple of weeks, the students were hooked. They cleared out a cupboard to create a makeshift darkroom and began to experiment with taking and printing their own images. This inspired the young photographers' first professional assignment – they took charge of the school photographs for that year. They photographed every child in the school, then developed, mounted and sold the pictures to parents. The photographs were so good that the company who developed them asked if they would be interested in using their facilities. They did not realise the children were around nine years old at the time.

Staff may worry about expensive equipment being in children's hands. However, there are child-friendly 'tough' digital cameras now (for three- to seven-year-olds) and most children are adept at using such equipment as it mirrors phones, gaming devices and DVDs. Sending children away to photograph things that are important to them or to document a period of time, gives insight into their world and allows them to focus and record things that are important or interesting to them.

Using the work of other artists

'Engaging with artists' work offers children valuable opportunities to explore a range of creative ideas, concepts and techniques' (Cox and Watts, 2007: 136). The dilemma for many teachers, however, is how to use this work in the classroom.

Evidence suggests that, as discussed above, while artists' work is a feature of many art lessons taught to children aged from 3 to 11, its role is comparatively peripheral and teachers select works of art produced by a relatively narrow range of artists (Downing, 2005). Cox and Watts (2007) make the important observation that, while we expose children to a range of *authors* in childhood to extend and develop their own writing, we do not really expose them to a range of *artists* in a comparable way. Also, the authors we choose to show to children are writing *for* children whereas artists will not have considered the tastes and needs of children when they were creating their work. 'Essentially we are asking children to engage with work that is directed at people much older than they are' (Cox and Watts, 2007: 36). Therefore, the rationale for using that work has to be very clear.

The default activity has become one of showing and discussing a famous piece of art with the children then asking them to produce their versions 'in the style of' that artist. As early as 1992, Hughes commented that the act of recording or copying, over a prolonged period of time, may only serve to reinforce for the child the status of the picture as 'text' – that is, lacking in any exploration of any related experience. Therefore, we need to be clear about why and how we use artists' work if it is to have value beyond that of creating good visual displays for the school.

Children do need to know about the great artists, craftsmen and designers, but understand the historical development of their art forms, too (DfE, 2013b). The notion that art alters over time and it reflects the culture from which it came, can help children reflect on people, places and societies. This exposure will help them realise that, for example, not all drawing has to be realistic and art can be created in a multitude of ways, all of which have value.

It is a great pity that, in many primary settings, the cultural range of art is limited. This can have the effect of becoming almost a tokenistic response to 'culture'. Schools are now richly diverse, yet very rarely do teachers use this diversity within their classes to inform their art. For example, the Polish cultural art form of paper cutting (wycinanki) may have more relevance to many children than focusing on aboriginal art. The practice of looking at 'African' art still persists regardless of the fact that Africa as a continent is made up of hugely diverse countries, races, languages and cultural traditions. Seeing 'African' masks being made not only reinforces stereotypes but also does nothing for geographical and cultural understanding.

Allowing children to make connections between their own art and the art of artists, craftspeople and designers can inform their understanding of processes, application, skills and subject matter. If this is to happen, however, there needs to be an element of choice and originality. Children may learn about Van Gogh's application of paint and use of colour by copying *The starry night*, but then are they given the opportunity in follow-up work to explore these methods in their own work? The work of Andy Goldsworthy is often used with children. At best, such study is informed by a good understanding of the artist's intentions. If the children know why his work was created, then they are far more able to apply that to their own original work.

If children are exposed to a range of artists with a range of styles, then they need time and opportunities to synthesise this knowledge and make use of it in their own work. Even young children will have style preferences. If we are to encourage children to enjoy art past the ages of eight to ten, then we must build their confidence in their own abilities. An effective way of doing this is for them to develop their own style.

Supporting children as they develop and fostering the ability to apply their own critical skills in looking at works of art is essential if we are to nurture an enduring interest in art. To do this we need to make sure that artistic experience goes beyond the classroom. Seeing reproductions of paintings in books or posters is a poor substitute for the real thing. Gallery education can (engage, 2013):

Promote visual literacy – helping people develop the tools and vocabulary to experience and respond to art.

Unlock creativity – stimulating people to explore their own creative potential, to make art, and to pursue careers in the creative industries.

Bring cultural empowerment – building people's confidence with and understanding of artists, galleries, arts centres, art museums.

The most effective work comes from schools that have ongoing relationships with a local gallery. Then, children can visit for specific purposes, looking at specific work. There is little to be gained by trawling round an entire gallery or museum. 'The process of sustained looking encourages us to interrogate the familiar' (Cox et al., 2011: 141), so time is better spent looking in detail at fewer pieces, with the aim of articulating thought and opinion.

Planning for art

For some teachers, planning for art is exciting and of central importance. For others, it is marginalised and mainly accounted for by being 'tacked on' to other subjects. As there is little time allocated to the teaching of art for most teachers, we need to ensure that what time is devoted to it is planned so the most can be gained from it.

Flexibility is a quality that is essential in the primary teacher's armoury for planning, but it is also fraught with practical difficulties. Medium-term plans usually follow a pattern of six or seven lessons in sequence. This then restricts any ability to revisit or extend timings. The notion of revisiting is a powerful learning experience yet, as Cox et al. (2011: 110) agree, the impression is given 'that to repeat an activity would be a retrogressive step'. This goes against the very nature of art in that it takes time and is reworked.

This relates back to Fisher and William's (2004) points above concerning what creativity requires. The third point was gestation, yet how often do we allow children to develop their ideas and work? It is no wonder that they become disengaged from art when they have so little room to improve their skills. Once skills have been learned – for example, how to roll a coil and construct a coil pot, and having investigated coil pots in a range of contexts – then children can work in an open-ended way – creating a pot of their own choice (Penny et al., 2002: 47).

Planning for differentiation can challenge many teachers. If we are to correctly gauge a child's ability in art, then we need some insight into what they can create. This is usually decided by the work they produce in adult-led sessions. However, scrutiny of free drawing tells us far more about a child's ability, which should then inform our planning (see Assessing art, below).

A mistake that many teachers make is to *assume* levels of ability in art on the basis of the children's abilities seen in other subjects. Children may surprise you, since they may show ability in art that is at odds with their attainment in other subjects. This works both ways. For example, a child with ADHD who finds writing, reading and collaborative work very difficult, may be able to do detailed and expressive drawings at a level which is mature for his or her chronological age. Equally, a child who is gifted and talented in literacy and numeracy may struggle in art because he or she cannot bear the imperfection they perceive in their 'child-like' drawings.

Extension work does not always have to begin with drawing or creating; it can encompass taking thoughts further and using artwork as a starting point for other media. If children are frustrated by their efforts, then the creative use of ICT, including photography, can be useful. This is far more within the child's control. It appeals to concrete and literal thinkers, such as children on the autistic spectrum.

Some children may have deficits in imagination, some may have weak fine motor skills, some may be developmentally at a lower stage than their peers. These are the types of difficulties that teachers need to be aware of in order to differentiate effectively.

Planning for resources in art is a wide-ranging exercise and has exciting possibilities. The resources available to create inspiring and motivational art sessions are as wide as your imagination, but first-hand stimuli are always preferable. So, if the theme is 'the seaside', then plan to take a trip at an early stage. There is no substitute for this. Take videos while you are there. Bottle seawater, sand and seaweed to capture smells. When doing a lesson on texture, make sure you focus on the sense of touch. To do this, create an atmosphere of focus. For example, ask the children to close their eyes, keep silent and touch something softly, then more firmly, touch their cheek with the object and so on. This is the inspiration part of creativity. For example, when doing a lesson on texture using mixed media, one teacher surprised the children by bringing in her two pet rabbits. One had a smooth coat and one was a fluffy Angora. The children were able to experience the sensation of touch in a way that motivated them. The resulting work had depth and was varied because the children had physically and mentally engaged with the activity.

Make audio recordings, too, as well as taking photographs and videos. This will enable you to recreate the scene once back in the classroom. Remember that the best triggers for stimulating our imagination and recall are all of our senses. Always make sure that the context is one that the children can identify with. If you are in an inner city area of social deprivation, maybe your holiday photographs and images of a Greek island are not going to have meaning for many children. Ask them what their experiences are. If they are of British seaside resorts such as Blackpool and Skegness, then use these to create the context for the work.

Learning outside the classroom in any way is what most children remember. They remember active, engaging experiences. The work done in forest schools has a strong creative element. Here, children spend the day in woodland, mostly self-directed, exploring the environment, playing, creating dens, making constructions and talking to each other and the adults. The absence of resources encourages individual thought processes, the emphasis falling on the process and not on the product (Skone, 2010).

The adults in a classroom are, of course, also a resource. It can be testing for an unconfident teacher to plan for support staff in art. Sometimes the teaching assistant will be left to encourage children and give help where required. This can perpetuate practice that is unhelpful to the children. The adults need to have a common understanding of how the children's work will be approached and what constitutes advice (see Talk in art, below) in order for it to be effective. This is understood in such lessons as literacy and numeracy and so it should be in art.

When evaluating children's work in art, they are often insightful critics of their own work. The language they use in this process can be modelled by the adults. It is at this point in the programme that the success or failure of the creative process can often be at its most obvious. Robinson (2006) asserted that 'we stigmatise mistakes. And we're now running national education systems where mistakes are the worst thing you can make'. We need instead to aim for the children we teach to be able to see the value of trial and error in art, of being able to draft and redraft, and for some things to be more successful than others. However, this can only be done when there is the possibility of the final products being open-ended. If a whole class produces virtually identical pieces of work, then the children will continue to see themselves as failures if their work does not match the pre-ordained ideal outcome.

Assessing art

Assessing art can be a significant challenge for many teachers. Art lessons should have individual expression at their heart. Therefore, the question often posed is, 'How can one judge an individual response?'

It is difficult for teachers to maintain an objective approach to responding to children's artwork (Cox and Watts, 2007). Personal preference forms our responses to art, but we are all able to make judgements while taking away the 'Do I like it?' element.

It needs to be remembered that the purpose of the exercise should be to assess what the child has *learned*. We need, therefore, to gather evidence throughout the process and not simply judge the final product. This can be done via observation, discussion, self-assessment and looking at the final piece.

Teachers also need to be clear on their learning objectives, referring to levels of attainment. Naturally, children will not all progress at the same rate and at the same level, but this is often assumed in plans where it is thought the activity will serve to teach the children a skill. Instead, adults need to consider learning objectives that lend themselves to personalised learning as opposed to 'exposure = attainment'.

Providing children with personalised targets necessitates good prior knowledge of their work and abilities. Providing formative assessment can take place over a short or much longer period of time, but most children respond to feedback and guidance during the activity. The shift has to be made from giving feedback that simply tells the child his or her work is 'good', it pleases the teacher, to feedback acknowledging parts of the work which are successful and parts meriting attention. If this process becomes instilled, then children will respond by being increasingly self-reflective and comfortable with the language of assessment.

In the classroom   Feedback for assessment

Tom, a trainee teacher on a primary PGCE course, was supporting the class teacher in an art lesson. The eight- and nine-year-olds were asked to do a self-portrait using pencil.

There was some preparation in terms of the teacher asking the children to look closely in the mirrors provided and discussion on where the eyes are placed within the frame of the face. Then Tom was asked to move around the classroom, offering encouragement.

In reality, he said that his input consisted of comforting upset and crying children by telling them that their work was good, which had little effect as the children would simply say to him, 'No it's not!' This experience highlighted to Tom that not only do children need considerable preparation in order to complete such a task but also that preparation starts in the Early Years settings. There needs to be an exploration of materials and the building of self-belief in art. The children also need formative assessment that is considered and meaningful. His well-intended praise only served to frustrate them.

Tom targeted his ability to assess in art and developed his understanding of formative feedback. He became adept at using language carefully, asking the children's opinions as to what was successful or needed attention, and offering some solutions. He realised that blanket praise is meaningless and perpetuates the feeling that children have to create whatever vision the teacher has of what is a 'good' piece of work.

Managing art

'Setting up and maintaining a calm and controlled atmosphere, in which children can work imaginatively and express their ideas freely, can be a cause of anxiety for many non-specialist teachers' (NSEAD, 2013). The fact that art lessons can seem disorganised, with excitable and noisy children, can mean these lessons are not always encouraged or enjoyed, especially by practitioners who lack confidence or fear behaviour management difficulties. Therefore, the safe and effective organisation of the learning space needs to be given careful consideration.

Schools differ in the way they organise the time allocated to art in the curriculum. Some schools will allocate it a certain number of hours (or minutes) per week, some schools subsume art teaching time into other subjects and some will block off time per year for art – usually seen as an 'art week'. If art has its own specific time in the curriculum, then this can be when art skills are taught and developed. If art is constantly or only included within topic work, then children's skill levels are far less likely to develop and, ultimately, their enthusiasm for art will wane. Art weeks have merit in that art projects will have more time and energy devoted to them, and art will have more time to develop. However, this is undone if the art week is done once the 'serious' work has been completed. It sends the message to the children that making art is a 'fun' activity and not something intrinsic to their education.

Talk in art

This is an aspect of art that is frequently unappreciated in terms of its place and value. Throughout primary school and beyond, children need to have a dialogue alongside their practice.

As adults, we tend to fall into the trap of offering overly positive comments to children. This is hard not to do as we want to give them confidence. However, children quickly realise that much of this praise is hollow. They know if their work is good or not.

What we need to do is encourage children to be able to reflect on their own work and decide what is effective and what needs attention. We want children to realise that whatever they produce, it is individual to them and that is important. We do not want children to think there is a set 'right' way of doing everything. Talk has a fundamental role to play in this process.

- Talk *with* the children about what they are drawing. Ask them to tell you about their work. This is especially important when young children are doing free drawing.
- With observational work, offer advice and practical help. Remember that drawing is about *seeing,* so your comments can be based on what you see when you look closely.
- Ask the children to evaluate, comment and appraise.

Studies show that children's work matures and they gain greater pleasure and confidence if their work is done as part of this dialogue at home and at school. Narration has a place when working with children who have communication and/ or learning difficulties. As they draw (or construct) you can provide a dialogue, describing what they are doing. This affirms the process and vocabulary to them and has a positive impact on their confidence and attention span. This is a good role for a teaching assistant in these situations.

In the classroom   A change of approach in art

At a primary school in the East of England, standards in the core subjects have been generally good compared with schools nationally, but they have been disappointing when compared with similar schools. In response to these results, the school's leaders decided to focus on improving and extending the children's thinking skills throughout the school. By focusing on the characteristic of creativity for learning, which is concerned with reflecting critically on ideas, actions and outcomes, the headteacher and her deputy planned and led a series of staff development workshops. The staff spent time trying ideas, rejecting and adjusting. As a result of this activity, the school improvement plan was revised and a new approach was adopted that enabled the children to reflect on their own learning in order to improve their performance.

Throughout the school, the children are expected to reflect on their work and, where appropriate, discuss their thinking with their peers and teacher. In this way, the children begin to appreciate the learning process and take more responsibility for it. This results in higher levels of motivation and independent learning.

The teachers, too, gain valuable insights into the ways in which the children are learning and the problems they are encountering, all of which has a positive impact on assessment for learning in the school.

By the age of six or seven, all the children are provided with a learning journal, in the form of an A4 workbook. The children use their books, where appropriate, to describe how they have worked things out. They are also encouraged to annotate their work, showing how they solved problems or how they might improve their work in future. The school uses a child-friendly approach to enable the children to comment on their work:

I could improve by...

I think my work is...

I can do this...

But not this...

(NCSL, 2004: 10)

Reflective questions

- Think back to your own experience of art at school. What factors either encouraged your progress or inhibited it?
- Think about Rob Fairley's view that art is strongly connected with thinking. How much independent and original thought do children put into their art? How can you build on this aspect of creativity in art?
- Consider Fisher and William's (2004) four aspects of creativity. Reflect on providing these elements when you plan an activity.

Conclusion

It is a tragedy that young children start off with an instinctive enjoyment of making marks and building objects with a variety of materials, yet by the age of ten they are usually dismissive of what has by then been termed as 'art' and will say that they are not good at it.

Art education has a variety of processes and skills inherent within it. Each process demands some specific knowledge and will have different outcomes. Yet, there are certain threads that run through art education in primary schools and, if teachers both appreciate and are mindful of them, art can become far more valuable for children.

- Engage in non-judgemental dialogue with each child.
- Give children the time to draft and revisit.
- Give them the opportunity to work in groups.
- Build up art skills as you would skills in any other subject, by providing a 'vocabulary' before constructing 'sentences'.
- Be prepared to personalise your assessment and planning.
- Raise the ceiling of expectation for all children.
- Provide good-quality materials for good-quality work.
- See art as a subject in its own right.
- Consider your own creativity. Develop it and you will see it have a positive impact on your teaching.

Further reading

Eglinton, K. A. (2003) *Art in the Early Years*. Abingdon: Routledge.
This book is highly worthwhile for all practitioners in the primary phase. It has a good balance of theory and practical ideas and clearly articulates the reasoning behind the value of good art provision.

Fisher, R. and Williams, M. (2004) *Unlocking Creativity: A teacher's guide to creativity across the curriculum*. London: David Fulton.
If teachers are to be confident and effective teachers of art, they need to understand what true creativity is and how it can be facilitated. This book provides such a foundation. With this as a base teachers can develop their own creative approaches to art.

References

AccessArt (2013) Visual arts, teaching, learning and practice. Available online at: www.accessart. org.uk
Aimone, S. (2009) *Expressive Drawing: A practical guide to freeing the artist within*. Asheville, NC: Lark Books.

Burkitt, E., Jolley, R. and Rose, S. (2010) 'Art educational issues in the attitudes and practices that shape children's drawing experience at home and school', *The International Journal of Art & Design Education*, 29 (3): 257–70.

Clement, R. and Page, S. (1993) *Primary Art: Principles and practice in art*. Harlow: Oliver & Boyd.

Cox, S. and Watts, R. (2007) *Teaching Art and Design 3–11: Reaching the Standard Series*. London: Continuum.

DCSF/QCA (2000) 'Schemes of work'. DCSF. Available online at: http://webarchive.national-archives.gov.uk/20090608182316/standards.dfes.gov.uk/schemes3/

DfE (2013a) 'The National Curriculum in England: Framework document'. Runcorn: DfE. Available online at: www.gov.uk/government/uploads/system/uploads/attachment_data/file/210969/NC_framework_document_-_FINAL.pdf

DfE (2013b) 'The school curriculum, Primary National Curriculum, Art and design, Key Stage 1'. DfE website at: www.education.gov.uk/schools/teachingandlearning/curriculum/primary/b00198792/art/ks1

Downing, R. (2005) 'School art: What's in it?', *The International Journal of Art & Design Education*, 24 (3): 269–76.

Eglinton, K. A. (2003) *Art in the Early Years*. Abingdon: Routledge.

Eisner, E. (1972) *Educating Artistic Vision*. London: Collier-Macmillan.

engage (2013) 'What is gallery education'. London. engage. Available online at: www.engage.org/gallery-education.aspx

Fawcett, M. and Hay, P. (2004) '5x5x5 = Creativity in the Early Years', *The International Journal of Art & Design Education*, 23 (3): 234–45.

Fisher, R. and Williams, M. (2004) *Unlocking Creativity: A teacher's guide to creativity across the curriculum*. London. David Fulton.

Herne, S., Cox, S. and Watts, R. (2010) *Readings in Primary Art Education*. Bristol: Intellect.

Hickman, R. (2008) *Research in Art And Design Education*. Bristol: Intellect.

Hickman, R. (2010) *Why We Make Art and Why It is Taught*. Bristol: Intellect.

Malchiodi, C. (1998) *Understanding Children's Drawings*. New York. Guilford Press.

Matthews, J. (2003) *Drawing and Painting: Children and visual representation: 0–8*. London: Sage.

NCSL (2004) 'Developing creativity for learning in the primary school: A practical guide for school leaders'. Nottingham: NCSL.

NSEAD (2013) Primary Education. Available online at: www.nsead.org/primary/education/index.aspx

Odena, O. (2001) 'The construction of creativity: Using video to explore secondary school music teachers views', *Educate*, 1 (1).

Ofsted (2009) 'Drawing together: Art craft and design in schools'. Manchester: Ofsted. Available online www.ofsted.gov.uk/resources/drawing-together-art-craft-and-design-schools

Ofsted (2012) 'Making a mark: Art, craft and design education 2008–11'. Manchester: Ofsted. Available online at: http://www.ofsted.gov.uk/resources/making-mark-art-craft-and-design-education-2008-11

Penny, S., Ford, R., Price, L. and Young, S. (2002) *Teaching the Arts in Primary Schools*. Exeter: Learning Matters.

Power Drawing (2002) The Campaign for Drawing's website has resources, at: www.campaignfordrawing.net/power-drawing

Robinson, G. (1995) *Sketchbooks: Explore and store: Art and design for learning*. London: Hodder & Stoughton.

Robinson, K. (2006) 'How schools kill creativity'. Available online at: www.ted.com/talks/ken_robinson_says_schools_kill_creativity.htm

Roland, C. (2006) 'Young in Art: A developmental look at child art'. Gainseville, FL: Art Junction. Available online at: www.artjunction.org/archives/young_in_art.pdf

Room 13 (2012) 'The story of Room 13'. Available online at: http://room13international.org/about/the-story-of-room-13

Skone, J. (2010) 'Thinking creatively', *Early Years Educator*, 11 (10): 24–6.

CHAPTER 3

COMPUTING AND DIGITAL LITERACY

Helen Caldwell and Gareth Honeyford

Learning objectives

By the end of the chapter you should be able to:

- develop an understanding of how digital technologies can be used to teach computing as a subject and enhance teaching and learning across subjects
- reflect on the potential for using digital technologies to promote collaboration and help children engage in meaningful dialogues with each other and with the wider community
- develop strategies for taking into account teachers' roles, use of resources and assessment needs when planning lessons using digital technologies
- recognise that children can use programming tools to become makers rather than simply consumers of digital content.

Introduction

Computing and digital literacy. These three words encompass a treasure trove of tools and devices – laptops and netbooks, tablets and MP3 players, cameras, robots, visualisers and voice recorders, to name but a few.

What these devices share is the potential to bring learning alive by offering new ways for children and teachers to explore and collaborate. Reliable Internet access offers a window on the outside world, meaning that children are not restricted to the contents of the school library to find answers to their questions. They can find out by reading, listening or watching, and they can interact directly with experts or peers around the world. No longer limited to writing their thoughts on paper for their teachers, they can work together, creating professional-looking products and share them with wider audiences as soon as they have finished – making slideshows with sound, animated timelines, interactive blog posts, infographics, Google Earth tours, apps or computer games. The list of creative opportunities is growing all the time.

As Brighouse and Woods (2006: 114) point out, the chance for children to pursue their own questions along media-rich trails of information and develop interactive activities for others to use, makes their learning more personal, purposeful and engaging: 'The learning community can create, receive, collect and share text, images and sounds on a vast range of topics, in ways more stimulating, richer and more time-efficient than ever before.'

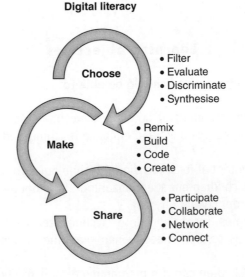

Digital literacy

Choose
- Filter
- Evaluate
- Discriminate
- Synthesise

Make
- Remix
- Build
- Code
- Create

Share
- Participate
- Collaborate
- Network
- Connect

Figure 3.1   Aspects of digital literacy

Our key themes in this chapter, then, are using technology to connect with people, create digital artefacts and capture evidence of learning in new and exciting ways, plus how this involves rethinking what lessons, teaching and learning look like. We will consider how this makes the use of technology special, both as a subject in its own right, computing, and as a tool to enhance and transform learning across the curriculum, and we will suggest how to balance these aims. We have deliberately avoided naming specific tools and software as these are continually evolving and because children need to learn to use a range of platforms and media. Heppell (cited in Le, 2013) echoes this idea when he says, 'Today technology can do anything you like and the tougher question is, "Well, what would you like learning to be like?"' As Figure 3.1 indicates, digital literacy can encompass a diverse and powerful range of skills for teachers and learners.

 ### In the classroom   Driving inspiration

An educational initiative, 'Driving Inspiration', brings together a paralympian, a disabled artist, a class in the UK and a class in Turkey, all of whom are using Skype to lead a joint discussion about Olympic values.

The Turkish children draw designs for an Olympic torch and children in the UK incorporate these into an online animation. Not only do the children take part in a joint artistic project but they also get the chance to learn about disabilities first hand and explore the themes of diversity and inclusion (Mandeville Legacy, 2011).

In the curriculum: computing versus technology-enhanced learning

Computing is unusual in that it is both a subject in its own right and is the tools used by teachers and children to serve other curriculum areas. You will come across terms such as *embedded technology* and *technology-enhanced* learning to describe its use in other subject areas. Think what it might add. It can be used to analyse videos of high jumps in PE, for example, annotate online maps to create an interactive tour of an historical expedition, program a maths game for younger peers or create a media trail around a locality using GPS waypoints. In each of these cases, you could argue that the technology enriches the experience and makes it more engaging. It also helps to capture the learning – that is, keep a trail or record of what has been created or noted, leaving you with something to return to the next day and use as evidence when assessing children's understanding of a topic. Alternatively, you might share it with a wider audience. Used in this way, technology can help you plan and document your classroom activities as well as enthuse your learners.

The difficulty with an entirely embedded approach is the likelihood of tools and devices being relegated to a less dynamic role, such as typing up handwritten stories. A completely discrete approach, however, can lead to disjointed tasks that have no meaningful context – pocket money spreadsheets and party plans spring to mind. What is needed is a balance between learning computing skills and applying techniques, as well as, importantly, a teacher who is able to make the most of opportunities for enhancing authentic learning by means of digital technology.

You will find, then, that you need to bear in mind the twin goals of *learning through technology* and *learning how to use technology*, allowing time for children to become familiar with the tools and software which will become part of their repertoire of transferable skills, as well as time to explore intrinsic topics, such as computer programming. When you use technologies in subject areas, there will often be two learning objectives: one relating to the subject topic and one relating to the use of the tools and devices. As children become confident users of a particular tool, the technology objective may become redundant as this is when, as Stevenson (1997: 18) describes it, 'ICT becomes like electricity – "invisible".'

Using technology for writing is a case in point. An imaginative teacher will look beyond colourful publishing opportunities using word art, clip art and fancy borders and, instead, explore ways in which they can benefit the whole writing process. Publishing online offers the chance to benefit from writing for a purpose and for a genuine audience rather than just the classroom wall. In this way, teachers can use technology to give an activity a 'real-life' feel, maybe as a blog post, a photostory or a video slideshow, a multimedia poster or an eBook. This can imbue a project with creative possibilities and personal choices.

Once the wider scope has been recognised, children have an authentic context for thinking about word choices and how best to organise ideas, as well as stronger motivation to correct spellings and punctuation. This prompts many children to take the initiative and invest time and effort beyond the lesson, to bring their ideas to fruition, especially if they are using free online tools that allow them to continue at home.

Another benefit for those who find writing a particular challenge is that simply removing the need to get writing right first time can give them the chance to produce work they are really proud of. They can try out alternative ways of capturing ideas, redraft without worrying about legibility and produce a finished piece that gives them the satisfaction of truly representing their thinking. The use of a wiki or online word processor provides opportunity for collaborative writing beyond the classroom, allowing children to switch between drafts with ease.

This is not to say that analogue tools such as paper and pens should not be part of the process. The writing journey can involve a mix of thought, talk, drafts, revision and responses, with technology helping children catch and hone their ideas in a classroom buzzing with a sense of shared purpose. In order to make this happen, however, you will need to help the children become familiar and fluent with the digital tools, just as you do with pens and pencils.

As a teacher, you will also need to be aware that there are risks as well as gains in sharing work with the world. It is essential that you repeatedly reinforce eSafety messages in this context and develop 'digital wisdom'. According to Naace (2012: 17), 'Digital wisdom is the ability to make considered, conscious decisions about the use of technology inside and outside school or a working environment.'

In the classroom   Pivotal scenes from history

Some eight- and nine-year-olds are learning about pivotal scenes from history. They are given the task of recreating Martin Luther King's 'I have a dream' speech, choosing from a selection of media tools to do so. One group chooses to create a stop frame animation, another uses an online tool to dramatise the speech, while a third group opts to make an interactive quiz, using visual programming software.

These approaches require the children to represent their knowledge about the topic in different mediums and, therefore, provide an impetus for checking relevant facts. They share their work on the class blog and pick up the theme again the next day by reading comments from parents together on the interactive whiteboard. Although the historical objective was uppermost in this lesson, in other lessons the main focus has been on the effective use of the tools.

The children are developing digital literacy skills by making considered choices about which tools best suit their purpose.

In addition to teaching through technology, we need to build knowledge about computer science as a subject in its own right if children are to learn the language of coding and programming. Not only are these important skills in a world where we all depend on technology, but they are also a great way to enthuse the classroom with opportunities to make and do. At primary level, computer science includes developing understanding of how computers are programmed and networked, how websites are constructed and coded and how data are stored. We also aim to give children an historical perspective, showing them how the field has developed over time and what new technologies are on the horizon.

By fostering understanding of how programs are constructed and what goes on 'under the hood' of computers and websites, we can help children see themselves as makers rather than simply consumers of digital content (Hope, in an interview with McLean, 2012):

> We need to be creators of technology, making games or fighting cyber-crime, rather than just passive users of it.

Prensky (2008) believes, 'the single skill that will, above all others, distinguish a literate person is programming literacy, the ability to make digital technology do whatever, within the possible, one wants it to do – to bend digital technology to one's needs, purposes, and will, just as in the present we bend words and images.' There is a chance, then, to solve problems by applying logical thinking skills. There is room, too, for developing technical understanding using kits such as the Raspberry Pi and exploring computing concepts away from the computer via 'unplugged' outdoor activities, using simple materials such as cards, chalk and string.

✍ In the classroom   Primary programming

Two children from each year group are trained as *digital leaders* within their primary school. They spend time learning how to use a selection of software and are given responsibilities for supporting the use of technology by acting as digital champions within lessons, testing out new software and even assisting at staff training sessions.

The digital leaders also help to run the Code Club with a teacher and a parent who has experience of computer programming. Children attending the club learn coding techniques using a free visual programming language called Scratch (see Figure 3.2) and then apply them to test challenges and solve problems. Their projects are posted on a website run by the Massachusetts Institute of Technology (MIT). They receive encouraging comments from around the world via the site and have the chance to remix and rebuild other contributors' programs.

The children's teacher is particularly proud of the progress made by Stephen – a pupil with behavioural difficulties – as a result of his involvement with the club. Stephen's idea was to create a set of musical motivators for the classroom using Scratch. He worked with a friend to design a background and turn photos into programmable sprites. They wrote scripts to animate these sprites using conditional statements such as 'repeat … until' and 'if … then', so that the users could control the sprites' responses to music. The children put their project through a user testing and debugging process, taking into account feedback from an audience of younger children, before launching it as a five-minute activity to begin the school day for the five- and six-year-old pupils.

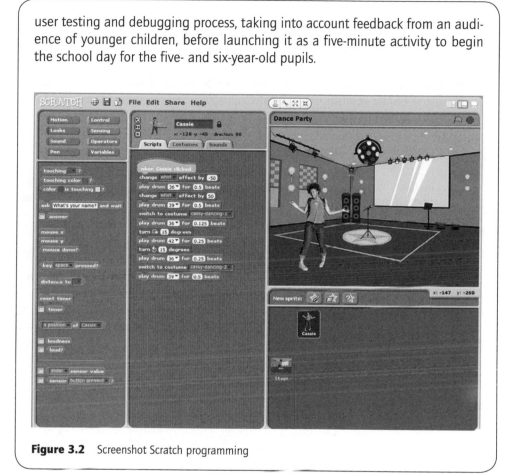

Figure 3.2   Screenshot Scratch programming

As the example above shows, visual programming tools such as Scratch offer opportunities for developing an understanding of how precise sequences of instructions are put together without the need to write complex code, allowing young learners to be creative and successful straight away. Such software enables children to make all kinds of things – interactive stories, animations, games, music, patterns or quizzes. You could use it to demonstrate geometry, coordinates or probability or control models made from building bricks.

Primary-aged children respond well to a problem solving approach to beginning programming. The term 'tinkering' describes the playful nature of this type of activity (The Tinker Factory, 2012):

> Tinkering is what happens when you try to do something you don't quite know how to do, guided by whim, imagination and curiosity. When you tinker there are no instructions – but there are also no failures, no right or wrong ways of doing things. It's about figuring out how things work and reworking them.

This creative cycle has much in common with Seymour Papert and Idit Harel's (1991) constructionist philosophy, in which children are guided to learn by doing and making, in collaboration with their peers.

Mitch Resnick (2007: 1) of MIT also notes that the development of early computing skills has much in common with play:

> Children imagine what they want to do, create a project based on their ideas, play with their creations, share their ideas and creations with others, reflect on their experiences – all of which leads them to imagine new ideas and new projects … our ultimate goal is a world full of playfully creative people who are constantly inventing new opportunities for themselves and their communities.

In practice, you will find that children learn to program at different speeds, but, given an investigative ethos, each individual will learn something new in each lesson. So, it is important to recognise the small steps of achievement for each child in each context and offer scaffolded support for those who need it by limiting choices, providing a template or suggesting just one aspect of a problem to solve. At the same time, you can encourage more able children to follow their own curiosity with the aid of help guides and videos.

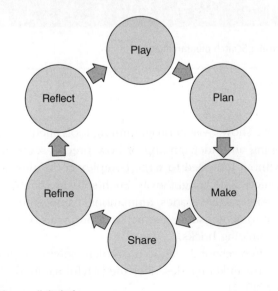

Figure 3.3   Computing as digital play

Approaches to primary technology: digital literacy

A real strength of the use of technology is that it offers children the chance to pursue independently their own lines of enquiry and choose how to present the results to an audience. They can share work they are proud of and receive meaningful feedback, which, in turn, enhances their self-esteem and drive. This has the potential to deepen understanding of curriculum content as the children make meaning together by participating in joint activities, talking and thinking about which information to use in their digital artefacts, which resources to include and whether or not their product communicates their message well.

In order to reach this degree of self-direction, however, children first need to develop the ability to frame appropriate questions and find answers using discrimination, whether they are collecting local data from the school community or globally from online sources. We all have access to more information than ever before via the Internet. This is both a benefit and a problem. Along with greater access to data goes the need to learn information literacy – that is, how to find, retrieve, handle and evaluate information, as well as assess the validity of sources.

As teachers, we need to help children to see that there is more to Internet research than 'cutting and pasting' from Wikipedia into a Word document. The key is to build experience of formulating questions, sift through sources to find relevant and reliable information, then use it in a meaningful way. In lower primary, children might navigate preselected websites and find answers to question prompts. By the end of primary school, most 11-year-olds should be able to select their own lines of enquiry and search terms, checking the accuracy of their findings. Concurrently, they need to learn to be safe and responsible digital citizens, acknowledging and attributing information sources and respecting licensing agreements. The twin skills of eSafety and information literacy must be threaded throughout this work from an early age.

If they are to become digitally literate, children need to learn to manipulate the material they find or generate using technology, whether it is computer code, words, numbers, images, sound or video, and remix and recombine it in meaningful ways. The goal is to be able to do this across a range of devices and tools, so that they are equally at home making an eBook on a tablet as they are collaborating remotely to program an animation on a laptop. As Naace (2012: 7) describe it:

> Having a high level of 'Digital Wisdom' will result in learners who can make decisions about using technology in interesting, creative and productive ways and involves having a 'bigger picture' of all the aspects of ICT and being able to make connections between them.

You can structure opportunities to learn these skills cooperatively through technology across the primary age range.

In the classroom   Red Riding Hood

In a class of four- and five-year-olds, the theme is Red Riding Hood. Technology is used in a playful way throughout the class – the children are taking photos of each other dressing up in the role-play area; one group is exploring leaves using the visualiser; another group of children are recording themselves retelling the story on tablets; others are programming a Bee-Bot to navigate a woodland trail. Three children are being supported by a teaching assistant to compose model sentences from the story and listen to them read aloud on laptops. The classroom is arranged to encourage independence, so there are sand timers for fair turntaking and the children have been taught routines for seeking help or to help each other. At the end of the session, the teacher shares snippets of video filmed over the last hour and invites the children to talk about what they have been learning.

At the other end of the school, 10- and 11-year-olds have spent a term gathering ideas for improving the school environment and are giving peer feedback on their presentations before they show them to governors and parents. One group gathered data on transport and put together an infographic predicting the impact of a car sharing scheme on the school's carbon footprint. Another group has used a 3D modelling program to design a sculpture trail around the school grounds. A third group proposes to demonstrate how voice-recording buttons might be used to make talking bulletin boards for children with reading difficulties in the school.

What these examples have in common is a commitment to using technology to enable children to make real choices about their learning, collaborate effectively with their classmates and help them capture, reflect on and share both their end products and key learning points throughout their work.

Planning: approaches

No other subject seems to evolve as quickly as computing and it can be a real challenge to keep abreast of new developments. In fact, it is literally impossible to be au fait with every new website, app and software package that presents itself.

One key to success in this fast-paced field is to have a systematic approach to curriculum planning, based on a well-designed scheme of work personalised to

Learning intention: Use visual programming techniques for story planning

Good	Great	Super
I can program a character to move around a landscape.	I can program a character to carry out a task to solve a problem.	I can design a scene and program characters to interact to tell a story.

Figure 3.4   Differentiated success criteria for programming skills

your school. This typically begins with a scheme identifying broad strands of learning and an overview of progress across year groups. These strands are then broken down into a series of learning intentions for each year group, backed up by key ideas, techniques and resources. The scheme can then be translated into a set of medium-term plans from which to draw down ideas for lessons and build in differentiated success criteria (see Figure 3.4) and cross-curricular links.

By having a clear set of realistic and achievable aims for each year group clear teaching sequences and planned progression across year groups, you can see where new tools and approaches might fit in, secure in the knowledge that they add to your children's learning in a relevant and meaningful way. This process can help give you the vision and confidence to integrate new digital tools into a robust overall scheme to create a rich blend of learning opportunities. It makes technology the servant rather than the master, supporting the learning rather than being included just because 'it's there'.

Your scheme does not have to be a static document – it is good practice to revisit it each year and allow a flexible and responsive computing curriculum to evolve as you come across new ideas and tap into collaborative spaces. The aim of your planning is to build a strong vision in dialogue with your colleagues and share your successful strategies. For it is in the hands of innovative teachers with a grasp of a range of technologies, in schools with a culture of sharing and strong leadership support, that the use of technology has the power to become transformational, creating learning that is not achievable in any other way.

Does this mean you need to be an expert in computing to be a good teacher? Not necessarily. It is essential, to have the drive to try new things and find ways to make them work. It is also important to acknowledge that teachers learn alongside the children. Although they may not be familiar with all the devices and tools used in the classroom, many children do bring a good deal of expertise with them from home and tend to approach tasks with a high degree of motivation and a 'can do' attitude. The teacher, as a more experienced learner, can help them to channel their learning effectively and promote an environment in which they seek advice from each other and solve their computing problems independently. This 'taught independence' allows the teacher to use adults in the classroom for targeted support rather than troubleshooting and can have huge benefits in areas beyond the use of technology.

Another way to avoid feeling overwhelmed by the pace of technological change is to join the online community of practitioners and see what works for others. It can be entertaining and reassuring to join in with social media groups and webinars, to share links and bookmarks and follow blog posts describing tried and tested strategies. It can then be even more satisfying when you go on to meet your online colleagues at events such as TeachMeets or local cluster groups to share good practice face to face.

Planning: role and pedagogy

A synthesis of research evidence on the impact of digital technology verifies that it leads to learning gains, but suggests that, in order to have the most impact, its use must be underpinned by sound pedagogy (Higgins et al., 2012). This means giving careful thought to your choice of technology and why it is the best tool for the learning situation in hand. Start with your learning objectives and then evaluate whether or not the technology adds anything. Does it help the children achieve something that they could not do any other way? Does it enable access to more content, allow for greater depth or offer alternative ways of exploring content through different media? Does it facilitate comments and input from a wider audience or give instant feedback on performance? Maybe it allows for learning to be more personalised and differentiated, giving children increased choice and control over the direction of their work? Perhaps it is simply more motivating and could act as a hook to engage them with a topic, facilitating 'pull' learning rather than 'push' learning.

The teacher's role is crucial in planning and guiding the use of technology for learning. You need to have the confidence to be a 'guide at the side not sage on the stage' and foster a culture of 'everyone learning together' in the classroom. Children's motivation to use technology is a real plus, but they need a teacher's input to harness, challenge and direct their learning, and help them reflect and extract personal meaning from it.

Nonetheless, there is a real opportunity to tap into their enthusiasm. Think about those children whose untidy handwriting and poor spelling makes them reluctant to put pen to paper at school and whose usual output is no more than a couple of sentences, under duress. Get them hooked on creative computing projects such as making interactive games, eBooks, apps or animations, where writing remains an integral part of the process, but is supported by other media, and often they will spend hours on projects outside school. Feedback from the wider community can give a tremendous boost to their self-esteem, too, and they may begin to apply themselves with an intensity and determination that surprises you – and them.

> ### In the classroom   Using an interactive whiteboard for media and modelling
>
> A Year 3 class is reading *Charlie and the Chocolate Factory*. They use the interactive whiteboard to watch an excerpt from the film and then brainstorm everything they know about the character of Willy Wonka using mobile devices around the room. The children are invited up to the board to drag and drop the resulting character traits into positive and negative boxes.
>
> As a whole class, they edit the words to make powerful phrases and the teacher models how to begin to combine these to write a character description. The children work in pairs to create an animated presentation, combining stills from the film with their descriptive phrases and choosing some accompanying music. Their presentations are shared on the interactive whiteboard using tablet mirroring at the end of the lesson and the teacher leads a discussion about how the combination of words, sound and images enhances the interpretation of character.
>
> In a follow-up lesson, the children use movie templates to make trailers for the film of the book and compose jingles using a music composition app.

The use of technology in the above example leads to a deeper understanding of the text. The high level of interaction helps develop shared ownership of the writing so that all feel they had an input and can use the model as a springboard for their own ideas.

Planning and assessment

Alongside the need to give careful thought to planning is the need to evaluate the impact of the use of technology on learning and the potential to use it as an assessment tool for gathering data to inform and improve your teaching. Robust, continuous assessment and feedback is particularly important as developing technological capability is more about processes than outcomes, more about the journey than the arrival. You can draw on a range of strategies to help your learners monitor their learning journeys and achievements and take some responsibility for their own progress.

As in all subjects, a good starting point is to identify the learning by displaying learning intentions and success criteria and use them to review and refine work. Technology can offer more than this, by giving you a host of ways to capture evidence of achievement. Sharing work in progress online via a learning platform, website or blog means that peer modelling and feedback via comments can become a natural part of the learning cycle. Once the children learn how to make quality comments and engage in meaningful dialogues, the sense of community adds an interactive dimension to their work. In addition, the chance to capture activity by means of recorded talk, film, images and responses makes the learning journey more visible than ever before.

Think about art apps, for example, that can record and play back drawing strokes or collaborative writing tools that record the drafting and editing process so children writing together on different computers can see each other's colour-coded contributions and use a chat window to comment on their evolving piece. Rather than relying on mini whiteboards, consider using personal response systems or 'clickers' via mobile devices to collect polls and display them as instant feedback charts on your whiteboard. Children might record explanations of maths problems or science processes as screencasts, allowing them to consolidate their learning and give their teachers an insight into their understanding. Another option is to create an online 'wall' on your whiteboard and ask the children to share 'what we know' and 'what we want to know' in relation to tackling a programming problem from their individual laptops or tablets. You might leave this brainstorming wall open over time for children to post answers to each other's questions and set the scene for a thoughtful summing up.

Tracking the progress of individual children poses a challenge when computing skills are taught within other subjects and may involve creative and collaborative working. You will need to devise a system for progress tracking that takes account of this and looks further than just the basic skills to identify the impact of technology on learning outcomes. For example, students at Rosendale School in South London have been exploring ways of 'tagging the learning' by assigning categories to personal learning reflections to capture how their understanding evolves over time. According to Tom Barrett (2012), a consultant with NoTosh, this idea has great potential:

> Imagine being able to search an archive of learning reflections captured by the children for the tags 'happy' or 'struggling' – we could tap into a unique view of a bubbling stream of learning right across school.

All of the tools described above increase our ability to tune in to learners' needs and respond by adjusting and refining our lessons. They also offer exciting ways to embed peer and self-review in the learning process so that children can reflect on their own progress – they could even be extended to involve parents.

In the classroom   Assessment

A science lesson for eight- and nine-year-olds on habitats and food chains begins with a review of the last lesson using a video recording of the plenary discussion. This is followed by a quiz on 'animals and their prey' using mobile devices and a pupil response app allowing answers to be displayed instantly.

The teacher uses this information to decide which areas to highlight. The children are directed to 'bunched links' of relevant websites and work in threes to research a food chain. They capture images and ideas as online sticky notes and rearrange them as they find out more. They finish by recording a screencast of themselves explaining and annotating a set of images on their chosen food chain. These are embedded as videos in the class blog and the children are encouraged to make meaningful comments on each other's work. They also use an online diary tool to record three things they learned today and share this over time with their parents. They earn customised online class badges to celebrate their achievements.

By taking this flexible and creative approach, teachers give children the ability to choose and apply relevant technologies for learning, rather than just learn competences or skills.

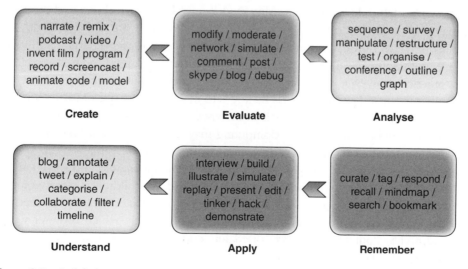

Figure 3.5   A digital taxonomy

According to Ofsted, in the best observed lessons, pupils are given the opportunity to collaborate and critically review their own work and that of others and, as a result, they are able to demonstrate their digital capability at a higher level: 'In essence, pupils need to know what aspects of ICT are available to them, when to use it and why it is appropriate for the task' (Naace, 2012). This idea is illustrated by linking Bloom's taxonomy of learning (Bloom et al., 1956) with some of the varied uses of technology. Bloom et al. offer a structure for considering a hierarchy of thinking skills in which knowledge and understanding are the basis for the higher-order thinking skills, such as analysis, evaluation and synthesis or creativity. Figure 3.5 illustrates how this might be applied to computing and digital literacy.

Managing the use of technology

When planning the use of digital devices, thought needs to be given to the organisation and use of equipment. You may find yourself restricted to a weekly slot in the computer suite or be lucky enough to have a bank of netbooks or tablets. Ideally you will have the option to access technology as a whole class when learning new tools, researching a subject or demonstrating a technique, as well as the option for individuals and small groups to turn to technology at relevant times to support their learning. Children should be able to access relevant devices, such as tablets, voice recorders or desktop computers, in the same way that they might choose pencils, scissors and glue when planning a project. It is useful, too, to have your own portable device for capturing evidence of learning indoors and outdoors, so that you can reflect on it as a class and plan next steps. In an ideal world, you will also have technical support to ensure that the technology is charged and ready for use, with software and updates installed for when you need them.

In practice, however, you are likely to find that access to such equipment and technical support is less than ideal. The key is to make the best use of the technology you do have available and plan well in advance for installations, updates, troubleshooting and unblocking of sites. Computing may or may not be a timetabled subject, but you will still need a scheme of work and robust plans. The use of technology flows much more smoothly if problems are anticipated and solved ahead of time. Trying to use a new tool for the first time with 30 children is never going to be effective. It is best to test software and tools in context, sort out the need for multiple logins, check the school's broadband speed, decide which browser works best and review content in advance for eSafety considerations. It is also a good idea to share the websites and tools you plan to use for the coming half-term with parents.

One helpful strategy is to pilot new software and hardware with small groups before using it with the whole class. This might be in a computing club, with gifted and talented children or those you have appointed as digital leaders (DLs). A DL programme may begin by inviting formal applications and selecting children to interview.

Successful applicants can then be trained in weekly lunchtime sessions until they are ready to take on responsibilities such as demonstrating software at staff meetings, solving technical issues, helping with whole-school blogging and clubs, hosting information sessions for parents and promoting eSafety within the school. They can be given badges to wear and earn online badges, as well as join in with a network of DLs across the country, using a safe social sharing site such as Edmodo. This is a fantastic way to promote computing within the school and help the use of technology to run smoothly, with the added benefit of raising individual children's self-esteem.

Increasingly, schools are exploring the bring your own devices (BYOD) option as another way to increase access and distribute available technology fairly to those who need it. Other schools instigate equipment loans schemes and ensure equality by supplying some equipment for free. For example, you might introduce BYOD by asking the children to bring in eBook readers for guided reading sessions. Children can discover that it may be a real benefit to make use of the sound support and the options to control the font and text size available with such devices.

You may also find that some children in your class with special educational needs are given their own technology to help them access the curriculum. For a child with a visual impairment it might be screen-reading software that reads aloud what he or she writes, for a child with dyspraxia it might be easier to control a keyboard than a pen, for a child with ADHD it might be using a writing framework on a tablet as a prompt and for a child with dyslexia it might by listening to and choosing from word suggestions on a computer to correct his or her spellings. Features such as text-to-speech, word prediction, wordbars, mindmaps and simple screen adjustments can make an enormous difference to learners.

The aim is to create a classroom ethos that supports flexible approaches to learning and encourages all learners to use technology in ways that suit them, without individuals feeling stigmatised for being different and needing support or thinking that they are missing out because they have fewer opportunities to use technology at home.

In the classroom   ICT for children with special educational needs

Katie is a seven-year-old girl with Down's syndrome in a mainstream school. She uses a tablet several times a day for short one-to-one sessions with her learning assistant (LA). They have a folder of familiar apps for practising specific learning targets based on letter sounds, sight words, numbers, colours and shapes. These have been personalised with familiar voice recordings, pictures and word choices.

(Continued)

(Continued)

Katie's LA says that Katie concentrates much better when using the tablet than during pen and paper activities and he thinks this is due to the sounds and animation, the game-like structure, the instant feedback and the way she is prompted by a sequence of steps to achieve success every time. Katie likes to be in control of the device and the pace of her learning.

A separate tablet folder has a selection of role-play apps for reward activities. Katie's favourites are the monsters' kitchen and the animals' hairdressing salon. These apps provide a context for developing her speech and language, as she talks about what she is doing, imagines what the characters might prefer and predicts the outcomes of her choices.

In this example, Katie's LA has made sure that there is a routine to reduce distractions by building in some choosing time. Whether you are using mobile devices for individuals or whole classes, it is important to be clear about your expectations and build this into your classroom management. An 'acceptable use' agreement between children, parents and teachers will take this issue into account, alongside guidelines for safety on the Internet and with social networking sites and emails, policies on using images, online publishing, copyright and data and identity protection.

Technology supporting talk

The use of technology can provide motivating and genuine contexts for developing talk skills and the reverse is also true: talk can be integral to the development of computing skills. Once again, you need to give thought to balancing two objectives: talk as a focus and talk as a tool for learning.

Imagine the potential range and quality of talk in a group of children programming a maths game for their younger peers and taking into account what they know, what themes would be appropriate and how best to make the design accessible to all. Also, think about the positive impact the talk is likely to have on the finished product. The combination of the use of devices and discussion is extremely powerful. Another example might be a trio of children using a puppet app on a tablet to retell a playground conflict by recording animation and voice. They choose the scene and main characters, and are guided to compose scenes illustrating the setup, conflict, challenge and resolution. Collaborating on these stories relies on effective communication skills and taking turns being the leader and director.

The benefits of these talk situations can be enhanced by recording the talk and reflecting on it later. Making sound recordings is an exciting area, with new possibilities developing as tablets and so on make it easier than ever to combine sound with other media. For example, there are apps that let children listen to a story and then record their own version as a page-turning book. Listening to themselves read gives them an insight into what their teachers really mean when they talk about expression, pace and punctuation. Other tools allow children to record their spoken responses to an image over time and then play back all the responses in turn. This is a fantastic way to respond to poems or paintings. Visual programming tools can enable children to create interactive projects for others to use based on manipulating sound recordings. These might take the form of a narrated story with branching choices or a themed question and answer session with a talking avatar.

Such scenarios provide opportunities for developing talk skills and modelling effective collaboration. They open up new ways to share and gather feedback. Crucially, they also offer opportunities to evaluate talk and identify ways to make talk work well as a tool for thinking, communicating and developing ideas.

Another exciting way to promote talk for learning by using technology is to take up the opportunity to connect online with wider audiences. The eTwinning movement offers a multitude of ready-made projects for working with schools in other countries involving the exchange of ideas and joint enterprises, supported by online talk. Some schools make the most of the opportunity to invite experts into their classrooms, too, via technology. For example, one school arranged an online series of lessons in how to produce video games, with input from well-known game designers across the Atlantic. Another school adopted a medical detection dog and followed his progress supporting a diabetic teenager via Skype and email, giving the children many authentic writing opportunities.

Technology can also help build communication skills for children who have speech, language and communication needs. This might be as simple as overcoming nerves by preparing a presentation in advance using a screencasting tool, capturing ideas using a lip-synched avatar, or using a teleprompting app on a tablet when talking to an audience. For a learner with more severe speech difficulties it might involve the use of a tablet device to indicate choices and speak words and phrases.

 Reflective questions

- How would you plan a computing or digital literacy project in your own classroom?
- What tools could you use to help elicit ideas and inspire children to research a topic and plan a digital product?
- How might you capture ongoing work so that children can weave in new ideas as they evolve?
- What computing skills will need to be taught and supported explicitly?

(Continued)

(Continued)

- How might you plan to publish and share your pupils' work?
- How does the use of technology add to the learning in your classroom?
- How might you gather evidence of impact?

Conclusion

This chapter has focused on how technology and computing can enhance learning from a number of perspectives: how the tools and devices can grab attention, motivate and engage children; help them make connections between ideas, capture and reflect on their learning; open up new channels of communication and exciting ways to collaborate; more accurately differentiate learning and make it much more personal; and offer myriad ways to create, make and do.

The key message we would like you to keep in mind is to focus on the pedagogy rather than the technology. Think carefully about how, why and when to use technology and computing and be aware of how both can amplify children's thinking and learning. If you are clear about this in your own mind, there will be a closer alignment of this area with your wider learning aims and the technology will become embedded as an intrinsic and indispensable tool. We would also urge you to enjoy building up your own toolkit of techniques, as your enthusiasm for the subject will be a catalyst for the children's learning.

Further reading

Barber, D. and Cooper, L. (2011) *Using Web Tools in the Primary Classroom: A practical guide for enhancing teaching and learning.* Abingdon: Routledge.
Considers how wikis, blogs, forums podcasting and social networking tools can be used safely to enhance teaching and learning, with numerous case studies of children as producers of knowledge, explorers and communicators.

Bazalgette, C. (ed.) (2010) *Teaching Media in Primary Schools.* London: Sage.
Provides strategies for embedding media education in the primary curriculum and helping children to become digitally literate by developing their critical awareness and using technology for creative expression.

Jesson, J. and Peacock, G. (2011) *The Really Useful ICT Book: A practical guide to using technology across the primary curriculum.* Abingdon: Routledge.

A highly practical guide on how ICT can be taught as a standalone subject and also used imaginatively to enhance the teaching of other subjects.

Laurillard, D. (2008) 'Digital technologies and their role in achieving our ambitions for education'. London: Institute of Education Publications.
Discusses an education-driven approach to the use of digital technologies and draws on key learning theories to develop a framework for incorporating them into the teaching–learning process.

O'Neill, S. and Howell, S. (2013) *Scratch from Scratch: For schools and clubs*. Available online from: www.saorog.com
An introduction to Scratch programming aimed at teachers with example projects broken down into specific tasks and skills.

Rising Stars (2012–2013) *Switched on ICT Schemes of Work*. Rochester: Rising Stars.
A flexible scheme of work for creative computing and ICT projects across the primary curriculum, developed in association with the London Borough of Havering.

Royal Society (2012) 'Computing in Schools: Shut down or restart?', Royal Society, 13 January. Available online at: http://royalsociety.org/education/policy/computing-in-schools/report
Reports on the Computing in Schools project, which investigated the teaching of computing in UK schools and influenced curriculum reforms, giving a higher profile to the teaching of computer science.

References

Barrett, T. (2012) 'Tagging the learning journey at Rosendale Primary School'. Available online at: www.dougwoods.co.uk/curation/tagging-the learning-journey-at-rosendale-primary-school

Bloom, B. S. (1956) *Taxonomy of Educational Objectives: Handbook I: The cognitive domain*. New York: David McKay.

Brighouse, T. and Woods, D. (2006) *Inspirations: A collection of commentaries and quotations to promote school improvement*. London: Network Continuum Education.

Higgins, S., Xiao, Z. and Katsipataki, M. (2012) 'The impact of digital technology on learning: A summary for the Education Endowment Foundation'. London: Education Endowment Foundation. Available at: http://educationendowmentfoundation.org.uk/library/2012/12

Le, T. (2013) *The end of education is the dawn of learning*. New York: Fast Company. Available online at: www.fastcodesign.com/1662358/the-end-of-education-is-the-dawn-of-learning

Mandeville Legacy (2011) *Driving inspiration*. Stoke Mandeville: Mandeville Legacy. Available online at: www.mandevillelegacy.org.uk/category_id__23_path__.aspx

McLean, H. (2012) *New ICT curriculum proposed by Royal Academy of Engineering and BCS, The Guardian, 13 November*. Available online at: www.guardian.co.uk/education/mortarboard/2012/nov/13/ict-computing

Naace (2012) *Naace Curriculum framework*. Available as a PDF online at: www.naace.co.uk/naacecurriculum

Papert, S. and Harel, I. (1991) 'Situating constructionism', in S. Papert and I. Harel, *Constructionism*. Stamford, CT: Ablex.

Prensky, M. (2008) *Programming is the New Literacy. Edutopia*, 13 January. Available online at: www.edutopia.org/programming-the-new-literacy

Resnick, M. (2007) 'All I really need to know (about creative thinking) I learned (by studying how children learn) in kindergarten'. *Proceedings of the 6th ACM SIGCHI Conference on Creativity & Cognition*. New York: ACM. Pp. 1–6.

Stevenson, D. (1997) 'Information and communications technology in UK schools: An independent inquiry'. London: Independent ICT in Schools Commission.

The Tinker Factory (2012) *About The Tinker Factory*. Available online at: www.tinkerfactory.net

CHAPTER 4

DRAMA

Jo Barter-Boulton and Jo Palmer

Learning objectives

By the end of this chapter you should be able to:

- understand how drama can be used in the classroom as a way of learning
- understand the position of drama in the curriculum
- apply straightforward drama techniques to your classroom teaching.

Introduction

In this chapter we will explore how drama can be used in the classroom as a way of learning. The word 'drama' can be confusing and possibly misleading as it means different things to different people. It is difficult to find one clear definition, but it is important that we have a shared understanding of the term as it is used when describing the kind of drama used in primary classrooms.

School-based drama in its broadest sense includes a wide range of activities for children, such as groups making up stories and acting them out in the home corner or imaginative play area or perhaps in the playground, where they pretend to be characters such as Spiderman or animals or famous footballers. This type of drama is known as fantasy play or imaginative play and is usually spontaneous, fast-paced and self-initiated. Children renegotiate roles and the storyline is unpredictable. Being involved in this type of dramatic activity helps children to develop a wide range of personal and social skills:

'I'll be mum, you are dad and you are the dog. Shall we have a picnic?'

'Can I be the dog now? Will you take me for a walk?'

Drama in schools can also be identified as a performance – perhaps a school play with an audience, costumes and lines for the actors to learn. Performance drama such as this, is carefully planned, often by the teacher, who directs the children. The play may be rehearsed many times in preparation for the performance in front of an audience and there is a final product in mind. The children are auditioned and have a script to learn. This can be a really exciting experience for children, but it can also mean that some are chosen for main parts while others are not. Of course, not all children want to take centre stage; some may shun the limelight, whereas others love this type of experience.

All of these drama experiences are beneficial to children, but the focus of this chapter is not on putting on a school play or preparing for a performance in a class assembly. Rather, it is on the importance of using drama in the classroom as a pedagogical approach.

It is in the classroom where drama can be used as a teaching and learning strategy in a creative, active and fun way, where the children are not only involved in thinking and problem solving but also can be engaged with emotionally. Classroom drama puts children in imaginary situations where they have to think and act as if they are someone else. These new situations can begin to challenge children's accepted opinions as they are confronted with new experiences and new people with problems and needs, helping them to make sense of their world and things around them. Using drama in this way in classrooms has been variously described by drama teachers and theorists as *drama in education*, *drama for learning*, *story drama*, *process drama*, *context drama*, *creative drama* and *classroom drama*. All of these terms mean more or less the same thing – that drama is being used as a way of learning, a learning medium.

Classroom drama uses a very child-centred approach, involving the children in working as a class or group to make up a story together in which they can explore characters, solve problems and find out more about what it is to be a human being.

Being involved in dramatic activity such as this relies on all of the participants having an ability and willingness to pretend. The children and teacher pretend they are different people in a different place with things happening to them. They pretend together that they are facing perhaps a moral dilemma, an unusual request, unexpected predicament or challenge. Together they have to decide what to do about it. Dorothy Heathcote (1984), one of the founders of the drama in education approach to teaching and learning, said it is 'like being able to put yourself in someone else's shoes':

> Let's do some drama today! Let's be pirates trying to find our buried treasure. We're on the ship sailing the sea but the only problem is we've lost our map! What can we do? Has anyone got an idea?

Using classroom drama in primary schools is exciting because it has no script as such and it requires no special equipment or acting talent on the part of the teacher or the children. The drama lesson is carefully planned by the teacher, however, with a clear learning objective in mind. It uses a range of drama techniques to enable the children to explore a story or situation. Although the lesson plan is fairly structured, the lesson itself develops almost organically, using ideas that flow from the children's imaginations. These ideas are collected then shaped and further developed by the teacher.

In the classroom   Silly Jack

The teacher planned a drama lesson based on *Jack and the Beanstalk* called 'Silly Jack'.

In the first activity, the teacher is in role as Jack's mother. She welcomes the children as friends of Jack's and shows them a note from her son saying that he has climbed up the beanstalk to the giant's castle. She tells the children she is worried about him. Do they know why he has gone? He hasn't come home. What should she do?

(Continued)

(Continued)

The children are very excited and all full of information about the giant and the beanstalk. Can they help to rescue him? Jack's mother asks for suggestions. How can they avoid capture? What should they take with them? Do they know the way? How will they get past the guard? Can they persuade the guard to let them pass?

The teacher listens to the ideas and uses the children's suggestions to help them formulate a rescue plan. The children use techniques such as mime to climb the beanstalk. They use a collective drawing technique to make a map to lead them to the castle. They also use a game called 'keeper of the keys' to practise creeping up to the castle without being heard. They use persuasive language, too, to convince the guard to let them in. They then use the freeze frame technique to show how they rescue Silly Jack and escape from the Giant.

This type of drama is *experienced* by the children as they take part in the lesson; it is this 'experiencing' that is so important. The children are in the story, they are the people, they are speaking in role and they have to make the decisions or give the advice. Such lessons have a unique quality and empower the children.

Although they are planned carefully and have a structure devised by the teacher, it is always the children who provide the ideas, suggestions and words to bring the plans to life. The teacher does not tell the children what to say. The talk is spontaneous, the discussions unplanned and the outcomes unpredictable. The children have to think quickly and find solutions. Otherwise, in the drama, something terrible might happen. For example, what if they cannot get past the guard? Will Silly Jack be found by the Giant? This dramatic tension is exciting for children and they can feel an urgency and a responsibility to make decisions.

One of the most exciting things about this way of working is that everyone works together in the story to create an imaginary environment in which they can all 'take on different roles'. When the teacher also pretends to be a character in the story, the technique is known as *teacher in role* (TIR). This allows the children to meet a whole range of different people who all have different problems and issues that they can help to solve. The teacher is completely involved in the lesson and the action, rather than acting as an observer or director. For example, setting a scene as follows:

Let's do some drama today! In our story we are going to find out what happened when some explorers were on an expedition in an unexplored jungle. I'm going to pretend to be Ms Collins, the Chief Explorer, and I am asking you to be famous explorers who have come to a meeting.

This, of course, necessitates the children and teacher suspending their disbelief for the duration of the drama lesson. The children have to imagine that the teacher is a dragon or perhaps a Roman soldier in the drama on any given day. Joining in with a pretend situation is usually not difficult for children as this kind of activity is closely related to the imaginative and fantasy play in which children from most cultures regularly engage, but it can be harder for adults to lose their inhibitions and play with the children in this way.

Some teachers are under the misapprehension that they need to be good at acting. This is not the case, as using drama involves taking on a character or role that can be indicated by the slightest change of voice, stance or action. Children respond really well to teachers pretending to be someone else. It is like a shared secret – 'we all know that you are really still our teacher, but we are willing to go along with your game and "believe" that you are a pharaoh as it sounds fun.' They can then learn about the pharaoh's life in role as one of the planners designing his pyramid, rather than just from reading about pharaohs in books. They can talk 'in role' (as the planners) to the TIR (as the pharaoh), choosing their language carefully so as not to offend him and using their skills to design a pyramid that pleases him.

This active approach to learning enables children to find out about people, situations and themes from *inside* the story. They *are* the people in the story. Things are happening *to* them and they have to react accordingly.

It is in the nature of most primary school teachers to 'have a go' at using different teaching and learning approaches and, once they have been involved in a drama session with children, teachers usually recognise what a powerful and fun approach it is.

In the classroom   Pirates and kings

In one classroom drama the children met the teacher in role as an unhappy pirate. The children questioned him and found out that he had lost his crew and his ship. They helped solve the problem by volunteering to be his crew and helped the pirate to become happy again by building a new ship for him and going on an adventure to find buried treasure. The children gave support and encouragement as well as practical solutions.

In another drama, the children met the teacher in role as a king who had to arrange a surprise anniversary party for his wife. They discovered that the king had never arranged a party before and did not know what to do. They helped

(Continued)

(Continued)

him to plan a wonderful party, showing him how to decorate the room and make cakes. This empowered the children by putting them in the teaching role and using their superior knowledge of parties.

Sometimes the children can solve practical problems for characters in a drama. In one, they helped Albert, a painter and decorator who had hurt his back and needed help to finish a job. In another, the children confronted a dilemma about the rights and wrongs of building a waste recycling depot near to a children's playground.

In drama, children are encouraged by teachers to think beyond their own point of view. They are put into fictional situations and encouraged to see the world from someone else's perspective or viewpoint. Sometimes this challenges what they may have always accepted or believed and makes them reflect on their views and understandings. If the situation is difficult or challenging, they will work together to sort things out.

One of the special qualities of classroom drama is that it is fiction. It may reflect reality, but the children are only pretending. The teacher can stop the fiction at any time and step out of the drama to talk about what is happening. The children can talk about and reflect on how they feel about the drama or the people and explore how this story relates to their real lives. It is crucial that the teacher helps the children to make links between the pretend fictional story and its characters and their real lives or real situations in the world.

Classroom drama is also a way of exploring difficult issues, such as, 'What can we do about bullying?', 'Is there a solution to global warming?', 'How can we confront prejudice?' Through drama, these issues can be explored while the children remain in the classroom, in a 'safe' fictional situation.

In the classroom   Real-life issues

In a class of eight- and nine-year-olds, the teacher was using drama to explore the issue of sibling rivalry, bullying and family relationships, using the fairy tale of *Cinderella* as the context.

The children met the teacher in role as Cinderella and asked questions using a hot seating technique to find out why she allowed her sisters to treat her so badly. They suggested some possible strategies she could use to persuade her sisters and, without the aid of a 'Fairy Godmother', empowered Cinderella to become more assertive and 'go to the ball'.

It was then the teacher's task to discuss what had happened and how the children had helped in this situation. It was also important to universalise their learning so the children could appreciate how this advice could apply to anyone who might find themselves in a situation where they felt disempowered.

Classroom organisation

Teachers sometimes shy away from using drama, fearing the children may 'mess about' or that there is not enough time on the timetable or space in the classroom or, perhaps, thinking they lack the right skills. We would argue that all primary teachers have the basic skills they need to use drama in a classroom.

The classroom itself is the best place to do this kind of drama work. Just clear away the tables to provide enough space for the children to sit in a circle and then the learning space is ready. If you have to use a bigger space, such as the hall, it is a good idea to mark off an area with benches. Children often have preconceived expectations of the hall, as, when they have PE or dance, they are told to use all the space. For drama, however, it is important to have a more controlled area. It is also important for the teacher to tell the children how they are going to gain attention when they are working – for example, by clapping or using a countdown.

Children become very involved in their work in drama, so you need to be clear about the 'rules of the game'. It is important that you make your expectations clear to the group with respect to behaviour and engagement. By reminding the children that the same classroom rules apply in drama as in all other lessons, they will then be in no doubt about the parameters.

It is also useful to tell them that they have everything they need to take part in the lesson and they will not need to use objects from the room to help them. You could illustrate this by miming some simple tasks, such as brushing your hair or cleaning your teeth, modelling to the children what is expected.

Drama in the curriculum

Drama is used as a teaching approach by many classroom teachers who value its flexibility, interactivity and creativity. Drama is identified as a curriculum subject at secondary level, but is not a subject in its own right in primary schools. It is now generally accepted by primary practitioners as a non-negotiable pedagogical approach.

There is certainly content to learn, particularly the terminology used to describe the ways of working (such as *hot seating* and *conscience alley*), but children soon learn what is meant and how to use these techniques. It is also important for teachers to know a range of simple techniques that they can use as needed. These techniques can be part of the creative teacher's toolkit, to be used as an alternative to watching a film clip, completing a worksheet or researching on the Internet.

As drama is such an exciting and interactive approach to teaching and learning, every child should be involved, not only within English lessons but also across the curriculum, where drama can support learning in a wide range of subjects, particularly history and religious education. You may sometimes decide to use drama techniques as short, one-off activities, perhaps within a literacy or history lesson – an approach that can appeal to inexperienced or less confident teachers. You could decide to use drama in an English lesson – to hot seat Humpty Dumpty, for instance, to find out more about him as a character. 'Why was he sitting on the wall in the first place?' You could choose to use a 'time machine' technique in a history lesson to find out about the feelings of World War II soldiers on the night before they crossed the English Channel on D-Day. These and other short drama activities will allow the children to deepen their understanding of particular characters or moments.

In English lessons teachers provide opportunities for children to participate in a range of drama activities to explore situations and characters perhaps linked to books and stories. Drama can be used to find out more about the motivations of characters, exploring their thoughts and feelings. It can also provide the teacher with the context for different types of talk and lead on very naturally to writing activities.

In the classroom   *Mary, Mary*

In an English lesson for five- and six-year-olds, the children were exploring the story *Mary Mary* by Sarah Hayes and Helen Craig (2004).

The teacher took on the role of the Giant, who was sad because he had no friends. The TIR was hot seated by the children and offered some advice. After the drama, the teacher discussed the Giant and how the children had helped him. This led on to a writing activity in which the children wrote in speech bubbles, giving advice to the Giant.

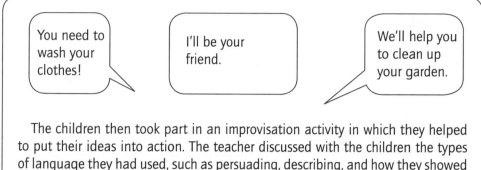

You need to wash your clothes!

I'll be your friend.

We'll help you to clean up your garden.

The children then took part in an improvisation activity in which they helped to put their ideas into action. The teacher discussed with the children the types of language they had used, such as persuading, describing, and how they showed they were 'being friendly' by the tone of voice they used.

Approaches to primary drama

The ways in which you use classroom drama will, to some extent, depend on the age of the children, your and their experience and confidence levels and the theme or content to be explored. Younger children may be introduced to drama activities by working in role and creating imaginary scenarios with the teacher or teaching assistant, who can sensitively join in with role-play situations in the home corner or imaginative play area. Often children and teacher decide together what they would like their play area to be and they will help the teacher to create the environment.

A sensitive adult joining in with children's fantasy play can provide a model for them about how to interact and respond, how to work together in a group and listen to each other's ideas. The adult can also help to add structure by providing ideas for a story, offering possibilities, suggestions or a new direction and even suggesting new characters. This does not mean that the story belongs to the adult, but they can help to open a child's thinking up to things outside their experience, possibly support children who are quiet and lacking in confidence and also extend and motivate the children's language use.

In the classroom   Growing

The theme for the term's work for a class of five- and six-year-olds was 'Growing'. The children and teacher discussed the possibility of changing their outside play area into different environments linked to this topic and decided on a garden centre that would include a pet and aquatic centre.

(Continued)

(Continued)

The children helped to design the garden centre, decided what tools and equipment were needed and helped to make resources using art and design and technology skills. The teacher and the teaching assistant helped the children to create the environment and filled the sand tray with compost to use as a potting bench. Plastic pots were collected and then there was a discussion with the children as to how they might be used – 'What jobs could the people who work in the garden centre do?', 'What kinds of people might visit the garden centre?' Props and items of costume were provided to help the children get into role.

The teacher joined in the children's play and demonstrated how to mime a range of jobs, such as digging and weeding. The teacher also modelled the correct terminology for equipment, such as rake, trowel, mower. The teacher and children discussed possible scenarios, such as a lady who is looking for a present for her friend and a man who has come to the garden centre to apply for a job.

The children were given time in groups to play freely in the garden centre as part of their daily programme and develop new characters and stories which were then shared with others.

On other occasions and certainly with older children, the teacher would work with the whole class and use dramatic techniques to structure a drama lesson to help the children explore characters and issues in a story drama. This might take a whole morning to complete or a number of sessions. The drama is developed using a range of techniques, such as hot seating, teacher in role and conscience alley. These are introduced to the children and used as appropriate in the context of the drama. It is important that you teach the children how to use these techniques so that they feel comfortable and know what is expected.

Some key techniques for drama in primary classrooms

Hot seating

Hot seating involves one person taking on the role of a character and being asked questions by the rest of the class. The person sits on a chair and speaks as though he or she was the character. It is useful with younger children if the person in role identifies when he or she is in role by wearing an item of clothing or carrying a prop.

To begin with, the teacher is usually the best person to sit on the hot seat to model the technique, as it can be quite a challenge for a child to know how to reply to the questions asked. Of course, teaching assistants can be briefed to take on the role and sit on the hot seat while the teacher manages and organises the children to ask questions.

Sometimes, the hot seat technique can be used as a way to provide information to a group. Then the teacher is the best or only person to do this.

In the classroom   Fairy 13

In the story of *Sleeping Beauty*, the teacher was in role as 'Fairy 13', as the children called her.

The children, in pairs, discussed what questions they would like to ask Fairy 13. This gave them ideas before the hot seating session began. The TIR then sat on the hot seat and was questioned by the children, also in role as the other fairies, about why she cast the spell on the baby princess. The teacher wanted the children to ask questions in order to learn about the motivations and emotions of the character.

By using this technique, children can be given information without being told by the teacher. Instead, they can discover it by asking carefully framed questions. The children decide individually or in pairs what questions they want to ask and can directly question the character on the hot seat to find out the answers. They have to think of the best questions and also the best ways of asking them. The children can ask the questions as themselves or in role, as others in the drama.

Teacher in role

In the classroom   TIR

In the story of *Sleeping Beauty*, the children were in role as reporters, questioning the TIR as the Prince about what he found when he entered the palace. This provided them with enough information to then write a newspaper report on the events.

Improvisation

Another familiar drama technique is *improvisation*. This involves the children pretending they are different people and acting and speaking in role. Unlike other forms of drama, an improvisation is not planned or prepared in advance, but is a spontaneous piece of dramatic activity. A teacher in role will often lead an improv-isation, though, to ensure the class stays on task and all are working together within the fictional world set up at the beginning.

In the classroom   Housekeeper

The teacher told the children they were going to meet a character who was going to be in the drama and they would have to listen carefully to what the character said so they could pick up clues to learn who they were going to be in the drama and what was going on.

The teacher then entered the group in role as a housekeeper in the palace at the court of Sleeping Beauty's father. She welcomed the children as local villagers who had applied for jobs in the palace. The children responded to the housekeeper in role as the villagers and were immediately involved in speaking as characters in the drama, quickly adapting their speech to the new context.

Conscience alley or thought tunnel

In this technique, the children look closely at a particular moment in a drama. It is usually used when there is a decision to be made by a character, but sometimes the children are asked to give advice to the character. It is important that the children are told what they will be asked to speak about and have a clear understanding as to whether it is advice that they will be giving or they will be speaking aloud the thoughts of the character.

In both forms of this technique, the children stand in two lines, facing each other and about a metre apart, forming a passageway for the teacher to walk slowly along. In a *conscience alley*, the teacher, in role as the character, walks from one end to the other, then turns to a child on one side and then to a child on the other and the children speak as if they were the character.

In a *thought tunnel*, the teacher, in role as the character, moves through the tunnel in exactly the same way, except this time the children are encouraged to speak aloud a word or line that they have prepared.

In the classroom   Prince

In the story of *Sleeping Beauty*, the teacher took on the role of the Prince as he walked along the thought tunnel, which was described as a pathway, overgrown with tangled briars, that led to the palace. The children created a tunnel for him to walk through by holding hands across the top of the tunnel.

As the teacher in role made his way along the path, the children called out warnings to him, saying, 'Take care!', 'Don't go in there!', 'Hurry up!'

The conscience alley and thought tunnel activities offer a different way to hear a character's thoughts and feelings spoken aloud. It also allows the children to learn more about the characters on a different, perhaps more emotional, level.

In the classroom   In the alley

In the story drama of *Sleeping Beauty*, the children formed a path to the palace and the teacher, in role as Fairy 13, walked along it on her way to the christening party to which she has not been invited.

The children spoke the fairy's thoughts – 'Why have they left me out?', 'It's not fair!', 'I am going to cast a spell on that baby.'

Alleys or tunnels can be curved, to represent contexts such as a winding path, or straight, to represent a corridor leading to an important room. However, straight lines enable children to see and hear each other more clearly.

Freeze frame

Teachers just starting to use the approaches described so far will often plan lessons carefully to make sure they address the particular learning needs of their group. For example, if the class is challenging, lively or new to drama, the teacher may choose to use a more controlled technique that limits the children's physical movement in the classroom. One of the most popular drama techniques that fits into this category is called *freeze frame*. It is sometimes called *still image*, *frozen picture* or *tableau*, but all these terms essentially represent the same approach.

The technique focuses on body language and facial expressions to portray emotions. Freeze frames are very flexible and used in a variety of ways, depending on the learning intention for the lesson. They involve the children imagining that they are people or sometimes objects in a three-dimensional picture, depicting a scene or a particular moment. The moment is frozen in time and can be likened to a photograph or a painting in which time has 'stopped'. Other groups are invited to look at the 'picture' closely and read what they can see.

This develops children's visual literacy skills as they have to read the signs provided by the people creating the image. Equally, of course, this means that the children creating the freeze frame have to be really careful as to how they create their picture. They have to consider how their body language, facial expression, proximity and positioning are showing exactly what they mean to convey.

In the classroom   Friendship

In a freeze frame created by a group aiming to show the friendship between two people, consideration was given as to whether showing the two people standing side by side, not touching, or face to face, shaking hands provided the most clarity for the observers.

Freeze frames can be created by small groups or by the whole class working together. For example, the whole class could work together to create a freeze frame of the birthday party for the Princess in the story *Sleeping Beauty*. A freeze frame can be created quickly or it can be built slowly, adding one person at a time. This slower image-building approach gives children time to think about and respond to what others are doing in the picture by placing themselves in a carefully chosen position that relates to the others. For example, if the class is creating a collective freeze frame of the christening scene in *Sleeping Beauty*, a child seeing someone else pretending they are setting up a table of food may decide to stand nearby, as if they are guests waiting to be served.

Figures in freeze frames can be spoken to by being tapped on the shoulder and asked questions about something that is happening or asked to speak their thoughts and feelings. Freeze frames can also be brought to life, so the characters interact with each other, improvising what is happening. This can be done using mime or it can be with added speech.

It is also possible for the children to create images and imagine they are pictures that are going to be in a book or perhaps photographs for a newspaper. They can decide as a group what would be written in a caption under the picture.

The teacher can use a digital camera or tablet to take a photograph of the freeze frame and the children can be encouraged to evaluate their work. These photographs can, in turn, be used to make a class storybook or wall display of the story, with the captions written underneath.

Mantle of the expert

The *mantle of the expert* technique puts the children into the role of experts on a specific area.

In the classroom   Bugs

A group of seven- and eight-year-olds were told that they were expert entomologists and were welcomed by the TIR to a meeting of the Royal Entomological Society. The TIR, as Chairperson, explained that, as they were all such well-known experts, they might be able to help with the search for a species of beetle becoming extinct in Fiji.

The children seemed to 'grow' into the role of being important experts and put forward ideas about what needed to be done in quite formal language.

When teachers are more confident or if they are working with older or more experienced classes, they may consider asking the children themselves to suggest how the drama might unfold and which techniques could be used. Of course, the more drama the children experience, the better they will be at understanding how it works and what value there can be in using the different drama techniques. Indeed, experienced groups will often devise their own techniques if an existing one is not quite providing what is needed.

In the classroom   Wolf dilemma

A class of nine- and ten-year-olds were working in drama on the story *Red Riding Hood*. This was the second lesson of a unit and the planned outcome of which was for the children to be able to put forward an argument for and against a decision.

The teacher asked the class which drama technique they could use to explore the inner thoughts and feelings of the wolf at the moment before he entered Granny's cottage. The class discussed the possibility of using a thought circle, but decided on using a conscience alley technique, as this was physically more appropriate, the shape echoing the curve of a woodland path.

(Continued)

(Continued)

The children stood in two rows representing the path to Granny's door and, while the TIR as the wolf crept along, they spoke his thoughts aloud – some encouraging and some discouraging him. They decided to add a controlled physical movement to their words, which they considered would add tension to the activity. Some chose to step forward, as if barring the wolf's way, while others covered their eyes as if to show they did not want to see him make a wrong decision.

Planning and managing drama in the classroom

Teachers structure and organise drama lessons to ensure that all children have access to the story and are taught how to take part in the drama techniques. Classroom drama is a very inclusive way of working as everyone can take part, bringing all their own thoughts and ideas to it, which can be shared and discussed. Indeed, children who find writing challenging may experience drama as a very accessible way of learning for them. Less confident children, too, will be given the opportunity to work in role as someone who might be far more confident than they are! Teachers will observe and monitor the children's involvement, making notes about particular children's engagement.

For a successful drama lesson, first of all you need to consider a number of factors.

- *How you want to use drama* Do you want to use selected drama techniques within lessons or do you want to plan and teach a whole-class drama lesson that will explore a story or poem in depth?
- *What you want the children to learn from using the drama approach* Is it to practise using language in context or is it to learn facts about the life of Florence Nightingale?
- *What space, time and resources are available to you* Is the room big enough?
- *Whether or not the children have had experience of drama* Do you need to teach them some drama techniques?
- *How committed you are to using and understanding the drama process* Do you know a range of techniques that you can choose from?
- *How you might enhance the drama* By using props, costumes, music, sound effects or pictures on an interactive whiteboard that could be used to display a picture as a backdrop for the drama.

In the classroom   Brick wall

With a class working on the story *Humpty Dumpty*, the teacher chose to use a picture of a brick wall on the interactive whiteboard and, during a hot seating activity, she sat on a stool in front of the screen to add to the children's experience.

Talk in drama

For children to become confident and competent readers and writers, they must be confident speakers and listeners. With this in mind, drama would appear to be an obvious starting point to encourage talk in the classroom, as talk is such a key aspect to this pedagogical approach. The responses from the children result in what is known as *dynamic drama talk*. Talk in drama allows children the opportunity to experience the diversity of spoken language and use it in context. This therefore supports them in developing speaking and listening skills through activities such as paired, group and whole-class tasks.

When using TIR, the talk will be between the teacher and the children in the first instance, with the teacher setting the scene and introducing the character to the children. Questions should be planned and asked by the teacher that will encourage the children to respond in a thoughtful manner, exploring different solutions to problems presented to them. It is important that the questions are open rather than closed, allowing exploration to take place.

Children's responses to the questions asked by the TIR can then be explored in the drama. The children can be involved in paired, group or whole-class activities, possibly even a combination of all three to do this. In each of these groupings, different language demands are put on the children. Asking questions of the TIR is an excellent way for them to discover more about a character or situation. They could also make suggestions and help to determine the direction the drama takes. Children can also be involved in group discussions focusing on their reflections on the effectiveness of the drama, enabling them to evaluate and justify their thoughts and ideas. Even though the teacher, in the first instance, will lead the drama when in role, the children will take more ownership as it develops.

In the classroom   Being evacuated

The teacher of a class of 10- and 11-year-olds was in role as a child being evacuated from London during World War II. The scene was set and the TIR explained how he was feeling worried about being evacuated and leaving his family behind. He then posed a question, asking the children if he should go or tell his parents that he wished to stay in the city.

A group discussion took place, during which the class worked together to persuade the evacuee to go to the countryside. The teacher, still in role, actively listened to the children's advice and chose to leave the city as a result, making it clear he still had concerns about leaving his family behind, but acknowledging the realisation that going away was the safest thing to do.

(Continued)

(Continued)

The teacher came out of role and explained that the children were going to meet the evacuee again, after the evacuation had taken place. It was also explained that they would hot seat the evacuee to see if they felt the right choice had been made and how the child had felt about being away from home. The children worked in pairs to plan questions to ask the evacuee during the hot seating activity. They were reminded of the intentions of the activity, ensuring that their questions were focused.

The teacher then returned in role as the evacuee and was hot seated. As the drama unfolded, some children decided to change their questions, as a result of the responses of the TIR – possibly because their questions had already been asked or had been answered in another route of questioning.

Through this drama activity, the children were developing skills in speaking, listening and reflective thinking. This was demonstrated by their ability to evaluate their questions and adapt them as the drama progressed.

Another way in which talk can be used effectively within a drama is by means of a debate. In this format, the children can practise using persuasive language in context. Providing them with opportunities to rehearse using vocabulary verbally, rather than expecting children to know how to use this language in written form, immediately enables the more confident use of new language. As with any teaching method, good practice will see the class teacher modelling this to the children and, therefore, being in role. Indeed, all adults may have a role to play to allow opportunities for appropriate language to be modelled.

Teachers always encourage children to use vocabulary in context and drama is an extremely effective tool for providing children with opportunities for this. Using techniques such as role-play, hot seating, debate and having role-play areas allows the children to practise and rehearse vocabulary learned within taught sessions, in context and in a safe and stimulating environment.

In the classroom   Trial

A teacher of seven- and eight-year-olds set up the classroom as a courtroom after studying the traditional *Red Riding Hood* tale. During previous lessons, the characters of the story had been explored by means of hot seating, freeze frames and TIR.

The teacher set the scene for a trial that was to take place in the court-room. The Wolf had been arrested for breaking into Grandma's house and behaving in a threatening manner towards both Grandma and Little Red Riding Hood.

The children were organised into groups – those who were to be the prosecution, those who were the defence, witnesses and the jury. The teacher was in role as the judge, with the teaching assistant in role as a jury member.

The children had to work in small groups to discuss and plan the arguments to put forward in court. By carrying out the trial, the children were able to practise using persuasive language in context as they had to persuade the judge and jury. As well as this, they were able to practise using questioning in order to obtain the information required to strengthen their argument.

How you might plan your own drama to explore *Sleeping Beauty* with seven- and eight-year-olds

It is useful to begin by deciding what your learning outcome will be. In this lesson, let's say we want the children to understand that everyone should be made to feel welcome in their community.

To plan such a lesson, it is sometimes useful to work backwards from this point and consider which drama techniques it will be best to use. Jot down ideas – you can structure them into a lesson later. Consider using a range of drama techniques to give the children different opportunities. Some techniques are more physically demanding, while others demand more speech. Some are individual activities, while others involve children working in groups. It is for you to decide which activities to use and in which order, taking into account the needs and experience of the children you will be working with. Similar ideas could be used with younger or older children. Drama lessons are always very adaptable and certainly one based on a traditional tale such as this can be used throughout a primary school.

Always have in mind what it is you want the children to be doing and also learning from the activities. It may be that your focus will be on using persuasive or descriptive language, practising speaking in role or analysing a character's motivation. All of these are possible within a drama. It could spoil the drama, however, if you tell the children at the beginning what the learning objective is, so it could be more valuable to discuss this at the end of the drama. The lesson might follow a plan such as that shown below.

A drama lesson based on *Sleeping Beauty*

1 *Storytelling* Familiarise the children with the main events of the traditional story. Perhaps use an oral storytelling session and record the key points on a story mountain.

2 *Narration* Start by narrating the beginning of the story – baby born, party organised, invitations written and sent to the important people in the land.

(*Writing activity* Write the invitation either as shared writing activity or individually.)

3 *Overheard conversations* The children are asked to work in role as fairies/guests. They work in groups of four to discuss what they think about the invitation. The teacher walks around the room listening in to their conversations – could be in role as the fairy who has not been invited. Give her a name – Grottilda?

(*Art activity* Draw or paint pictures of themselves in role as fairies/guests.)

4 *Telephone conversations* The children work in pairs – one as Grottilda and one as her sister. She has overheard conversations about the party and is cross she has not been invited. The pair make plans for revenge.

(*Writing activity* Conversation written in speech bubbles.)

5 *Ritual* The children work in role as the fairies who have been invited to the christening. They decide on a present for the baby. Each fairy presents a gift to the TIR as the Queen (holding 'the baby'). The children have to consider how they walk and speak.

For example: 'Here is the flower of youth. May you remain young forever.'

'Here is a silver cup for your milk.'

(*Writing activity* The children write to describe or draw their gift for the baby.)

6 *Thought tunnel* Good versus bad – allows us to hear the good and bad thoughts of Grottilda on her way to the party. The children stand in two rows, representing the corridor to the ballroom, and speak her thoughts as TIR walks along it.

7 *Freeze frame* Create the moment at the party when Grottilda arrives. The children decide where their characters will stand, such as protecting the baby. TIR as Grottilda enters the scene and puts the curse on the baby.

8 *Narration* The teacher narrates how it was fortunate that one fairy had not yet given her gift and was able to change the spell to prevent her death and

allow her to sleep for 100 years instead. Narrate that the King banishes spinning wheels. Life goes on until her eighteenth birthday, when the Princess explores an unknown part of the castle and comes across the room with an old woman spinning. Curious, she enters the room ...

9 *Alter ego* Organise the children to work in groups of four – one in role as Grottilda, one as Beauty (they decide how to sit or stand), the two others standing behind them and taking on the roles of their alter egos, speaking their inner thoughts.

10 *Conscience alley* The teacher walks down the alley, while the children speak aloud the fairy's thoughts. Why did she behave in this way? Consider how she was feeling and why she made the decision to put the curse on the kingdom.

11 *Narration* The forest grew around the castle. Everyone was asleep. The Prince comes riding by. He had heard the story and chopped through the undergrowth with his sword.

12 *Freeze frame* What did the Prince find? TIR as the Prince. As he walks around, he touches each person and wakes them (though not waking Beauty yet!)

13 *Soundtracking* The children create a soundtrack of realistic sounds they would hear as the kingdom wakes up – yawning, birdsong, a fire burning, people moving, talking. Orchestrate this, starting with one small sound and building to a crescendo as all comes back to life.

14 *Narrate* The Prince kisses Beauty and she awakes to the sounds. They discuss what Grottilda has done and options about what to do. Decide to talk to her.

15 *Guided walk* Where and how will the children be able to challenge Grottilda? Perhaps the TIR as a good fairy or Prince or Beauty? Take the children, in role as other good fairies, on a journey to Grottilda's home. When they reach her home, the teacher changes role to Grottilda. The children have to persuade her to change her ways.

16 *Hot seat* TIR as the bad fairy. The children are to develop their own questions to ask her. They are to use persuasion to make her see that she has done wrong. She has also been badly treated – she doesn't belong to the community. How can the children suggest that things could improve?

17 *Review* Ask, 'What have we learned about in this drama? What has this got to do with our own lives? Can we understand why Grottilda behaved as she did?'

Possible further developments

18 *Teacher in role* As the Queen, the children in role as courtiers. The Queen has a new baby and does not know what to do about inviting the bad fairy to the

(Continued)

(Continued)

christening because of what happened before. The courtiers have to support the Queen in reaching a decision. The children should begin to recognise and make the Queen aware of how the bad fairy was/is feeling and why she behaved as she did.

19 *Teacher in role* As the bad fairy, having received a letter from the kingdom inviting her to a celebration of the new baby's birth. The children as the bad fairy's servants to discuss what she should do.

20 *Conscience alley* Should the bad fairy put a curse on the new baby? No, she has changed her ways.

By taking part in the above lesson, the children will have explored the story from the inside, used language in a variety of ways and solved the problem of the bad fairy by working together.

Reflective questions

- What other writing activities could be inspired by a drama lesson such as *Sleeping Beauty*?
- Are there any cross-curricular links that could be developed?
- Which story do you think could be explored using drama techniques in this way?
- Do you think drama could be used to teach other primary school subjects, such as science and geography?
- How could ICT be included in drama lessons?
- How can you ensure that all the children have been involved in the drama lesson?
- How could you use a teaching assistant to help with assessment in a drama lesson? What would you want to assess?

Conclusion

Using drama to teach and learn in primary classrooms is accepted as good practice by primary school teachers across the world. Teachers who use drama in this way will be able to give many examples of how children have not only enjoyed the lessons but also produced quality work in other associated subjects and areas of the curriculum such as art and writing. Have a go and do some drama!

Further reading

Ackroyd, J. and Barter-Boulton, J. (2013) *Drama Lessons: Ages 4–7*. London: David Fulton.
Ackroyd, J. and Barter-Boulton, J. (2013) *Drama Lessons: Ages 7–11*. London: David Fulton.
Baldwin, P. (2008) *The Practical Primary Drama Handbook*. London: Paul Chapman.
Neelands, J. (2000) *Structuring Drama Work*. Cambridge: Cambridge University Press.
Toye, N. and Prendiville, F. (2000) *Drama and Traditional Story for the Early Years*. Abingdon: Routledge.
Toye, N. and Prendiville, F. (2007) *Speaking and Listening Through Drama 7–11*. London: Paul Chapman Publishing.

References

Hayes, S. and Craig, H. (2004) *Mary Mary*. London: Walker Books.
Heathcote, D. (1984) *Dorothy Heathcote: Collected writings on education and drama*. London: Hutchinson.

CHAPTER 5

ENGLISH

Gill Chambers, Kate Coleman and Gareth Davies

Learning objectives

By the end of this chapter you should be able to:

- understand the three modes of English and the relationship between them
- identify the key features of coherent planning and teaching of primary English
- recognise appropriate and creative strategies for classroom practice.

Introduction

English is a unique subject in the curriculum. It is a discrete subject with its own content, but it is also a means of communication by which all learning across the primary curriculum is facilitated. English can therefore be seen as the beating heart of the curriculum.

The key skills of speaking and listening, reading and writing are central to how we communicate with each other, how we learn, how we develop and how we understand the world around us. Without English we would not be able to express our simplest thoughts or feelings. From our earliest moments we reach out to others and try to make them understand us. This is done, first, by making sounds, cries and gestures and then increasingly by using language – a formalised and recognisable system of sound communication – as we gradually acquire it. The English language is also the most widespread language on the planet and, as such, is a global means of communication. To communicate clearly we must therefore learn how to use English effectively in its standard form, so that we can exchange thoughts, ideas and comments clearly with others, as well as appreciate how it can be used creatively.

English is the window through which children can peer, learn and wonder at the world, its creatures, peoples and their relationships and its problems. By means of literature, children can experience many different situations, emotions and issues; they can empathise with the characters involved, learn from their mistakes and successes, and gain access into their own and others' cultures. Literacy can empower children by 'conferring the skill not just to read and write but to make these processes genuinely transformative' (Alexander, 2010: 269).

This chapter sets out essential aspects of teaching and learning in English. The teaching of English can help children to reach out to the world by increasing their expertise in understanding and manipulating the language. This permits them to communicate clearly with others, solve problems, understand other areas of learning and deepen their involvement in their world, while also conferring on them power, allowing them to exert some control over their lives.

English in the primary curriculum is a core subject, made up of the three modes of speaking and listening, reading and writing, all of which need to be addressed, both individually and within other contexts across the curriculum (Cox, 2011). This may seem a huge task, but, as English is our normal mode of communication in school, all subjects will utilise the three modes as a matter of course. When specifically teaching English, the aim is to provide children with opportunities to improve their knowledge, skills, understanding and ability to utilise the language in a meaningful and proficient way. You therefore need to be passionate about the subject, have a very good understanding of it yourself and be aware of a range of teaching and learning styles and strategies in order to vary your approach and ensure that children are engaged in their learning.

In the classroom   Reading a novel

This example illustrates how the three modes of English can be woven into a lesson or series of lessons.

A group of eight- and nine-year-olds were about to start reading a novel. An image of the book's cover was projected on to the board and the children were asked to think about it quietly on their own for a minute. What did they see? What did they think about it and what did they feel about it? What did they think of the title?

They were then asked to discuss their thoughts with a partner and agree what they would then share with the whole group. The class then pooled their thoughts and ideas, building up a communal idea of what they thought of the cover and what the book might be about.

This exercise involved the children in thinking and forming their own opinions; speaking and listening, first with a partner and then with the group; predicting what the story might be about, and considering why that particular cover design had been chosen. The children then wrote down their predictions to compare with the actual story later. They were given a framework to help them with this:

- I/we think the characters ...
- I/we think the story will be about ...
- I/we think the cover is/is not interesting because ...

After reading the first section of the novel, these predictions were revisited, compared to what had happened in the story to that point and amended. In subsequent lessons, the children considered how the characters felt and why they did things or behaved in certain ways. They used drama to recreate and extend elements of the story – for example, creating a still image or freeze frame (photograph) of an incident and then considering what the characters might have been thinking at that moment in time. They also wrote diary entries for some characters and letters, which helped them understand and empathise with the characters.

In the classroom   Moon poetry

A group of five- and six-year-olds were asked to look at the Moon in the evening and think of words to describe it. The next day, the teacher asked them to share their words and added some of her own. These were collected on the board.

While sitting in a circle, the children were each asked to finish the sentence 'The Moon is ...' by choosing a word or words from the collection. The teacher then read a poem that was projected on to the board and asked the children to look for the descriptive words and suggest alternative but interesting words. The teacher wrote down their suggestions.

The teacher then demonstrated how a poem about the Moon might start:

The moon is ...

A twinkling nightlight

A slice of yellow lemon ...

She then asked the children for suggestions for the next line. The children worked in small groups and individually to write their own poems following the given format.

In this example, the children are working individually and cooperatively; they are reading a text type – poetry; they are extending their vocabulary by creatively thinking about a subject; they are speaking and listening to each other; they are writing both as a group and individually.

English in the curriculum

The framework document for the 2014 National Curriculum in England (DfE, 2013: 13) sets out the overarching aim of the subject as being:

> to promote high standards of literacy by equipping pupils with a strong command of the written and spoken word, and to develop their love of literature through widespread reading for enjoyment.

English is organised in different ways depending on the needs of the children, the priorities of your school and the needs of the local community. Your teaching of English will need to be inclusive, meeting the needs of those with special educational needs and English as an additional language as well as those who are gifted and talented, for example (Medwell et al., 2012). There will be a mix of discrete literacy teaching, guided and independent reading, phonics sessions, handwriting practice, spelling and research and writing opportunities linked to other areas of the curriculum. These will be designed to enable children to meet national standards of attainment and levels of progress commensurate with their age and ability.

What do we teach?

How is teaching organised?

As Figure 5.1 shows, the three modes of English are taught using a variety of approaches. There is no specific statutory curriculum time devoted to the teaching of English, but

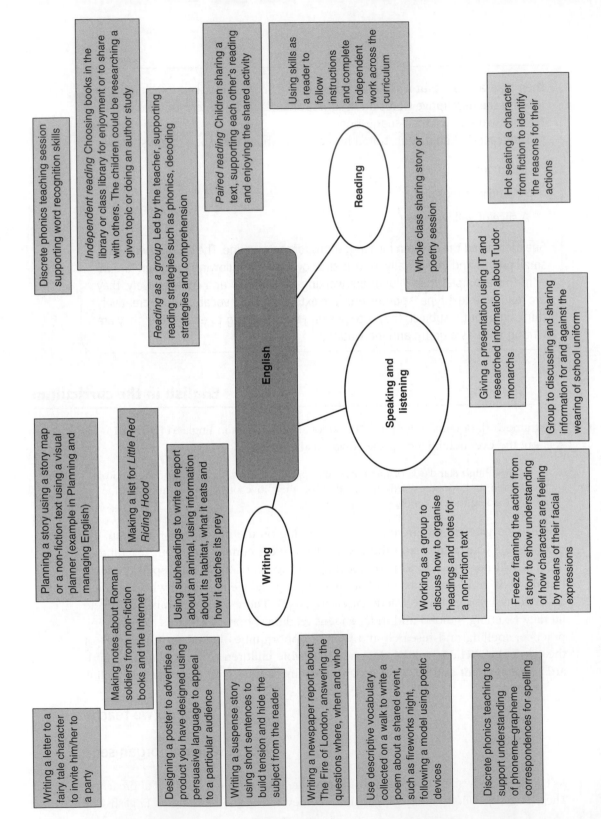

Figure 5.1 Spider diagram of examples of teaching activities

schools usually arrange this as a daily session of about one hour, with additional time for daily phonics sessions for four- to seven-year-olds. Time is also allocated to reading as a short, often daily, activity, split into whole-class, independent or guided reading sessions, with other opportunities to share stories and poems with the whole class.

Many schools have developed creative curriculum models, where discrete teaching works alongside 'theme' days, with longer periods of time used for drama, world book days or writing workshops to inspire feelings of there being a purpose to reading, analysis and writing. You will find further information about this under Planning and managing English, below. This arrangement enables children to make links across the curriculum with subjects such as history, science or geography, and for children to see a purpose to their writing.

Within each English session, you would choose a variety of strategies (as shown in Figure 5.2) to ensure the most purposeful mix of reading and exposure to the range of text types – fiction, poetry and non-fiction. You would involve the children in the analysis of the features needed for writing each text (such as specific grammar structure, word choices and layout) and the skills of planning, drafting and redrafting. You would also include opportunities across the week for handwriting teaching and practice, phonics or spelling teaching and reading opportunities. These strategies would include whole-class, shared and guided work with a small, matched ability group, as described in Figure 5.2. By working with the class, then with small ability groups, you can target the learning appropriately for all the children.

 In the classroom   About the farm

The teacher used shared writing with the whole class to plan part of a recounting of a farm trip. This enabled her to show the children how a plan should be organised. Some children then worked independently to complete this work, while others who needed support were assisted in a number of ways, being given:

- guided support by the teacher, working with a group to recall and order events
- visual prompts – photographs of activities, such as, feeding the pigs, riding on a tractor and collecting eggs
- the opportunity to work with a partner
- word banks of time connectives, such as 'first', 'next', 'after that'.

During the rest of the week, the teacher worked with other groups or individuals to help them improve their first drafts by thinking about descriptive words and sentences. This made the optimum use of teaching time, ensuring that she intervened in the learning when specific children needed it.

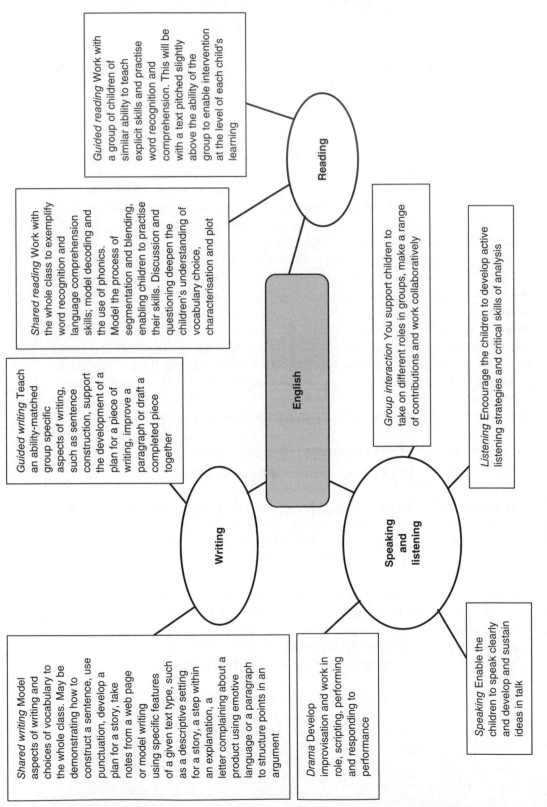

Figure 5.2 Strategies used to teach the three modes of English

Progression in English skills

In early primary classes, learning builds on the progress children have made in their Early Years settings in relation to speaking and listening, reading and writing. Your daily literacy sessions will build on and consolidate skills that the children can then apply to other areas of the curriculum.

Speaking and listening, from five to seven years

As children develop, their language will be the principal vehicle for learning. It underpins their understanding of reading, writing and learning across the curriculum (Clipson-Boyles, 2012).

Throughout this phase, the children will need to listen attentively, recognise the rules that govern talk, sustain conversations and compare ideas and views with others. Retelling events and stories supports children's understanding of structure and allows them to experiment and plan their own stories and recounts of personal events. Drama and role-play, too, are crucial to developing problem solving skills, understanding characterisation and extending vocabulary. You will learn more about this in Chapter 4, on drama.

In the classroom   The garden centre

The role-play area in the classroom was turned into a garden centre. The children chose to play in this space and adopted the roles of customers and garden centre workers.

As workers, they answered the telephone, took orders and helped customers to select plants to buy. The 'customers' asked advice about their gardens and engaged in talk about everyday topics, such as the weather and the plants. In doing this, the children used vocabulary related to size, shape and colour. Adults joined in with this role-play talk and extended the children's contributions and vocabulary by means of questioning. The children were also encouraged to create scenarios within the garden centre to aid sequencing in storytelling or work together to solve problems.

Reading, from five to seven years

As children move through the early primary years, they develop an understanding of the alphabetic code for English, which supports them as they decode words.

They learn to recognise sound–letter (phoneme–grapheme) correspondence and read a range of common words, so developing their ability to read simple sentences.

In order to inspire children's engagement with reading and apply their emerging skills, they need to experience high-quality fiction, poetry, non-fiction, visual and multimodal texts (Cremin, 2009). Reading aloud and sharing texts, too, enables children to develop an understanding of the structure, rhythm and tone of language and so improve their comprehension. Systematic teaching of word recognition also supports children in self-correcting, as they apply the alphabetic code and make good use of segmentation and blending. Their knowledge and understanding of context and syntax enables them to check for sense and use expression, so improving their fluency and comprehension.

In the classroom   Understanding a text

In a class of five- and six-year-olds, during shared class reading of a big non-fiction book about favourite toys, the teacher modelled the segmentation of words containing phonemes taught during recent phonics sessions. Parts of a word were covered to show how it could be segmented into individual phonemes and then uncovered as the children blended and then read the whole word. For example, 'd u ck', 't e dd y'.

The teacher also asked questions, such as, 'What material is the teddy made from?' and 'Why is fur fabric used?' This allowed the children to show their understanding of the text.

By the end of the early primary years, most children are independent readers, reading with increasing fluency and the routine ability to apply their phonic skills. They use this developing skill and understanding to read for their research, evaluate what they read and pose questions about the content.

Writing, from five to seven years

At the beginning of this phase, children's developing grasp of the alphabetic code supports them when spelling simple words and allows them to tackle more complex words, using phoneme–grapheme correspondence. As they progress, the children will be able to compose a sentence using one idea, planning and then writing it. Some will be able to use a capital letter and full stop, applied from their reading experiences. Reading will also support their understanding of story structure, as some will construct a simple story or recount events from their own experience.

Patterns from shared stories will also be used in the children's own writing. They will increasingly write for different purposes using a range of forms, such as lists, captions and information texts.

By the end of this phase, the children will be planning and writing a range of texts based on their reading and analysis. Their stories will be structured, with descriptions of the characters and dialogue. As their fine motor skills develop, most children's handwriting will be correctly orientated and show the right form and proportion.

Speaking and listening, from 7 to 11 years

Speaking and listening are critical skills that impact learning across the curriculum. Children will need to develop their ability to talk with others, joining in small group discussions, and to organise their work.

As they progress through this primary phase, the children will increasingly be able to sustain conversations and explore their views critically, collaborating on activities. Context will enable the children to vary their language so it is appropriate for their role and viewpoint – for example, when being persuasive or justifying a point of view. They will need to use language to resolve conflict, give and receive constructive feedback and explain their findings.

In the classroom   Rainforest

A group of nine- and ten-year-olds used research findings to argue the case for a village that was to be destroyed by loggers in the rainforest.

They used persuasive vocabulary to articulate their points of view and organised them to ensure their argument was valid. This was based on research from non-fiction, film/TV extracts and the Internet, which enabled the children to make links with their reading, write a plan and present their case.

Reading, from 7 to 11 years

There is a move from a phonics approach, used in the lower primary years when decoding words, to the use of comprehension cues. Children's reading will increase in fluency and they will use evidence from the text to articulate their viewpoint, making inferences about characters and their feelings. By the end of this phase, children will be reading longer texts where exposure to complex sentence construction will demonstrate constructions not usually found in speech.

Children of this age will articulate how word choice affects the reader and analyse the themes or effect the author has tried to create. Navigation of text will be efficient, enabling the children to retrieve and find information by skimming and scanning text. Misunderstandings will be clarified in the process of rereading.

By the end of primary school, children will also have had experience of evaluating bias and checking the accuracy of what they read.

In the classroom   Guided reading

A group of eight- and nine-year-olds in a guided reading session explored a character's actions within a story.

The teacher's questioning encouraged them to find evidence in the text to support their opinions and enabled them to discuss and justify their thoughts based on their readings of the text. For example, 'Why do you think the boy felt worried?' and 'Which words in the text told you this?' The children were encouraged to comment on the author's choice of words and sentence construction, which revealed their understanding of the text.

Writing, from 7 to 11 years

Across the upper primary phase, children will become more secure in writing simple and compound sentences. They begin to create balance and variety in their sentence starts, creating interesting effects. As they progress, they will use complex sentences, employing subordinating conjunctions, such as 'if', 'so', and 'when', to start sentences. Their word choices, too, will create different effects and be appropriate to the text type concerned.

In the classroom   Writing about spiders

In a shared writing session, the teacher modelled to a class of seven- and eight-year-olds how to write the main body of an explanation text about how a spider caught its prey. The teacher showed how the writer used connectives such as 'when' and 'so' to explain how the spider built a trap to snare an unsuspecting prey. This supported the children in writing their own text and extended the learning of a specific text type. Expectations were also clarified as to the content that was needed.

By the end of primary school, children should be writing with increased control and fluency. Paragraphing will be used to organise points and punctuation and commas will be used within sentences in ways that show they have an understanding of sentence construction. Within narrative writing, children will employ their growing vocabulary to create effects and use dialogue and action to engage the reader.

Planning and managing English

The organisation of the English curriculum, as outlined in the previous section, will influence a school's approach to planning the subject. All planning has the children at its centre.

Table 5.1 is an example of a long-term planning map for eight- and nine-year-olds, showing the topics that will be covered during any one year. The children can be involved in the decision-making regarding what is included in such planning. Similarly, they can contribute to daily lesson planning that is informed by the assessment of the previous day's lesson.

Many schools have a long-term map of themes that naturally lead to a focus on certain genres throughout the year. For example, a topic on the Tudors would be ideal to link with biographical writing or newspaper reports, creating a *Tudor Times*. In both examples, the children would need to be taught the key features of each genre, plus the historical facts and then merge this learning together in the final outcome.

In Table 5.1, such linked learning in English is mapped, so that the teachers can achieve a balance of the genres focused on during the year. The same exercise would be done for all year groups to ensure that a similar balance of fiction, non-fiction and poetry would be achieved throughout the primary phase.

Table 5.1 Example of a long-term planning map for eight- and nine-year-olds

Term	Autumn 1	Autumn 2	Spring 3	Spring 4	Spring 5	Spring 6
Theme	History detectives	Fire and ice	Explorers	Tudor times	Reduce, reuse, recycle	The Earth and beyond
English-linked learning	Stories with historical settings	Poetry Explanations	Stories set in imaginary worlds	Information texts Biography Newspaper reports	Persuasion Plays	Poetry Information texts

Medium-term or unit planning

For medium-term planning, you need to identify the key learning objectives and curriculum links central to the plan. You also need to consider:

- prior learning in this genre and expectations for this year group
- the children's interests
- school initiatives and priorities in English
- the place of continuous learning, such as phonics, spelling and handwriting
- resources – including key texts
- the classroom environment
- opportunities for outdoor learning.

At this stage, you may focus more specifically on units of English work about a particular genre. These can be standalone or cross-curricular, as described above.

The term *unit planning* refers to a blocked period of time in class when there is a specific study made of a particular genre or theme, such as instructions or shape poetry. Within a unit approach, the teacher begins by familiarising the children with the genre via a range of reading experiences. Teaching then progresses to focusing on the key features of that genre, such as its particular vocabulary, grammar or way in which it is laid out. Finally, the children work towards an outcome, to show that they have an understanding of the genre and can apply this learning. *Outcomes* could be, for example, a written piece, on paper or on screen, a practical activity or a presentation to an audience. The teacher determines how long a unit will last. It may be a week, two weeks or more.

There are many published schemes that support this unit planning process, including those available on the Internet from resource sites and forums. With such a wealth of information available, it is up to the individual to make a professional decision as to the quality of the source and its suitability for use in a particular classroom.

The sequence illustrated in the model shown in Figure 5.3 acknowledges the interrelationship between the three modes of English, as previously discussed, and supports the progression from reading to writing. Teachers who have considered this model when planning say that it reminds them of not only the value of rich speaking and listening experiences but also how reading scaffolds writing.

Under your guidance, the children are encouraged to be borrowers and explorers of language and texts, and to use the 'treasures' that they gather in their own writing. Throughout the process, show the children how to take part in such activities, by modelling a good example of what the genre looks like in everyday reading and writing. For example, in demonstrating how to write instructions for making pizza, you would refer to the imperative verbs such as 'knead', 'roll' and 'sprinkle' and be sure that the children know the appropriate layout for a recipe (see Table 5.2).

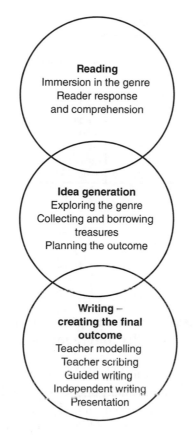

Figure 5.3   A model of good teaching

Adapted from the UK Literacy Association/Primary National Strategy (2004)

Talk is a key feature of all stages of this process. During the reading phase, the focus will be on discussing the text. Teachers need to ensure that the children understand the vocabulary and the thoughts, viewpoint or messages that the author is trying to convey.

Our task during the idea generation phase is to help the children to unpick the genre and generate ideas for their own writing. One analogy is to compare this to peeling away the layers of an onion to discover what is underneath or lies within each layer. The ideas are then captured from this analysis so that the children have something to refer to during their own writing. This may be creating a poster of rich vocabulary or a bulleted checklist of points to remember. Through talk in this phase, these ideas are then captured in a plan. Plans may take many forms – a visual diagram, for example, a story map or a spider diagram, a sequence of sticky notes or a skeleton frame.

Table 5.2 A skeleton plan for instructions

Title:	
What you will need (write a list here)	
What to do (tell the reader how to make your pizza) 1. 2. 3. 4.	**Useful verbs** weigh knead roll sprinkle chop
Put a photo of your pizza here	

In the classroom   Example of a unit plan for myths and legends

This practical example shows you how the model for good teaching shown in Figure 5.3 translates into what actually happens in the classroom.

The teacher had planned a four-week unit of work on the 'Myths and legends' theme for a class of nine- and ten-year-olds. Ongoing teaching and learning, such as spelling, handwriting, guided reading and library time, are discrete sessions throughout the unit. This is what happened.

Week 1

The children were immersed in a mythical world. The teacher told stories to the class and the children read a range of myths and watched carefully selected film clips. The class started to put together a display to show what they already knew about myths. This consisted of characters, settings, key events and rich language. This was added to as more myths were explored during the week.

Week 2

This week focused on drama and, instead of a daily English session, the teacher collapsed the time available during two mornings to allow for an extended drama session. This enabled the children to explore character, setting and plot and develop their understanding of the text.

By the end of Week 2, the children had a good understanding of the key features of a myth and were ready to begin to use this as a model to create their own.

Week 3

The children used what they had learned about myths in Weeks 1 and 2 to plan their own myths. They created story maps of the journey of the 'hero' character. These were drawn on large pieces of paper or produced using computer software. They depicted the quest of the main character as he or she travelled through a series of settings and overcame trials and barriers to reach the final goal. The children annotated their map with key vocabulary and jottings to capture the elements of character, setting and plot. Using their map, they then rehearsed their story orally via storytelling pairs or small groups.

Week 4

The children developed their plans into the final written outcome – their own myth. They were given a choice as to what this could look like on the page or on screen. For example, some children chose to create a hyperlinked choose-your-own adventure-type story using ICT, while others opted for a comic strip format. The children shared their work with each other, children in other classes and their parents. The teacher displayed the stories in the classroom, some were shared in the library and some were posted on the school's website.

Short-term planning

This planning is informed by the medium-term plan and details the day-to-day teaching and learning. It is a working document and changes can be made to it according to the outcomes of the learning that occurred the previous day. Teachers often refer to their short-term plan as a visualisation of what the lesson will look like in practice. It helps teachers consider what the lesson might look like, feel like and sound like for learners.

In the short-term plan shown in Table 5.3, the teacher has decided to focus on dragons to ignite the children's interest and excitement. The plan shows what three days' planning within a themed unit could look like. There is more to include than is shown here – for instance, when and where to incorporate ongoing teaching and learning, discrete phonics or guided reading. Days four and five are focused on the children creating and presenting their own dragon guide on paper and on screen.

Table 5.3 Example of a short-term plan

Year Group: 3	Term: 2	Cross Curricular Links:	ICT opportunities:
Theme:	Date:	Heating and cooling	Film clips
Dragons		PSHE – feelings	Drafting, editing and presenting written outcomes
		Art – design a dragon	

Curriculum references

Unit genre/text type: Poetic descriptive sentences; instructions and explanations (information texts)
Length of unit: 2 weeks. This unit is part of a cross-curricular theme week on dragons

Resources
A range of picture books about dragons with rich description – shared in storytime
Pet shop leaflets giving guidance on how to look after pets
Film clip

Unit outcomes
Dragon descriptions using poetic sentences – a postcard to Professor Hilda Tarragon
'How to look after a dragon guide' – leaflet, poster or web page

Assessment opportunities
Self- and peer assessment against success criteria
Mini plenaries during session
Teacher assessment of final outcomes

	Learning objectives	Success criteria	Teaching	Guided/focus group	Independent groups	Plenary
1	To identify how a writer uses effective vocabulary to build pictures in the reader's mind	Collect words that authors use to: • tell my friend why I have chosen these words • write some descriptions of my own using effective vocabulary	Shared reading/writing	Differentiation via intervention	Differentiated learning activities	Review/ reinforce learning and feed forward

Teaching – Shared reading/writing

Mantle of the expert – read a letter from Professor Tarragon, the famous dragon explorer, asking the children, in role as dragon explorers, to record descriptions of new dragons they find
Use a chosen book or books as a model
Shared reading with an evocative soundtrack in background to create mood

Key questions
What do you think/see?
How does the author paint pictures in our minds?
Collect memorable words and record them
What else does the author do to create images for the reader? Identify alliteration and similes

Guided/focus group – Guided word collection, using a chosen text or texts, categorising how the dragon looks sounds, moves
Record on large piece of paper

Independent groups – Using a range of texts, identify words and phrases the author uses to describe the dragons and add to this by creating own descriptions – with alliteration and similes

Plenary – Share collections and evaluate
From this, create success criteria for writing

Year Group: 3   **Term: 2**   **Cross Curricular Links:**   **ICT opportunities:**

Theme: **Date:**   Heating and cooling   Film clips

Dragons   PSHE – feelings   Drafting, editing and presenting written outcomes

Art – design a dragon

| 2 | To know how to use effective vocabulary in own descriptive writing

To know how to improve writing | Choose the best words for my writing

Use alliteration to make my writing interesting

Use similes to create pictures for the reader

Show how I have improved my writing | Display success criteria generated yesterday. Model writing a description using this and give a running commentary on the decisions you make as a writer

Children's ideas are asked for part of this composition and the teacher scribes these. Introduce model:

• My dragon is …
• My dragon eats …
• When she/he flies, sleeps, …
• My dragon tells me …

Together we …
Children discuss their dragon in talk partners and orally rehearse sentences | Improve example written by teacher
List of how to improve
Write own description | Children each write a description of their dragon
Differentiated scaffolds:
For some groups, offer a writing frame for structure
Word banks
Sentence starters | Mini plenary mid-session
Share writing and discuss effective vocabulary and how children have improved their writing
Share final outcomes |
| 3 | To know the key features of an information text | Talk to my friend about how an information text is organised

Plan my own information text | Continue the idea of the mantle of the expert – Professor Tarragon thanks the children for their postcards. They will be added to a new dragon database. However, she would like their help again, this time to write a guide on how to look after a dragon

Share the pet shop leaflets and discuss what needs to be done to look after pets. Mark organisational features in the text
What would this look like for a dragon? Talk partners
Watch a film clip to support discussion. Share some initial thoughts | Guided talk to reinforce shared session

Teacher scribes spider diagram plan | Spider diagrams – how to look after a dragon | List of what needs to be considered – such as scales, to be jet-washed and polished weekly |

Creating a short-term plan

Approaches to short-term planning vary from school to school, but the following are elements that are commonly found.

Speaking and listening

Opportunities for children to take part in a range of activities that develop 'talk for learning' skills are built into a short-term plan. During any week, the teacher will identify specific tasks as assessment opportunities for speaking and listening. For example, during shared learning on Day 1, the teacher plans to focus on partner talk and children's ability to listen to the contributions of others, take turns and speak clearly to an audience.

Learning objectives and success criteria

Learning objectives capture the intended learning for the session, whereas the success criteria are the steps to be taken to achieve success and allow the children to self- and peer assess how they can achieve the learning. It is good practice to involve the children in developing the success criteria.

Differentiation

The teacher considers the different ways in which learning can be supported and provides additional scaffolding for some groups and individuals, such as writing frames, word banks and visual prompts. It is good practice to identify a guided or focus group during the English lesson. The focus of the group work is determined by the assessment.

Assessment

Assessment opportunities are identified at the medium-term planning stage and then embedded within lessons at appropriate points. There is ongoing self- and peer assessment by the children against the success criteria for each lesson. It is useful to organise for a mini plenary to occur during the lesson. These are ideal opportunities for the teacher to check understanding, for further ideas to be shared and the lesson to be adapted accordingly.

Resources

The time taken to find quality resources is time well spent. For the dragon example discussed here, the teacher has wrote the letters from Professor Tarragon herself, collected a range of stories about dragons and identified appropriate film clips.

Classroom environment

In the dragon project, the teacher, with the help of the children, turned an area of her classroom into a dragon's lair and the classroom displays were on the theme of dragons, including collages of dragons, the postcards to Professor Tarragon and a collection of books on dragons for the children to browse during reading time.

A 'working wall' was also developed. This was a cumulative display, added to each day as the children explored the genre. Such displays may include examples of the focus text, such as poetic sentences, collections of rich vocabulary, pictures of dragons, examples of children's work in various stages of drafting and success criteria checklists.

Reflective questions

- Reflect on the various ways in which you have seen the teaching of English organised. How is the teaching of reading and writing supported by the school?
- Look at an example of a short-term plan you have created. Reflect on what the lesson looked like, felt like and sounded like for the children in your class.
- Think about a memorable lesson that you have observed or taught. What made it memorable and what impact did the lesson have on children's learning?

Conclusion

English lies at the heart of all learning in the primary classroom – it is the bridge that links learning across a range of contexts. English teaching and learning is an exploration, an adventure into the language. Its origins and structures are also a journey through real and fictional worlds, the past, present and future. Ensure you prepare the children for the future by teaching the skills of English well. Find out what excites and interests them, keep up to date with new literature and developments in the subject and be hungry for new ideas. Purposeful talk and immersion in high-quality children's literature are central to all rich learning environments and it is your expertise and passion that will ignite children's enthusiasm for learning in English.

Further reading

Bower, V. (2011) *Creative Ways to Teach Literacy*. London: Sage.
A practical guide to teaching narrative poetry and non-fiction, with relevant case studies and a host of creative ideas to try out in the classroom.

Cox, R. (ed.) (2011) *Primary English Teaching*. London: Sage.

Written by lecturers from teacher training institutions, this book provides a useful and comprehensive introduction to primary English teaching. The text is very accessible and bridges theory to practice for the reader.

Joliffe, W. and Waugh, D. (2012) *Teaching Synthetic Phonics in Primary Schools*. London: Sage.

A thorough overview of the pedagogy and practice of systematic synthetic phonics. There is a balance of research and practice and consideration of the place of phonics across the primary age range and curriculum.

Jones, D. and Hodson, H. (eds) (2006) *Unlocking Speaking and Listening*. London: David Fulton.

This book endorses the value of speaking and listening as a foundation of the primary curriculum. There are useful case studies that bring classroom practice alive for the reader.

References

Alexander, R. (ed.) (2010) *Children, their World, their Education: Final report and recommendations of the Cambridge Primary Review*. Abingdon: Routledge.

Clipson-Boyles, S. (2012) *Teaching Primary English Through Drama*. Abingdon: Routledge.

Cox, R. (ed.) (2011) *Primary English Teaching*. London: Sage.

Cremin, T. (2009) *Teaching English Creatively*. Abingdon: Routledge.

DfE (2013) 'The National Curriculum in England: Framework document'. Runcorn: DfE. Available online at: www.gov.uk/government/uploads/system/uploads/attachment_data/file/210969/NC_framework_document_-_FINAL.pdf

Medwell, J., Wray, D., Minns, H., Coates, E. and Griffiths, V. (2012) *Primary English: Teaching theory and practice*. London: Sage.

UKLA/Primary National Strategy (2004) *Raising Boys' Achievements in Writing*. Royston: UKLA.

CHAPTER 6

GEOGRAPHY

Ken Bland

Learning objectives

By the end of this chapter you should be able to:

- understand the nature of the subject of geography in primary school
- understand the role geography plays in the curriculum
- be aware of a range of resources to support learning primary geography.

Introduction

What is our knowledge worth if we know nothing about the world that sustains us, nothing about natural systems and climate, nothing about other countries and cultures.

Jonathan Porritt, Forum for the Future (GA 2009b)

As Jonathan Porritt indicates, geography helps children to understand and explain things in their world. When studying geography, children practice mapwork and enquiry skills in their classroom and, in the local area, geography also allows children to evaluate their own feelings about a place and so start to learn more about themselves. Michael Palin (2008) hints at this self-discovery when he states that geography is 'a fusion of the power of the imagination and the hard truths of science.'

Geography is a very important subject for children and adults alike, but how can this be demonstrated in the classroom? One simple example is that you could ask the children where their food comes from, as many children are unaware of how food is grown and where. A simple approach would be to have labels showing where the goods from one supermarket come from. Alternatively, you could opt for a practical approach. Many schools are starting to have school gardens and this will demonstrate, in a very practical way, how food is grown. If space for a vegetable plot is not available, then your school could grow potatoes in canvas bags, with class competitions to measure the total number and weight of potatoes grown by each class. The pupils can then cook the potatoes and enjoy with perhaps butter and mint that has been grown in the school garden.

Another excellent way to introduce geography is to look at topical news items. Take, for example, the bush fires in Australia in early 2013 or weather events, such as Superstorm Sandy in 2012, which affected the Caribbean and eastern USA. The images, photos and eyewitness accounts (via tweets, blogs and social media sites) can all be downloaded as the stimulus for the lesson. Then you can explain how the storm occurred or ask the class to investigate this via appropriate websites.

The interplay between human and physical geography can be clearly seen in such studies, but then you can extend this by bringing in economics and economic development. Look, for example, at the impact of the storm on less developed islands, such as Haiti, the defences, infrastructures and buildings of which were not able to withstand the storms.

In a similar vein, you can look at the impact of earthquakes of a similar size or magnitude on more developed countries such as Japan and less developed countries such as Haiti. In the latter, the impact on buildings and loss of life is usually much greater.

Geography helps to explain these sorts of events and, in geography topics, children study the interplay between the physical and human environments. Geography lessons often focus on local issues, too, and the example below looks at sustainable housing in a new development in Northampton.

In the classroom   Sustainable housing development at Upton

A Year 6 class visited Upton estate in Northampton to study a 'sustainable' housing development. The learning intentions for the children included developing their geographical and enquiry skills, as well as their knowledge and understanding of environmental change and sustainable development.

The teacher chose Upton as it is a pleasant new build that contrasts with the rural locality of their village. Upton's importance is that it is an area of sustainable housing that is recognised nationally as an example of good practice. There are some unusual features to the housing itself and the environment. For example, there are 'ditches' that run down the middle of many streets as a means of controlling the runoff of surface water when there is heavy rainfall.

Prior to the visit, the class used Digimap for Schools, Google Earth and Up my Street on the Internet to investigate the estate. When the class visited Upton, the children undertook an environmental quality audit and focused on the social and aesthetic views of the houses in Mill Pond Drive, comparing them to the traditional eighteenth- and nineteenth-century Northamptonshire ironstone houses and 1930s local authority housing developments in their own village.

While your school may not be able to visit Upton, this process can be applied to a development near your school or you can investigate Upton from your classroom as a virtual field visit (available online at: www.northamptonshireobservatory.org.uk/docs/doc_Uptoncasestudy.pdf_113342150306.pdf).

Geography in the primary curriculum

The framework document for the 2014 National Curriculum in England (DfE 2013: 198) sets out the purpose for studying geography as follows:

> A high-quality geography education should inspire in pupils a curiosity and fascination about the world and its people that will remain with them for the rest of their lives. Teaching should equip pupils with knowledge about diverse places, people, resources and natural and human environments, together with a deep understanding of the Earth's key physical and human processes. As pupils progress, their growing knowledge about the world should help them to deepen their understanding of the interaction between physical and human processes, and of the formation and use of landscapes and environments. Geographical knowledge provides the tools and approaches that explain how the Earth's features at different scales are shaped, interconnected and change over time.

This statement gives a good indication of the value of geography as a subject and its relevance to primary-age children.

On a practical level, in geography, all schools have to decide whether to follow a topic- or subject-based curriculum. Some schools have adopted the International Primary Curriculum (available online at: www.greatlearning.com/ipc), for example, in which geography is part of a wider topic. Other schools opt for a topic-based approach, in which a number of subjects are included in a topic such as 'Water'.

While decisions about planning are made at school level, it is important to consider your own opinion on the 'subject' v. 'topic' debate. There are advantages and disadvantages on each side. For example, within a very broad topic, geography is often relegated to having a minor and superficial role, such as drawing a map of the area. Also, sometimes within broad topics the links between individual lessons can be very tenuous.

On the other side of this discussion, some teachers suggest that teaching via a subject-based curriculum inhibits children's investigations and interests as they do not see the world in subjects but in a more holistic manner. Teachers need to consider these issues, but, whichever curriculum model is adopted, there remains the need for teachers to base their teaching on what is good practice in geography.

Good practice in geography

Geography may be defined as the study of people and places and how these interact. As Scoffham (2010: 9) indicates:

> Traditionally, there are two main branches of Geography. Physical geography focuses on the earth's surface and the processes that shape it, and covers topics including landscapes, rocks, oceans, climate and habitats. Human Geography is the study of people and places. By exploring themes such as settlement, population, transport, agriculture trade and industry, Geographers investigate the ways we live our lives. They look for patterns and connections and try to identify future trends. However, a focus of particular interest and concern now is the state of the natural environment. Environmental issues, which are inextricably bound up with the relationship between people and their surroundings, are central to geography.

Before you can start to plan geography lessons and schemes of work, it is important for you to consider what is good practice in geography. Consideration needs to be given to the following issues.

Integration of skills themes and places

Good practice in geography occurs when there is an integration of geographical skills, topics and places. This can be seen in Figure 6.1.

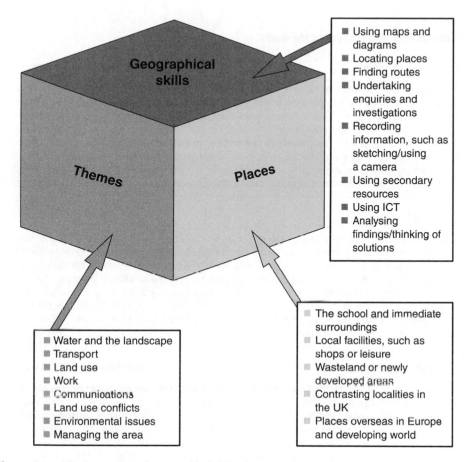

Geographical skills
- Using maps and diagrams
- Locating places
- Finding routes
- Undertaking enquiries and investigations
- Recording information, such as sketching/using a camera
- Using secondary resources
- Using ICT
- Analysing findings/thinking of solutions

Themes

Places

- Water and the landscape
- Transport
- Land use
- Work
- Communications
- Land use conflicts
- Environmental issues
- Managing the area

- The school and immediate surroundings
- Local facilities, such as shops or leisure
- Wasteland or newly developed areas
- Contrasting localities in the UK
- Places overseas in Europe and developing world

Figure 6.1   The integration of geographical skills, themes and places (Scoffham, 2010: 308)

Getting started using artefacts

Scoffham (2013) suggests using everyday objects to start teaching geography in a creative way. Figure 6.2 lists some great examples and how they can be used to aid learning.

Using geographical questions

A sequence of lessons and activities should be planned around geographical questions, such as, 'What is this place like?', 'Why is this place as it is?', 'How is this place changing?', 'How is this place linked to other places?', 'What is it like to live in this

Artefacts that tell the story of the world

1   A bottle of water   *Concepts: Water and the environment*

We depend on water in lots of different ways. We drink, cook and wash in it. Water irrigates crops, helps to run factories and provides the power to make electricity. Although seas and oceans cover nearly three quarters of the Earth's surface, Fresh water represents less than 3 percent of the total. Most fresh water lies deep underground or is frozen in the polar ice caps. Nevertheless, there is enough to meet our needs. The problem is that supplies are unevenly distributed and drought and erratic weather conditions are affecting people in many parts of the world. Obtaining supplies of clean drinking water is essential for health. Bottled water is one of guaranteed quality. The label will also indicate the source, opening up a discussion about the water cycle, rivers and weather patterns.

2   A fossil   *Concepts: Rocks and mountains*

Fossils have been a key source of evidence for piecing together the story of life on Earth. They also show that the rocks that are now at the top of high mountain ranges were once under the sea. Children love collecting rocks and fossils and they make an excellent addition to any geography display. Ammonites, belemnites and other small sea creatures from the Jurassic period are quite common in many parts of the country. Fossilised dinosaur bones feature in museum collections and new finds are reported in the media from time to time as they are discovered. Extend the collection to include minerals and brightly coloured stones. You may not be able to identify them all at but a simple collector's guide will certainly help.

3   A pair of woollen gloves   *Concepts: Weather and seasons*

The weather in the UK is notoriously variable. The interaction between warm air from the equator and cold air from the poles means that there are continual changes. Children are particularly responsive to the weather and enjoy learning more about it. There are plenty of opportunities for practical work. Recording the weather on a day-to-day basis links strongly with science while seasonal changes are revealed in longer-term patterns. A pair of gloves represents the winter just as a sun hat or sunglasses can symbolise the summer. Finding out what causes the seasons and how the seasons affect plants and creatures takes the work to greater depths.

4   A map of the London Underground   *Concepts: Maps, routes and journeys*

Geographers are particularly interested in where places are and how they relate to each other. Maps are a powerful way of representing such spatial information. There are many types of map ranging from the personal maps we carry in our heads to the formal maps found in atlases and gazetteers. The London Underground map has become a classic because it is brilliantly effective at showing the sequence of stations and links between lines. If children are exposed to different types of map, it gives them models they can copy and adapt. There are a surprising number of occasions when you need to find out where places are. Finding out the answer and speculating over routes and connections can be a highly creative process.

5   A cuddly toy   *Concepts: Habitats and biodiversity*

Children have a deep-seated empathy for the natural environment and tend to be fascinated by living creatures. Finding out about animal habitats is one way of exploiting their interest.

Celebrating the variety and wonders of the animal kingdom is also an excellent starting point for wider investigations. Four thousand million years of Earth history have given rise to great diversity. Sadly, many creatures are under threat, particularly due to human pressure and climate change. The cuddly toys that many children have treasured since they were toddlers symbolise not only their interest in animals but also issues to do with biodiversity. There are plenty of links to geography. Bears, for example, are found around the world – koalas in Australia, brown bears in the Rockies, polar bears in the Arctic. Identifying these places and finding out about their climate is an integral part of any study.

6   An energy-efficient light bulb   *Concepts: Energy and global warming*

One of the great challenges at the present time is to find ways of reducing carbon emissions. Scientists warn that without radical measures we face the prospect of damaging global warming and climate change. The humble energy-efficient light bulb could be part of the solution. These bulbs use a fraction of the power of incandescent bulbs, last much longer and give out roughly equivalent amounts of light. Other measures to save energy at home, school and work could make a really significant difference to our carbon emissions and be part of a battery of strategies to combat climate change. However, time is not on our side as levels of atmospheric carbon dioxide need to be drastically reduced to have any meaningful impact.

7   A banana   *Concepts: Food trade and global inequalities*

Much of the food that we eat comes from other countries. We import grain from the USA and Canada and fresh fruit and vegetables from the Mediterranean. Some other products such as tea, coffee and pineapples come from the tropics. Bananas make a particularly interesting case study. Supplies are shipped to the UK from the Caribbean, central Africa and parts of southern Asia and distributed to shops and supermarkets from warehouses. Some bananas are grown under fair trade agreements that ensure the producers receive a reasonable payment for their work. Others are sold on the open market where prices fluctuate. Finding out about the terms of trade raises questions about global inequalities. It also reminds us how we are linked to other people around the world through the food chain and how we depend on them for our survival.

8   A mobile phone   *Concepts: Communication and the future*

Mobile phones have not only become cheaper and more versatile in recent years, they have also become more powerful. As well as sending messages, mobiles are important for navigation and a significant number of internet searches are to do with location. The traffic is not all one way. Any mobile that contains a battery is tracked by satellite, effectively monitoring the whereabouts of the vast majority of people in economically developed countries. Thus the children in your class are not only going to benefit from the information about the world that is now, literally, at their finger-tips, they are also going to have to come to terms with the privacy implications and learn how to cope with information overload. As a communication tool the mobile phone has eliminated distance and opened up enormous possibilities for intercultural dialogue. In this sense it is profoundly interesting to geographers.

Figure 6.2   Many everyday artefacts relate to everyday geographical concepts (Scoffham, 2013: 10–11)

place?' These and similar questions indicate the distinctive nature of geographical study and show how geography is different from other subjects. Questions such as: 'What do you like about a place or feature?' and 'How will you change a place?' have no incorrect answers and so are inclusive.

Another good approach is to ask the children what they would like to know about the topic. Having considered this, the children can formulate their own questions to supplement the ones devised by the teacher. Many teachers make the lesson objectives, the learning that is expected and any key questions explicit to pupils at the beginning of each lesson and refer to these frequently during it. As an extension of this, it is desirable for children to also identify what they want to achieve when studying a topic. These individual objectives can be seen as enhancing the lesson objectives set by the teacher. This approach can also increase the interest and motivation of the pupils. When planning lessons, there is a need for a strong emphasis on the children learning by discovery and enquiry.

Work outside the classroom

Geography lessons and schemes of work should try to involve work outside the classroom wherever possible. Such work could be within the school grounds, within the local area or wider area around the school.

Some schools visit a local field centre where the staff organise the visit for the school. Alternatively, many teachers attempt, using the Internet, to create a virtual field trip where pupils visit a locality by using their laptops. There are clear advantages to undertaking a real field visit, of course, but time, cost and distance will limit the possibilities of this essential experience for the children, so it is perhaps realistic to encourage the use of virtual field trips.

One advantage of virtual field trips is that they encourage research skills, so you may wish to go on them as a class. For example, you could arrange a class visit such as the 'Let's Visit Coll' example later in this chapter or set as homework for the children to visit a place of their choice.

Use of resources

Geography lessons need to be supported by being able to access a good range of resources. In some cases these may be physical resources, but at other times they will involve ICT.

Geography teaching should make use of the excellent resources available on the Internet, such as videos and photographs of places and themes. The children can produce their own resources, too – by taking photographs or videos relating to a local issue, for example.

Geography should be a practical subject wherever possible. So, for example, for a topic on soils, the lesson should involve experimenting using soil samples. Geography is closely linked to science at times and the issue of what is a *fair test* is as appropriate for geography as it is for science.

Links with other subjects

To link geography with other curriculum areas, it is possible, for example, to use fiction and stories set in a particular locality to introduce a topic. There are many examples, but *Handa's Surprise* (Brown, 2009) offers children the chance to see how a child lives in an environment different from their own. Such stories can be used to link geography and literacy and so enhance the children's experiences of both.

In the book, Handa puts seven tropical fruits in her large hat and, as she walks towards her friend, animals take the fruit. Handa is oblivious to this, but luckily, at the end, a goat charges into a tangerine tree and fills her hat with fruit again.

In the classroom   *Handa's Surprise* and a class of five- and six-year-olds

A higher-level teaching assistant (HLTA), working with a Year 1 class, planned, with the class teacher, a series of lessons on Kenya and, as a starter to the scheme, used *Handa's Surprise*. The HLTA used ideas from *The Early Years Handbook* (de Boo, 2004) in her planning.

Handa's Surprise was read to the class and the children were asked to say where they thought Handa lived. The HLTA used a map on the interactive white-board and an inflatable globe to discover where Kenya was in Africa.

The pupils asked questions such as, 'Is that where Handa lives?', 'Does Handa go to school?' The class then tasted the fruit and developed their language by, for example, using words such as 'sweet', 'juicy', 'tasty', 'soft' and 'chewy'. The class then, for the rest of the scheme of work, looked at a locality study in Kenya based on a part of Nairobi.

Geography and the Early Years Foundation Stage

Geography is taught across the primary curriculum and builds on the 'understanding the world' part of the Early Years Foundation Stage (DfE, 2012). Thus, geography can be seen as an important part of children's development. The Geographical Association (2009a) suggested the following as key ideas underpinning geography's place in the EYFS:

Young children are best able to make sense of their place in the world when:

- They are inspired to think about their own place in the world, their values, and their rights and responsibilities to other people and the environment and are given opportunities to actively participate
- Their wealth of knowledge, understandings and feelings about people and places are drawn on by practitioners
- They are supported and encouraged to construct their own meanings about people and places
- They are encouraged positively to identify with other people and places
- Practitioners recognise that children's sense of identity is rooted in the places they live and play
- Their home areas, families and communities are valued; and
- They actively experience a range of high-quality, stimulating environments.

Such teaching and learning is effective when children are involved in structured play. The following example, from a lesson in a Reception class, comes from an Ofsted (2009) report.

In the classroom   Structured play in Reception

In the starter activity, the children had been issued with flight tickets for their journey to Mexico. Carlos (an imaginary character) left them messages under his poncho and sombrero. The use of Carlos really held the children's imagination. Visual images on the interactive whiteboard and the storyline involving Carlos had been used very effectively to introduce children to the village in Mexico. Their perceptions about what the village might be like as well as questions about their journey were used well. Pupils knew what they had flown over to get to Mexico and discussed their journey home in the final part of the lesson. They all mimed packing their bags, putting on their seatbelts and flew back (noises and arms like aeroplanes) on their long journey. They knew they had flown over the Atlantic Ocean and had to land in England. The final stage was used effectively to share findings and enable the children to begin to make comparisons with their home town. Expectations and levels of challenge were high but all the pupils responded well to these. The teaching, supported by the teaching assistant, was dynamic and inspirational. Both the teacher and the teaching assistant constantly encouraged and supported the children's learning and made excellent use of opportunities for the children to talk in pairs. At the end of the lesson, the teacher ensured that the pupils knew what they had learnt and how and what they would be learning next.

Teaching geography – getting started

Weather

The weather is a common topic in primary schools, chosen because it offers the possibility of taking a practical approach and it is always relevant. Weather recording, for example, is usually part of the topic, whether in the form of simple observations or using home-made or more sophisticated weather instruments.

The topic of weather often integrates physical and human geography. So, for example, the children will look at the causes of, say, rainfall, but will also look at the impact on humans of too little or too much rainfall.

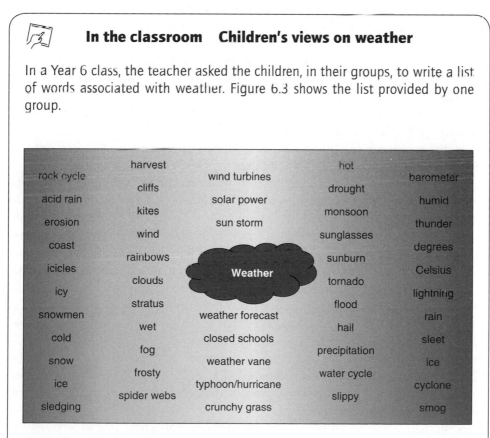

In the classroom   Children's views on weather

In a Year 6 class, the teacher asked the children, in their groups, to write a list of words associated with weather. Figure 6.3 shows the list provided by one group.

rock cycle	harvest	wind turbines	hot
acid rain	cliffs	solar power	drought	barometer
erosion	kites	sun storm	monsoon	humid
coast	wind		sunglasses	thunder
icicles	rainbows	**Weather**	sunburn	degrees
icy	clouds		tornado	Celsius
snowmen	stratus		flood	lightning
cold	wet	weather forecast	hail	rain
snow	fog	closed schools	precipitation	sleet
ice	frosty	weather vane	water cycle	ice
sledging	spider webs	typhoon/hurricane	slippy	cyclone
		crunchy grass		smog

Figure 6.3   Words associated with weather

(Continued)

(Continued)

The teacher used the lists to devise the topic on weather that would cover the next half-term. The groups kept their posters and were encouraged to think of extension activities to investigate.

Mapwork

Mapwork is an important part of geography and is taught either as a standalone lesson, integrated into a theme or in the form of a study of a particular place.

The children will often start by drawing maps of their desk or tabletop and then move on to mapping the classroom. In doing this, the concept of scale – either as standard or non-standard measures – is introduced, along with grid references. Progression involves, first, using letters and numbers to label the grid, then using numbers only. Cardinal points can be added, using the mnemonic 'Never Eat Shredded Wheat'. A scale, title and a key are then added to complete the map.

This builds on work the children will have completed in Reception, when they will have used play maps and models. At what age, though, do children develop this ability to recognise and reorder their known environment as a map, and so develop an awareness of their surroundings?

A good way to answer this question is to give preschool children an aerial photograph of an area and ask them to identify the features they can see. They often will see roads, buildings, rivers, railway tracks and so on. By doing this, they are showing that they are able to 'read' an iconic or picture map. They are able to use their play experience, along with their developing knowledge of the journeys they make as part of their lives. If you ask a preschool child to describe or draw a journey he or she knows well, such as a visit to the local shops, you will begin to collect information about what age it is that children develop such spatial awareness.

Coleman and Balachin (1965) suggested that spatial awareness be termed *graphicacy*, and considered it to be a fourth 'ace in the pack', an additional basic skill alongside numeracy, literacy and oracy. It is a form of visual literacy and may be described as an essential form of communication and a life skill. In developing their graphicacy skills, children use signs, symbols, diagrams and photographs. They will also use maps, atlases and globes.

An alternative way to introduce maps is to start a collection of a wide variety of maps. These can be depictions of real or imaginary places and it is useful for the children to add to this by also collecting maps from their homes and local area. You can ask the children to answer the following questions in groups as a way of encouraging them to focus on the detail of the map itself.

- What does the map show?
- How does it represent features?
- What area does it cover?
- When was it produced?
- What is the scale?
- Who would use it?

As mentioned above, very young children can use maps and mapwork starts in nursery or Reception. What maps should be used in primary schools, however? The Ordnance Survey produces maps at a range of scales and schools should have the following range of maps for use across the primary age range:

- 1:1250 (50 inches to one mile or 1 cm to 12.5 metres)
- 1:2500 (25 inches to one mile or 1 cm to 25 metres)
- 1:10,000 (6 inches to one mile or 1 cm to 100 metres)
- 1:25,000 (2.5 inches to 1 mile or 4 cm to 1 km)
- 1:50,000 (1.25 inches to 1 mile or 2 cm to 1 km).

(More details about these scales are available from the Ordnance Survey at: www.ordnancesurvey.co.uk)

Distant places

Teaching children about places other than the local area of the school is an essential part of any level of geographical study. In the primary curriculum, however, there is an emphasis on the study of 'localities'. These small-scale areas are similar to the scale of the local area of the school. For example (DfE, 2013: 199), at Key Stage 1, children should:

> use simple fieldwork and observational skills to study the geography of their school and its grounds and the key human and physical features of its surrounding environment.

 In the classroom   Let's visit Coll

A Year 3 class in Northamptonshire looked at the Isle of Coll and, working in groups, planned a visit to Coll for five different characters. They had studied the scheme of work 'An Island Home', based on the Katie Morag books by Dr Mairi Hedderwick (2010), and information about the island of Struay.

(Continued)

(Continued)

There were 30 children in the class, including two who were considered to have special educational needs. There was a teaching assistant who was present in the lessons.

The teacher planned the work for Monday afternoons, to continue for four weeks in total. The teacher wanted to encourage groupwork and allow for learner choice. In the first lesson, the teacher reread the Katie Morag story of the New Pier and then asked the class to look at the resources she had collected for Coll. These included a photo pack of Coll ('Discover Coll: The Real Struay'), the Katie Morag stories, five Ordnance Survey maps at a scale of 1:50,000 and a range of photographs of Coll downloaded from the Internet generally and the Visit Coll website (at: www.visitcoll.co.uk).

The teacher gave a number of photographs of characters to each of the five groups in the class and the groups had to create a character and a reason for the character wanting to visit Coll. These characters included a scout leader, a young teacher, a mother and father and their two young children, a 30-year-old daughter and her retired father and, finally, two retired female teachers. The teacher encouraged the group to invent a life story for each of these characters.

The first lesson was to plan the journey from their town to Oban (the nearest ferry port to Coll) and then they had to book a place to stay. In the second lesson, the groups had to research Coll and plan a week's stay for their character and book the ferry. At the end of this lesson, the characters boarded the ferry and 'went' to Coll. In the third lesson, the groups enjoyed their week's stay 'on' Coll and looked at the differences between Coll and their home town. The final week's lesson involved each group presenting a book on their visit to Coll.

Approaches to teaching a locality study

Teachers can use a range of activities to introduce a locality study. Here are some examples.

- Plan a journey from the local area to the locality using maps, globes, atlases and airline timetables.
- Set up a passport control and airport lounge in the classroom and issue each child with a passport. This works really well when a number of classes are studying different localities at the same time, so they can get their passports stamped when they visit other classes.
- Show the links between the local area and the locality to be studied.
- Ask the children to say or draw what they already know about the country of the locality to elicit the current awareness of the group.

- Usually, start the locality study after a brief introduction to the country as a whole.
- If possible, arrange a talk by a person who has been to the locality.
- Use a fiction book set in the locality as a stimulus.
- Collect photographs and videos from the Internet.
- Plan a virtual field trip to the locality using the resources available on the Internet.
- Show a range of photographs of the locality and encourage the children to ask 'Where am I?' This may challenge stereotypes held by the children.
- Use newspapers from the locality (see www.aldaily.com).
- Where possible, it is interesting to use artefacts from the country.
- Look at the locality through the eyes of a child.
- It is important to look for similarities between the locality and the local area before starting to look at the differences. This approach will tend to reduce negative views held or developed by the children.
- It is important to study a locality of a similar size to the local area so like will be compared with like.
- It is important for teachers to challenge discriminatory views.
- When studying localities, it is important to not just focus on problems but also look for solutions.
- Enable the class to feel empathy for the people who live in the locality.
- Vary how the topic is covered by doing a locality day or week.
- In Key Stage 1, have Barnaby Bear or any soft toy 'visit' the locality. With older children, why not introduce another character who texts the class from his or her mobile phone. Perhaps he or she could also be on Twitter and the class can follow the tweets.
- Perhaps the most satisfying approach is when the class links with another school in another locality.

Levels of planning

Schools will have a policy statement for geography and a long-term or Key Stage plan for the subject that provides an overview of the topics to be covered. In addition, schools have medium-term plans or schemes of work and short-term or lesson plans. Schools sometimes use nationally available schemes of work or published schemes, such as SuperSchemes, published by the Geographical Association (www. geography.org.uk). By far the most satisfying professionally is for schools to produce their own schemes or at least adapt an existing one.

How to plan a scheme of work

How do you start to plan a scheme of work? You can start by considering the following questions.

- Can you and the children research what is available for the chosen topic?
- Can you identify what you are trying to achieve in terms of the overall objectives?
- Is a practical application possible?
- Is a wide variety of resources available?
- Is fieldwork possible? If not, is a virtual visit possible?
- Can 'experts' on the topic be used?
- Is the topic a one-day, 'short', half-term or continuous topic?
- Does the topic link with other subjects?
- Does the topic build on the children's earlier knowledge and skills?
- Will the topic allow pupils to use geographical terms?
- Does the approach represent good practice in geography?
- Are the children allowed to choose part of what they do?
- Does the approach allow group and individual work and is it inclusive for all learners?
- Is there a balance between teacher- and child-led work?

There is a danger, whatever scheme is used, that it becomes 'set in stone', so all schemes need to be revised on a yearly basis. More experienced teachers do not plan all the work at the start of a topic – they let the children have some input into what is covered.

The first lesson involves some initial assessment of what the children already know about the topic and what they want to find out about it. Some of these ideas can be used in the subsequent planning of the topic. It is also helpful if, when children work in groups, they investigate as a group one aspect of the topic and then feed back what they have found out to the class as a whole, along with the work from the other groups.

Resources

The Geographical Association has a wide range of resources for developing geography in primary schools. In addition to the public pages there are members' pages. It is advisable for primary schools to join and subscribe to the journal *Primary Geography*, which is published four times a year.

When the school joins, it will be given a login number and password that will allow access to all past copies of the journal, along with copies of the *GA Magazine*. Students on courses of initial teacher training should contact their academic librarian or geography tutor as the majority of universities provide access to this member page via their institutional subscription.

In the classroom   Applying for a Primary Geography Quality Mark

A local school in Bedfordshire is proud of the geography taught there and has decided to apply for the Geographical Association's Primary Geography Quality Mark.

In preparation for the visit by the assessor, the subject leader for geography asked the other teachers, teaching assistants and the children, to contribute their views on how geography is taught and learned in the school. The subject leader used the questions below with her colleagues and devised a separate task for the children to complete on what they liked about geography.

Section 1: What is geography like in your school?

This section asks you to look at what the learning environment looks like and what you are trying to provide for the children in your geography curriculum and how the children feel about it. *You will need to communicate the excitement and richness of the geography that the children experience.*

1 Achievement is high and pupils make good progress in relation to age, ability and prior experience.
2 Assessment is seen as an essential tool in planning learning and monitoring the children's progress.
3 Fieldwork, active enquiry learning and the use of ICT has a clear impact on the way children learn geography.
4 The effective teaching of geography is seen as the key to engaging pupils with creative and critical thinking about 'people and place', local and global change, sustainability and possible futures.
5 The teaching of core geographical knowledge underpins children's learning about the world.
6 Geography supports other curriculum areas, contributes to the enjoyment and achievement of learners and to whole-school initiatives.

Section 2: How effective is subject leadership and management?

This section asks you to look at how effectively you are developing the subject and setting a clear direction for the development of geography in your school,

(Continued)

(Continued)

influencing your colleagues and the school's culture and reaching out beyond your school.

1   There is a 'vision' for geography that is helping to shape the way that the subject is taught. This vision informs the geography policy and guides the writing of schemes of work based on the National Curriculum. It has the clear support of the headteacher and subject leader.
2   The subject leader formulates clear and relevant development targets to guide teaching in the school. Subject monitoring is focused on ensuring curriculum provision has a clear impact on the children's progress and identifies the professional development needs of teachers.

The subject leader also looked at 'A different view: A manifesto from the Geographical Association' (2009b), and also reviewed the latest Ofsted (2009) report on the teaching of geography, then decided to apply for the Primary Geography Quality Mark. The school was successful in being awarded a bronze category and the subject leader has now prepared an action plan, as part of the school development plan, to apply next year for the silver award.

Subject knowledge

The Geographical Association provides lots of support for subject leaders in geography (at: www.geography.org.uk/eyprimary/geographysubjectleaders). One of its tools is a subject audit. You can assess yourself using the questions below.

- Do you have any educational background in geography as a subject?
- Do you have any personal interest in geography?
- How would you rate your awareness of the National Curriculum for geography?
- How do you perceive the geography lessons that you have taught?
- How confident would you feel if a school-based mentor, teacher training tutor or headteacher observed one of your geography lessons?
- If you were responsible for geography throughout the school, what would be your main objective(s)?
- What is/are the main constraint(s) on the teaching of geography in schools?
- How could this/these be improved?
- Highlight something that you have done regarding geography that gave you a real 'buzz' and sense of achievement.

Having completed this audit, create an action plan for how you can improve your expertise in teaching geography in a primary school.

Reflective questions

- How can I engage children in their study of the Earth?
- How can I develop children's enquiry skills in an effective way?
- How can I plan for good geography?
- What are the key features of an effective scheme of work?

Conclusion

This chapter has provided an introduction to the nature of geography and how to teach it in primary schools.

Geography as a subject provides an excellent opportunity for children to be more aware of their world and allows them to understand their place in that world and the world itself. Geography is also a unique subject, forming a bridge between humanities and the sciences. As the world-renowned journalist, Simon Jenkins (2007) indicated, 'geography in the widest sense of the concept remains to me as the queen of the sciences. It holds the key that unlocks the coherence of the physical world'. He continues this justified praise for geography by noting, 'It is geography that explains why each of us are located where we are, in neighbourhoods, nation, continent and planet, and how fragile might be that location. Without geography's instruction, we are in every sense lost – random robots who can only read and count'.

The Internet has transformed the world and our involvement with it, but to surf the world is not the same as to experience it. Therein lies the value of geography in schools as it allows children to understand topics as diverse as global warming, the location of a football ground and of Everest. With all the world to consider, which topics will you choose to teach?

Further reading

Pickford, T., Garner, W. and Jackson, E. (2013) *Primary Humanities: Learning through enquiry*. London: Sage.

Considers the nature of good geography and this is illustrated by showing the relevance of geography to children and in the revised primary curriculum. This is achieved by looking at a number of themes such as fieldwork, the integration of geographical skills, themes and places and the use of geographical questions when planning and teaching in the primary school. Geography's place in the primary curriculum and its links to the Early Years Foundation stage curriculum are outlined. In addition map work, fieldwork, the teaching of distant places, weather and the use of resources are discussed.

References

Brown, E. (2009) *Handa's Surprise*. London: Walker Books.

Coleman, A. and Balachin, W. (1965) 'Graphicacy: The 4th ace in the pack', *Times Educational Supplement*, 5 November.

de Boo, M. (ed.) (2004) *The Early Years Handbook*. Sheffield: The Curriculum Partnership/ Geographical Association.

DfE (2012) 'Statutory Framework for the Early Years Foundation Stage'. Runcorn: DfE. Available online at: www.foundationyears.org.uk/wp-content/uploads/2012/07/EYFS-Statutory-Framework-2012.pdf

DfE (2013) 'The National Curriculum in England: Framework document'. Runcorn: DfE. Available online at: www.gov.uk/government/uploads/system/uploads/attachment_data/file/210969/NC_framework_document_-_FINAL.pdf

Geographical Association (2009a) 'Making Connections: Geography in the Foundation Stage: A position statement from the Geographical Association'. Sheffield: Geographical Association.

Geographical Association (2009b) 'A different view: A manifesto from the Geographical Association'. Sheffield: Geographical Association. Available online at: www.geography.org.uk/adifferentview (there is also a video).

Hedderwick, M. (2010) *Katie Morag and the New Pier*. London: Red Fox Picture Books.

Jenkins, S. (2007) 'The assault on geography breeds ignorance and erodes nationhood', *The Guardian*, 16 November. Available online at: www.theguardian.com/commentisfree/2007/nov/16/comment.politics

Ofsted (2009) 'Geography: Learning to make a world of difference'. Manchester: Ofsted. Available online at: www.ofsted.gov.uk/resources/geography-learning-make-world-of-difference

Palin, M. (2008) 'Geography action plan at Speaker's house', *Mapping News*, 33: 4–5.

Scoffham, S. (ed.) (2010) *Primary Geography Handbook*. Sheffield: Geographical Association.

Scoffham, S. (ed.) (2013) *Teaching Geography Creatively*. Abingdon: Routledge.

CHAPTER 7

HISTORY

Mary Bracey, Paul Bracey and Sandra Kirkland

Learning objectives

By the end of the chapter you should be able to:

- explain the principles of teaching and learning history in primary school
- consider how misconceptions can affect learning
- appreciate the range of approaches and resources available to support learning primary history.

Introduction

History encourages children to ask questions about the past, whether these relate to their own lives or the wider world. Hoskins (1969: 14), an historian who pioneered using the outdoor environment to find out about the past, exemplifies the wide range of opportunities history presents for teaching and learning in the primary years when he says, 'A commonplace ditch may be the thousand-year-old boundary of a royal manor; a certain hedge bank may be even more ancient … a certain deep and winding lane may be the work of twelfth-century peasants, some of whose names may be made known to us if we search diligently enough'.

Children can develop their understanding of the past by looking at their own past and asking questions of a person from their community. They can also make use of a vast selection of material evidence related to the past, including objects and pictures, written evidence or music from different times and the local environment. Children's understanding of the past becomes progressively more refined as they make use of a rich array of resources to build up their subject knowledge. It is your responsibility to research and plan lessons and activities in order to make this possible. In this chapter, we will provide some valuable ideas and practical suggestions to help you plan for exciting and innovative learning opportunities.

In the classroom   Using artefacts relating to Victorian and Edwardian washdays with five- to seven-year-old children

The children explored washdays of the past using a range of genuine and replica resources, including flat irons, cotton clothing, different soaps, two washboards, a range of wooden pegs, as well as photographs and pictures showing women in sculleries and kitchens.

The children began their learning journey by using their senses to investigate the artefacts. They closed their eyes and used their sense of smell for the soaps. None of the children recognised the soaps' smell as that of a washing product. In a later session they looked at modern products for washing clothes and they talked about how soap could be used to do this. The children used their sense of touch to investigate the washboard (hidden in a feely bag). When feeling the washboard, some of the children were able to suggest adjectives to describe it. Even when they could finally see the washboard, they did not recognise it as something for washing clothes. One six-year-old child felt the ridges on the

---

washboard and suggested it might be a musical instrument. Perhaps an understandable misconception, this was built on in subsequent learning by looking at pictures and descriptions of washdays from secondary sources to establish how the washboard was used.

Using the artefacts was a good starting point and stimulated the children's interest. The opportunity to handle the objects offered a unique experiential opportunity. Handling the flat iron, for instance, made them realise how heavy it was; rubbing clothing on the washboard helped them experience how quickly their arms became tired. As a result, the children began to understand how labour-intensive washdays were in the past and how different the whole process was from their own personal experiences today.

What misconceptions do children have about the past?

The ways in which children learn are complicated and misconceptions occur naturally when they instinctively try to relate their new experiences to their existing knowledge and understanding. The following statements provide some examples of these in the context of learning history

- 'You've got it all wrong. I have seen pictures of cavemen fighting dinosaurs' (an 11-year-old child having an animated discussion about the emergence of early people).
- 'Great fire of London. Was that when you were a little girl, Miss?'
- 'The Vikings must have won because they had longboats and Spitfires' (a drawing in which a child portrayed the Saxons being defeated by the Vikings).
- 'This teddy is older than that one because it is scruffy' (six-year-old child confusing the condition of an object with its age).

These examples raise issues about how the past can be misunderstood. It is possible to pre-empt some misconceptions by giving thought to the way the work is structured. For example, contextual and/or visual impressions of Viking and Tudor times can be compared to help develop an understanding of continuity and change. However, issues arise unexpectedly in any topic and if you spot and then use these opportunities constructively, such moments offer the perfect chance for children to test their misunderstandings and use the process to support their learning. For example, the child who thought that Spitfires were used by the Vikings was applying knowledge quite logically based on what that child knew about warfare in the twentieth century. Rather than simply telling the child that this was wrong, it is possible to use the moment to get the child to investigate aspects of the Vikings in order to test the hypothesis. This provides a productive way of meaningfully constructing the child's knowledge of the past.

What is the place of history in the primary curriculum?

According to the National Curriculum framework document (DfE, 2013: 204), history teaching should:

> help pupils gain a coherent knowledge and understanding of Britain's past and that of the wider world. It should inspire pupils' curiosity to know more about the past. Teaching should equip pupils to ask perceptive questions, think critically, weigh evidence, sift arguments, and develop perspective and judgement.

What is taught, as well as how it is taught, and the relative importance of content and skills, have proved contentious issues that have drawn attention from politicians, the media, academics and those of us more directly involved in what is taught in primary classrooms. At the same time, the advantages and disadvantages of teaching history as a discreet subject or as part of a topic that embraces different aspects of a child's learning have also been widely debated. An integrated approach can, of course, provide effective links between curriculum areas and provide an exciting and tightly focused approach to learning that, many teachers would argue, has advantages over a curriculum taught by means of discreet subjects, as suggested in the new curriculum proposals. The example below illustrates this effectively.

In the classroom   Creating models of air raid shelters with 10- and 11-year-old children

The children used pictures, diagrams and first-hand historical accounts to support this task in design and technology, which they then used as a resource to explain what life was like during the Blitz (see Figure 7.1).

Figure 7.1   Model of an air raid shelter (with thanks to the children of Yelvertoft school)

The rich opportunities that this activity provided in both subjects can be applied elsewhere by using similarly linked learning opportunities across other areas of the curriculum. Examples would include the location of Saxon and Viking place names related to the study of settlements in geography. Historical fiction, such as *Goodnight Mr Tom*, or fictional stories produced in the past (such as *Beowulf*), can draw on and develop both history and English skills.

However, ill-defined topic work can be problematic. Ofsted (2011) observed that in one school which had been inspected: 'Pupils' perceptions of history were unclear in some primary schools where a cross-curricular framework had been introduced … [However] including history in a thematic approach did not of itself undermine the integrity of the subject. Integrated work succeeded where the development of the knowledge and thinking of each subject was emphasised' (Ofsted, 2011: 33).

Whether history is taught as a separate subject or as an element within a topic is an interesting issue to consider, but of more critical importance is the quality of the planning, teaching and learning, which can draw out the key qualities of the subject and promote the associated knowledge and subject-related thinking skills.

What is history in classrooms about?

History involves exploring the past. This raises questions about what is learned and has implications for the development of relevant skills. Consider the views expressed by the fictional schoolmaster, Thomas Gradgrind (Dickens, 1854: 47):

> Now, what I want is facts. Teach these boys and girls nothing but facts. Facts alone are wanted in life. Plant nothing else, and root out everything else. You can only form the minds of reasoning animals upon facts: nothing else will ever be of service to them.

This approach to learning presents knowledge as if it were something contained in a sealed box and assumes that the 'facts' are both predetermined and meaningful in their own right. It provides no opportunity to question misconceptions, as we have suggested above, or explore the unknown with the passion demonstrated by the historian Hoskins at the start of this chapter.

Even if we just teach facts, we cannot say that what is taught is unimportant or value-free. Debates over what should be taught reflect concerns as to how this is believed to affect the way in which children see the world. When this includes a canon or list of specified individuals as subjects, and particular events, these may be essentially intended to shore up a sense of national identity. Whether or not this is an appropriate use of history is debatable, but perhaps of more interest is whether or not it is effective.

Several research studies have questioned the effectiveness of depending on children's acquisition of dates and events. Research undertaken by Wineberg (2000) found that poor memory of historical events has been a problem since the early twentieth century, regardless of the teaching approaches used. Another study that investigated how children build up their understanding of the past was initiated by the following concern (Foster et al., 2008: 2):

> memory of discreet items of information may be a poor indicator of their ability to use knowledge of the past for orientation in time. We cannot tell from tests of 'key facts' whether children leave school with a coherent framework of knowledge linking past, present and future which they can use to make sense of the world.

This study found no evidence to suggest, beyond family and personal history, that history was a major factor in influencing identity and suggested that it would be wrong to conclude that students need a fixed national identity around which they should unite.

A major concern is how far children are able to understand the way in which different parts of the past link together in order to gain an understanding of the past (Ofsted, 2011). Children may know about the Vikings and Victorians, but they are often unable to locate them within a broader map of the past. For example, a study with six- and seven-year-olds undertaken by Hodkinson (2003) argued that it is not enough to use temporal concepts such as 'long ago' or 'a very long time ago'. Both are ambiguous and confusing for children. Precise measures, such as decades and centuries, need to be used to promote an understanding of the past. Developing a sense of chronology is of particular concern, as a means of providing a framework to which children can relate their understanding of the past. Thus, sequencing and timeline activities are commonly used to develop this skill.

In the classroom   Using timelines with four- to seven-year-olds

A sense of chronology was developed with four- to seven-year-old children by encouraging them to make a timeline of their own life. This required support from parents/carers, who were asked to provide their children with a small range of photographs of them, from their earliest baby photographs, followed by pictures taken in school. The children collected the pictures and talked about them with their parents/carers before bringing them in to school.

During the activity, the children tried to put the photographs in the correct chronological order and were supported by the teacher, providing scaffolding when necessary. The five- to seven-year-old children learnt about chronology when studying the Fire of London, the events in the life of a famous person and grouping toys from different periods in history.

A class timeline was built up, to which were added events and vocabulary such as '50 years ago', 'more than 100 years ago' and 'about 400 years ago' was used. By using chronology-related activities, the children were able to deal with number and time concepts that some of them would otherwise have found challenging.

As children progress into the upper primary years, their understanding of the past needs to become increasingly sophisticated.

Chronology can be taught in a number of ways, such as producing timelines on the wall or a history washing line across the room, together with a range of approaches considered later in this chapter. Closely associated with chronology are concepts such as change, cause and effect and studies of past situations, which provide insights into the ways in which the past has unfolded. The child mentioned earlier who thought that the Vikings had used Spitfires to defeat the Saxons clearly had misconceptions relating to change and did not have a sense of period. To avoid this, in upper primary classes, the children can compare aspects of people's lives, such as travel, homes and work at different times, to develop an overview of the past. Within specific topics, too, such as 'migration' or 'treatment of the poor', there is scope to compare and make links between the experiences of groups of people at different times.

The way in which children construct their understanding of the past is critical for learning about this or other aspects of their historical understanding. We argue that this should cover consideration of a diverse range of experiences, including rich and poor, people from different ethnic communities and genders (Claire, 1996; Bracey et al., 2011). Cooper (2012: 14) points out that the study of the past can relate to a range of contexts if they share a common approach:

> History may be broad or in depth. It may be about an individual, about social groups, economic or social movements, local, national or global … But history is not just a story or a list of events. Whatever content an account of the past may focus on, it must be investigated through the process of historical enquiry.

How can children begin to build up their understanding of the past through historical enquiry? We can only try to establish what happened in the past and, for this, children need time to explore, observe and discuss what they see and think. They then need to be able to share their possibly incomplete understanding with their teacher and peers.

This may appear daunting for you as a teacher, especially if your own knowledge of the past is limited, but it is possible if you prepare well. As a starting point, it is essential that you have researched the period or topic. At the same time, it is important to appreciate that you are unlikely to know everything and you are almost certainly going to develop your expertise in the process of planning and teaching the subject. It is also important that you consider the potential range of resources that you could use – both within the classroom and outside, including members of the community, the locality, museums and sites and re-enactment companies. This provides a menu from which you can pick things that will develop the children's subject knowledge and understanding.

It is also useful to have an insight into history topics that your class has undertaken in the past in order to relate the current topic to any relevant previous learning. You can begin by finding out what the children know and eliciting any early misconceptions. You can also locate what they are learning within a wider timeframe. You could begin this process by locating their new topic on a timeline in the context of previous periods in history that they have studied and making visual comparisons between them. The proposed chronological approach for teaching history in upper primary classes should further facilitate this.

Through historical enquiry, children can find answers to their questions in order to build up a provisional idea of the past without assuming it is a jumbled mass of dates and facts that can be passively swallowed up. Turner-Bisset (2005: 26) defined questioning as:

> the force that drives historical enquiry … from open, speculative questions which may spring either from the children or the teacher, the children can generate further questions which refine the focus of the enquiry or open up further themes.

This enquiry-based approach requires a key question for the topic, followed by six or seven supporting questions as a focus for specific lessons or groups of lessons. Such questions can start with 'How?', 'Why?', 'What?' or 'When?' This firmly establishes the principle of there being a process that is at the heart of learning. It is useful to consider some ways in which both the questions and the process can be used effectively to engage children in their learning. For example, Riley (2000: 3) recommended that teachers should look at how well their key questions not only provide an historical focus but also engage children by providing 'something with a more obvious puzzle element, that can be used to intrigue pupils and connect one set of facts with another.'

This principle could be applied to devising questions at primary level by thinking of key questions for topics as well as individual lessons. Consider the following key questions for medium-term plans

- What happened in Tudor times?
- What caused the Fire of London?
- The Fire of London – was the baker to blame?
- Elizabethan times – all banquets and fun?

We hope you agree with us that the last two would provide a more intriguing start to a topic than the first two!

The same approach should be applied to individual enquiry questions within the scheme. With respect to the first given below, why bother asking the question when you have been given the answer? The second question is intentionally open-ended, with opportunities for the children to develop their own ideas.

- Why was Mary Queen of Scots beheaded?
- Why did Mary Queen of Scots have so many enemies?

You may well think of more effective questions, but, in both cases, the alternative questions attempt to introduce a degree of mystery and intrigue that is lacking in the examples listed first.

Here is a further example. The following set of questions were raised with 9- to 11-year-old children in the context of the cross-curricular topic 'Enterprise', under the heading 'How enterprising were the Victorians?'

1. Who were the Victorians?
2. How can we tell that the Victorians were enterprising?
3. What does the Great Exhibition tell us about the enterprising Victorians?
4. Why did the Victorians build factories?
5. What impact did enterprise have on the lives of children?
6. How enterprising were reformers?
7. Was George Cadbury enterprising?
8. How enterprising were the Victorians? What was the effect of this on their lives?

Approaches to primary history

With younger children, history tends to be broadly based, asking and answering questions about personal, family and local contexts, together with stories, events and people in the recent and distant past from Britain and around the world. As the children's knowledge becomes more refined, however, they explore and draw links between different times and spatial contexts. They should also consider how the past has been represented and interpreted in different ways, such as in museums, films, souvenirs and books.

Key questions can provide the focus of your enquiry and, from this, the children can develop their knowledge and understanding by focusing on historical objectives drawn from those described in more detail below. Any question will inevitably include many of these different aspects of history, but one or more will usually stand out as a focus for the work. By developing subject knowledge as a result of setting historical objectives, the children will be able to look for answers to questions in a more systematic way. They provide the driving focus for selecting activities and represent what you want the children to achieve. They are based on the following.

Chronological understanding

With younger children, this includes placing events, pictures or objects, such as toys, in chronological order and using simple words related to time, such as 'before and after'. The use of timelines related to their lives or those around them, together with people and events studied also provides a means of supporting their development of an understanding of the past. Similarly, having read through the life story of a person, the children can be given cards with key events, from which they can pick out and sequence the key events in their lives. For example, this exercise was used by Claire (2008) to enable children to gain an overview of the life of Walter Tull, a footballer and the first black officer in the Army during World War I.

Should timelines be straight lines, though? A thinking skills technique can be used to encourage children to think of, for example, the high and low points in Walter Tull's life. A smiley face can be put at the top of a piece of sugar paper and a sad face at the bottom, with the original timeline down the middle. By moving the cards towards the top of the page, the children could produce a wavy timeline, which would provide opportunities to consider Walter Tull's changing fortunes and concepts of changes and situations as well as chronology.

As children progress, particularly into upper primary classes, they need to relate events, people and changes to different times in the past. A number of studies have argued for the use of timelines around rooms and school halls, developing them with the children as they learn different topics. Measuring duration and changes, both between and within periods of history, provides a sense of the significance of different times, events and individuals. It is useful to locate periods of history within a broader picture of the past by having timelines and using pupils as human markers for a large timeline (Sossick, 2011; Wallace, 2011).

Understanding events, people and changes

This includes finding out why people did things or why things happened and having a sense of what it was like to live at different times in the past.

In lower primary classes this could include topics such as 'Why should we remember Walter Tull?' or 'The Fire of London: Was the baker to blame?' It could also include looking at life at different times – comparing living in a castle with a home today.

As children progress into upper primary classes, the objectives become increasingly demanding, so they are required to find out about the specific features of different times. This is likely to include the lives of men, women and children, the social, cultural, religious and ethnic diversity of societies, together with the reasons for and results of events, situations and changes within and across periods of history.

Historical interpretation

This relates to how people look back at the past and perhaps best represents the way in which most children and their parents encounter the past. An example is the English Heritage living history event at Kenilworth Castle, shown in Figure 7.2.

Figure 7.2   English Heritage living history event at Kenilworth Castle, showing players as Queen Elizabeth I and Robert Dudley, Earl of Leicester

Useful resources might include the perceptions of historical events or periods of history presented in films, such as costume dramas, school textbooks, museum displays, souvenirs, travel catalogues, role-play, re-enactments or historically based adverts. Many of these will be encountered naturally, even by young children.

As children progress they should be encouraged to question why people, periods of history and events have been represented as they have, not simply take things at face value. This in itself can provide a wonderful basis for a topic. For example, you could start with an image of Victorian times shown on a Christmas card, in a costume drama, re-enactment or a visit to Cadbury World, then study aspects of Victorian life, including slums, children's working conditions and the workhouse. This could lead on to discussing why these more relevant depictions did not find a place on the front of the card! Depictions of Luxor at Las Vegas provide a comparable, if more contentious, representation of the Egyptians, while Yorvik goes some way towards challenging stereotypical perceptions of the Vikings.

Historical enquiry

This objective is at the heart of the process of learning history – that is, children being able to ask and answer questions from a wide range of sources.

Cooper (2012) draws on the work of Piaget and Bruner to argue that young children tend to draw randomly from their experiences at home and school, but, progressively, they relate them to information about the natural world before moving on to being able to make abstract propositions. Therefore, we need to provide relevant experiences and information as children move through primary school.

The following exercise demonstrates how a group of older primary school children were able to link their direct experiences to a deeper knowledge and understanding of context and enquiry related to a specific time in the past.

In the classroom   ... or out of the classroom!

Using a walk through Yelvertoft village as an historical enquiry

A group of 10- and 11-year-old children were asked, 'What evidence can we look for to find out what Yelvertoft (a village in Northamptonshire) was like in World War II?'

The children began by comparing a map of the village from the wartime with a recent map to identify the buildings that had survived and still existed from then and coloured them in.

Following this, they were asked how and where they might find evidence of the war. They suggested looking at building styles, dates on buildings, the war memorial, gravestones, a plaque in the church and one child mentioned a building that had housed prisoners of war. This was followed by an investigative walk through the village, helped by a long-standing member of the community, who was able to add extra information. The knowledge some children had about the properties they lived in also supported their enquiry.

Organisation and communication

The key consideration here is that children of all ages should be involved in selecting and communicating their ideas in different ways, including, for example, discussions, drama, displays, drawing, extended writing, using ICT skills to create a film or making models based on researching the past.

These skills and methods need to be taught within a broadly based framework of the past, covering the recent and distant times from local, national, European and world history perspectives – a job that becomes increasingly complex as their knowledge, skills and understanding develop.

Getting started: stimulating interest and building on what the children know

When starting a new topic you, as the teacher, will have insights into the questions that you want to be explored, together with the context of the topic. What about the children?

They may well have existing ideas that are grounded in their own experiences and images of people, places and topics from outside the classroom and some of those ideas may be historically inaccurate or only partially understood. These misconceptions need to be identified and either discussed or used to support targeted planning. It is therefore important to reference the children's prior learning when beginning a new topic or lesson.

Sharing the key question and objectives, whether created for or developed with the children, provides them with a focus for their learning and conveys what is expected from them. Turner-Bisset argues that it is important to spend time devising creative approaches to inspire children, meet their needs and encourage their own creativity. This takes time, as it involves a 'shuffling of ideas and repertoire to devise the best possible teaching approach for what is to be learned' (Turner-Bisset, 2005: 174). Table 7.1 provides examples of starter activities that can provide a creative hook for learning about the past.

Table 7.1   Some stimulating starter activities to encourage creative approaches to learning

Well-known stories and nursery rhymes	*The Three Little Pigs* – materials used for houses at different times in the past – straw, wood or brick *Mary, Mary, Quite Contrary* – Mary Tudor's persecution of Protestants *Ring a Ring o' Roses* – the impact of the Plague
Pictures	Raising questions while looking at a picture of Victorian working children as the basis for an historical enquiry; using a local postcard as a basis for comparing past and present
Film or TV extracts	Using archive government propaganda films encouraging parents to evacuate their children during World War II or the opening scene from the film *Gladiator* (2000), with parental consent, could provide an introduction to Roman warfare
A story as a stimulus	An extract from *Coming to England* (1995) by Floella Benjamin can provide an introduction to the experiences of people migrating to this country
Letters and diary extracts	A letter based on Beatrix Potter's book can be used as a starting point for studying her life Extracts from Samuel Pepys or Anne Frank's diary can be used to promote historical enquiry questions
Artefact	Showing a Viking bone mug or sixteenth-century reed lamp to stimulate questions about their use
Visits/visitors	A visit to a local castle, local or national museum, from a member of the community or watching a role-play or re-enactment (these can take place at the start, middle or end of a topic, but, as a starter, can be used to encourage children to generate questions)
Drama	Freeze framing to depict a scene from the Fire of London or the Irish potato famine, for example, followed by the teacher hot seating a character from the events in order to initiate an historical enquiry

In the classroom   From stimulus to enquiry: examining a Victorian photograph of the seaside

Figure 7.3   The esplanade and beach at Weymouth in Dorset (reproduced by permission of English Heritage from www.heritage-explorer.co.uk)

We used a Victorian photograph of the esplanade and beach at Weymouth (English Heritage), from the digital National Monuments Record with children across the primary school. It is interesting to see both similarities and differences in the approaches used, which allowed for progression according to the children's needs in the two primary phases.

Lower primary classes

As a starting point, before using the picture, the children were reminded of basic question words that they could use, which had previously been covered in literacy sessions. The children had prompts available for the question words.

The six- and seven-year-olds then worked with their learning partners, looking at the photograph (A3 size). They were asked to think of some questions about the photograph that they would like to have answered. By having talk partners,

(Continued)

(Continued)

the children formulated and developed questions together and could support each other, with some questions naturally leading to others. Having a partner and sharing their questions gave some of the less confident children an opportunity to fully participate.

Working with the teacher, the five- and six-year-olds could be directed to try to think of questions starting with different question words. The teacher also worked as a scribe and was able to help them to compose questions when necessary. Following this introductory lesson, the children used photographs, pictures, books and the teacher, sharing information in order to try to answer the questions and learn more about Victorian holidays. The exercise also involved putting the Victorians on to a class timeline, with Victorian times being described as more than 100 years ago.

Upper primary classes

As a starting point, the children were shown the picture and given copies to share with their talk partners to discuss what it told them about going to the seaside in Victorian times. Some children showed very good observational skills and paid great attention to the details, such as the writing on the adverts. This included children across the ability range as it helped that the picture gave them a focus and the responses were open-ended.

The children then worked in pairs to raise questions about the photograph that they wanted answers to, using the details they had noted.

We discussed the picture as a class and used the working wall to display some question words. After devising their own research questions, the children used both textbooks and the Internet to answer them. The questions raised included, 'Did the Victorians ever sit down and relax on the beach?' and 'What is a bathing machine?' Some children found that they had to refine their questions by linking them to a broader theme in order to support their research.

The children evaluated the stimulus to enquiry process and some indicated that, once they had a starting point to find information, this acted as a catalyst for further research. The children were aware of the questions being researched and also helped each other.

This exercise shows how children's understanding is developed by the process of undertaking an historical enquiry, the process becoming increasingly complex as the children progress through primary school.

The key thing these activities have in common is that they show how children can use a stimulus, then apply process-based skills, together with speaking and listening, to help construct their knowledge of the past. Several different approaches can be used within a lesson or group of related lessons on a topic. For example, the research task undertaken by the older children looking at the picture of the seaside made use of a range of processes – observing, questioning and reflecting. It also made use of all aspects of speaking and listening for learning in history.

We would like to end this chapter by focusing on the value of talk as a means of learning about the past, shown in the following example.

In the classroom   Learning history by talking about the past

The opening two paragraphs of the story of Walter Tull (Claire, 2008) were read to a class of five- to seven-year-old children as a starting point and they were given copies of the illustration on page 5 of the book.

The children discussed with their talk partners what they thought was happening in the picture and what they had learned from listening to the reading of the text and looking at the picture. The older children recorded this on the reverse of the photograph and the others worked in a group with the teacher to use the clues.

The classroom furniture was moved around, with the tables placed in straight lines, and adults took on the roles of the head of the orphanage and the housekeeper. Very thin porridge was presented to the children as gruel – they did not have to eat it, but were reminded (in role) that if they did not, they would only be getting bread and cheese for tea and there was a lot of work to do before then. The children were expected to be very polite to the teachers in their roles – to sit in silence, listen to instructions and follow them immediately.

The children were split into groups and given some chores, such as ironing (using cold, but authentic, flat irons), cleaning using rags and cold water to clean some areas of the classroom, and dusting using other rags to dust around the room. After lining up in silence, the children were given a short playtime and played some traditional playtime games.

Hot seating was then used to encourage the children to think and talk about the experiences of Walter Tull and the other children in the orphanage. They

(Continued)

(Continued)

asked the adults questions, such as, 'Why did we only have cold water for washing?', 'Why could we not have sugar on our gruel?' The children were also given the opportunity to sit in the hot seat themselves and talk about their experiences.

To sum up, the lesson began with teacher-directed talk, then the children were given the opportunity to develop and share questions and responses in a follow-up hot seating activity. In the second activity, the children had opportunities to share their learning through talk and build this up collaboratively into a class discussion related to continuity and change.

Many of the activities that we have mentioned in this chapter, including freeze framing, questioning, using objects and artefacts, involve various forms of talk in order to share and promote learning. The links between talk, thinking and learning across all subjects in the curriculum are clear. Indeed, Alexander (2010) argues that Dialogic Teaching can be used to support children's development and learning. The five characteristics of talk in Dialogic Teaching are that it is:

- *collective* teachers and children address learning tasks together
- *reciprocal* teachers and children listen to each other and share ideas and alternative viewpoints
- *supportive* children feel free to share their ideas
- *cumulative* teachers and children build on their own and one another's ideas
- *purposeful* teachers steer classroom talk to meet specified educational goals.

 Reflective questions

- How can I engage children in their study of the past?
- How can I use historical sources effectively?
- How can I deal with children's misconceptions about the past?
- How can I help children to develop their framework of the past?
- What activities can I use as hooks for children in learning about the past?
- How can I use talk to promote learning in history?

Conclusion

This chapter has provided an introduction to the nature of historical enquiry as a means of enabling children to construct their understanding of the past. This includes developing an appreciation of a framework of the past, as well as exploring different stories, events and people within it. Accessing this via challenging and intriguing questions, together with appropriate teaching and learning processes and resources, can make history meaningful, valid and rewarding. We are aware that this has been a brief introduction to how history is taught and learned and we trust that you will have found things to reflect on and develop for yourself in this chapter. We recommend study of the Further reading list below.

Further reading

Cooper, H. (2012) *History 5–11: A guide for teachers.* London: David Fulton.
This provides a first-rate appreciation of the nature of history in primary schools, together with insights into current thinking and research.

Davies, I. (ed.) (2011) *Debates in History Teaching.* Abingdon: Routledge.
This text considers a range of issues in history teaching and provides a good basis for exploring these in depth.

Foster, S., Ashby, R., Lee, P. and Howson, J. (2008) 'Usable historical pasts: A study of students' frameworks of the past: Full Research Report ESRC End of Award Report' (RES-000-22-1676). Swindon: ESRC. Available online at: www.esrc.ac.uk/my-esrc/grants/RES-000-22-1676/read
This critical study provided insights into the way in which children construct the past.

Ofsted (2011) 'History for all: History in English schools 2007/10'. Manchester: Ofsted. Available online at: www.ofsted.gov.uk/resources/history-for-all
This is essential reading in order to consider the strengths and key issues in history teaching.

Turner-Bisset, R. (2005) *Creative Teaching: History in the primary classroom.* London: David Fulton.
This combines a very good insight into theoretical issues associated with historical knowledge and creativity with practical application.

References

Alexander, R. (ed.) (2010) *Children, their World, their Education: Final report and recommendations of the Cambridge Primary Review.* Abingdon: Routledge.
Benjamin, F. (1995) *Coming to England.* Harmondsworth: Puffin.
Bracey, P., Gove-Humphries, A. and Jackson, D. (2011) 'Teaching diversity in the history classroom', in I. Davies (ed.), *Debates in History Teaching.* Abingdon: Routledge. Pp. 172–86.

Claire, H. (1996) *Reclaiming Our Pasts: Equality and diversity in the primary history curriculum*. Stoke: Trentham.

Claire, H. (2008) *Walter Tull: Sport, war and challenging adversity* (Key Stage 1 Teaching Pack). Northampton: Northamptonshire Black History Association.

Cooper, H. (2012) *History 5–11: A guide for teachers*. London: David Fulton.

DfE (2013) 'The National Curriculum in England: Framework document'. Runcorn: DfE. Available online at: www.gov.uk/government/uploads/system/uploads/attachment_data/file/210969/NC_framework_document_-_FINAL.pdf

Dickens, C. (1854) *Hard Times*. London: Penguin.

English Heritage, photo of esplanade and Beach Weymouth, National Monuments Record, English Heritage. Available online at: www.heritage-explorer.co.uk/web/he/search.aspx?crit=esplanade&start=1&cid=26&tid=269&rt=0

Foster, S., Ashby, R., Lee, P. and Howson, J. (2008) 'Usable historical pasts: A study of students' frameworks of the past: Full Research Report ESRC End of Award Report' (RES-000-22-1676). Swindon: ESRC. Available online at: http://www.esrc.ac.uk/my-esrc/grants/RES-000-22-1676/read

Gladiator (2000) Directed by Ridley Scott. Hollywood: Universal DVD.

Hodkinson, A. (2003) 'The usage of subjective temporal phrases within the National Curriculum for history and its schemes of work: Effective provision or a missed opportunity?', *Education 3–13*, 31 (3): 28–34.

Hoskins, W. (1969) *The Making of the English Landscape*. London: Hodder & Stoughton.

Ofsted (2011) 'History for all: History in English schools 2007/10'. Manchester: Ofsted. Available online at: www.ofsted.gov.uk/resources/history-for-all

Riley, M. (2000) 'Into the Key Stage 3 history garden: Choosing and planning your enquiry questions', *The Historical Association*, 99: 8–13.

Sossick, M. (2011) 'Big timelines, bigger pictures: Supporting initial teacher trainees to think big about chronology', *Primary History*, 59: 31.

Turner-Bisset, R. (2005) *Creative Teaching: History in the primary classroom*. London: David Fulton.

Wallace, N. (2011) 'A living timeline: Getting Knebworth House's visitors to understand where the distant past is', *Primary History*, 59: 36–7.

Wineberg, S. (2000) 'Making historical sense', in P. Stearns, P. Sexias and S. Wineberg, (eds) *Knowing Teaching and Learning History*. New York: New York University Press.

CHAPTER 8

LANGUAGES

Paul Gurton

Learning objectives

By the end of this chapter you should be able to:

- use a range of activities to facilitate language learning
- adopt appropriate teaching approaches to use in language learning lessons
- integrate language learning into other curriculum areas
- structure language lessons to ensure progress.

Introduction

Learning another language enables children to widen the scope of their communication skills, gain insights into their own and other cultures and improve their understanding of how their own language works. Like music and drama, it can improve children's self-confidence and self-esteem and, because much of the early learning involves oral work, repetition, songs and games, it can also be more easily accessible to children who may not yet be fluent readers or writers or may struggle in other areas of the curriculum. Many young children, particularly, enjoy foreign language lessons. They regard languages as a 'fun' subject. When asked why, they say things like:

> 'It's fun – you get to play games'
>
> 'It's different because you get to do different things – in other subjects you just sit at your desk all the time'
>
> 'I like making sounds – J (in Spanish) is so cool! It's like Darth Vader after a hot curry!'
>
> (seven- and eight-year-old pupils from a Walsall primary school)

The challenge for you as a teacher is to make foreign language learning relevant and interesting and ensure that progression is planned for. There is always the problem of where to begin; older children will often complain of starting from scratch or covering the same ground again. This is also true at the start of secondary school. This can be demoralising and demotivating, so it is important, from the beginning, to build on previous experience and ensure progression.

This chapter will focus on practical and enjoyable ways to teach languages, bearing in mind two fundamental principles of language learning:

- ensuring correct pronunciation and understanding of spelling in the target language (phoneme–grapheme correspondence)
- teaching basic language structures as the building blocks, to enable the children to add words and phrases to convey more complex meanings, have simple conversations and ask questions.

If children are not taught the phonics of the target language, they can get into habits of pronunciation that are hard to break later on, as they try to pronounce words they are reading with English pronunciation. Equally, language learning is not simply about 'parroting' new words with no link to underlying language structures. Jones and Coffey (2006: 2) put it very clearly when they say:

> While teachers sometimes talk of children parroting words and phrases – a natural part of the early stage of language learning – children have the cognitive flexibility and physiological apparatus to become competent and creative language users.

In the classroom   Children's ideas about learning another language

Children aged nine and ten years in a school in Staffordshire were asked to talk about why we learn other languages. Some of their ideas were:

'It's rude not to be able to speak to someone in their language'

'It helps you understand and speak when you travel abroad'

'You can share it with everybody'

'It gets you to understand about your own language – when you think about it they are quite alike – vier is four in German and Allo is Hello.'

The history of language learning

Language teaching will become statutory in English primary education for the first time in the 2014 Primary National Curriculum, although, in Scotland, French has been taught as a statutory requirement in Primary 5 and Primary 6 (ages 9 to 11) since the 1990s.

There has been progressive development towards ensuring such provision since the announcement of an 'entitlement' to language learning for all children in the National Languages Strategy (NLaS) document (DFES, 2002). However, there is a varied picture when it comes to national provision. While French and Latin had always been widespread in private preparatory schools, the majority of State primary schools in England had not offered a language in curriculum time. Where they had, it was because of the passion and enthusiasm of a particular teacher or headteacher or sometimes a response to a local authority initiative. Despite the relative success of the Joint Schools Council-Nuffield Foundation pilot project 'French in the primary school' in the 1960s and 1970s, by the 1990s, language teaching in English primary schools had practically disappeared.

From 2002 onwards things changed in England. The publication of the 'Key Stage 2 Framework for Languages' (DFES, 2005) and QCA (2007) schemes of work for French, German and Spanish have provided useful planning and guidance and were accompanied by a number of commercial schemes that are now in regular use throughout the country. By 2010, the National Centre for Languages (CILT) was reporting that 90 per cent of primary schools were including language teaching in their curriculums.

Some schools may lack a clear vision or rationale for language teaching. Languages may be taught by class teachers, language coordinators, supply teachers, teaching assistants or local secondary school staff, which means that what is provided is dependent on which teacher is available. Many schools, however, have embraced the new initiative with open arms, securing International School Status and introducing children to a variety of different languages, using creative approaches to make links between this area of study and their English, geography, history and PSHE and citizenship curricula. They have been able to participate in British Council-funded Erasmus and Comenius projects. This has enabled children and staff to be involved in exchange visits, leading to an enriched curriculum, European and sometimes international links and all the benefits such cooperation involves – that is, a more open and tolerant worldview for children, relationships between schools in different countries that in some cases will be sustained and relationships between children which have the potential to last a lifetime. It is still the case that, in many schools, languages are not taught effectively because of pressures of time and a shortage of teachers with the necessary expertise or confidence.

Table 8.1 Some activities

Activity	Integrating language teaching
Taking the register	Introduce the register in French, German, Spanish (or whatever language you choose): 'Bonjour Hayley ... Bonjour Mademoiselle/Madame/Monsieur' Individual pupils could take the lead on different days or the register can be taken using numbers
Basic greetings	An extension of the idea above, using greetings, too, at the beginning or end of every day, perhaps also after play or lunchtimes. Greet and say goodbye: buongiorno, arrivederci, ciao, or 'Ça va?', 'Oui ça va bien merci'
Counting up to 10 or 20 and back down, possibly extending to counting in twos, tens or hundreds	A class chant for all to join in or a paired activity where children say alternate numbers. Can link well to the mental/oral starter in maths
Number bingo	This needn't just be with handout sheets for individuals to mark off the numbers they have heard, but could be using an interactive whiteboard or children could be divided into teams and representatives of each team could run to the number on a hundred square in the playground. There are many variations
Colours	Flashcards and pronunciation practice could be followed by the use of simple books (*Brown Bear, Brown Bear, What Do You See?*, by Bill Martin Jr and Eric Carle, 1995) or a catwalk with commentary or dressing-up activities where partners have to describe what each other is wearing – 'Es ist grün'

Table 8.2   Teaching approaches

Approach	Description
Using a teddy or puppet	Best suited to younger children, though this works well with children up to eight or nine years as well. Talking to a teddy, asking it questions and responding to it takes some of the self-consciousness out of language learning and children really enjoy it. In one school I know, Chester (a monkey) is a critical part of language lessons for seven- to eight-year-olds
Song	As with learning in your native tongue, singing is a basic, enjoyable means of learning. Rhythm and melody activate a part of the memory that embeds the learning deep down – we all remember such songs well into our adult lives. Actions, too, can help lodge meanings and appeal to kinaesthetic learning. Examples of action songs include 'Head, shoulders, knees and toes' in another language – tête, épaules, genoux, pieds – or counting songs – Eins, zwei, Polizei, drei, vier, Offizier
Story	Repetition, common in storybooks for young children, helps embed learning of vocabulary items and simple grammatical structures. Perennial favourites such as *The Very Hungry Caterpillar* by Eric Carle, can help children learn days of the week, numbers and colours
Games	The possibilities are endless, from simple board games, where children count in the language (such as snakes and ladders) to Simon Says (Jacques a dit), which uses imperative verbs, or Kim's Game, for developing memory and observation skills. Like song and repeated text, these are motivating ways to reinforce learning and are nearly always enjoyed. Just ensure that pronunciation and grammar are a focus so that what is being reinforced is correct!
Partner and group work (avec ton partenaire!)	Whether learning introductions (¡Ola! Me llamo ... Tengo el pelo castaño), practising a description of someone else or simple role-play, this approach is a must for language teaching
Varying pace, pitch, tone	You can use and adapt games and activities derived from a synthetic phonics programme such as 'Letters and Sounds' (DfES, 2007) – 'making your voice go down a slide "whee"' (Aspect 6 – Voice Sounds) – or use activities from singing and drama, exaggerating pitch and tone. This is a very important approach to ensuring correct pronunciation while also making learning interesting. Other strategies you could use are tongue twisters for pronunciation or blending and segmenting (and word-talking) when teaching early reading and writing skills, which are too often neglected
Spanglish/Frenglish	There is nothing essentially wrong with using a mixture in lessons, as long as there is new learning. This approach, which may happen accidentally at times, may be used by a teacher when emphasising classroom routines or integrating new language into another area of the curriculum
Getting it wrong (accidentally on purpose)	Children love it when the teacher (or puppet) 'gets it wrong'. The pantomime approach (C'est jaune ... non c'est noir) is a great way to ensure full participation and is a stock in trade of good primary teaching

How early should we start?

There is much debate about how early to start language teaching. Young children are generally good mimics and do not have the self-consciousness of older children, so it makes sense to start language teaching early. It seems best to embed some basic understandings before children move on to secondary education.

Research suggests that young children may not have an *affective filter*, which makes them more comfortable in a language learning environment (Krashen, 1984). This filter is emotions, such as fear, anxiety or self-doubt, coming into play and interfering with the process of acquiring a second or additional language, causing difficulty in processing language. Krashen identifies two prime issues that can bring about the raising of the affective filter. The first is not allowing for a silent period (expecting children to speak before they have received an adequate amount of comprehensible input according to their individual needs). The second is correcting their errors too early on in the learning process. From studies of feral children, it appears that a critical period exists for the acquisition of the mother tongue – a theory known as the *critical period hypothesis* (CPH). This means that young children have an instinctive capacity for speech and the development of grammar that progressively declines as they grow older. There is controversy, however, as to whether or not this theory, which is usually applied to learning a first language or mother tongue, can be applied to learning a second or additional language or languages. It is also acknowledged that older learners are more efficient learners in other respects.

In the past decade in England, schools have started to teach basic greetings and sometimes vocabulary for basic classroom routines in other languages to children as young as four years of age. This learning has then been consolidated in lower primary classes by the introduction of the words for numbers and colours and the use of simple everyday expressions and requests. The 2014 National Curriculum envisages language learning beginning when children are aged seven to eight years, but that does not preclude some basic groundwork being laid earlier. This is a decision individual schools will want to consider.

In Tables 8.1 and 8.2, you will see some initial ideas for how to make language teaching an integral part of the primary school day. The tables provide some strategies, activities and ideas for using foreign languages in the classroom and for direct language teaching.

Awareness versus progression and competence

Over the last decade, when language teaching has been introduced into primary schools, it has often been using what is known as a *language awareness* approach. This places emphasis on sensitising children to a culture or number of cultures and teaching learners how to learn languages, focusing on a number of core linguistic structures and making comparisons or contrasts between them. It is often characterised by the learning of two or more languages in the upper primary years or sometimes in different terms of the same year. Because most of the discussion takes place in English in such situations, it is better suited to non-specialist primary school teachers.

The *language competence* approach contrasts with the language awareness approach. For example, it has been adopted in Scotland where only French is taught in primary schools. The language competence approach is an overt one that aims for the children to make progress. The language itself is the focus of each lesson and this approach is therefore almost always limited to the learning of one language. It places demands on the teacher's linguistic knowledge and it is essential that due account is taken of the language likely to be studied at a receiving secondary school. This model informs the 2014 National Curriculum, in which languages are given as a compulsory subject for 7- to 11-year-olds.

Languages in the curriculum

Whole class once a week versus integrated

While the proposed Framework document for the 2014 National Curriculum in England (DfE, 2013) does not specify the amount of curriculum time to be allocated to teaching a foreign language, the 'Key Stage 2 Framework for Languages' (DfES, 2005: 9) 'works on the basis that schools will plan for no less than 60 minutes per week of dedicated "language time"'. This means that a language may possibly be taught for 10 to 15 minutes per day, two sessions of 30 minutes or three sessions of 20 minutes. However, the document also stresses the importance of teachers finding 'opportunities during the week for children to use their newly acquired language skills' (DfES, 2005, 2: 9), citing classroom routines and general literacy learning as two areas into which language learning could be integrated.

These guidelines have been interpreted differently. In some schools, languages are taught by a visiting or supply teacher who works with the class while the class teacher is receiving planning, preparation and assessment (PPA) time. This can lead to a lack of opportunities for the children to follow up or practise new skills and vocabulary unless there is adequate planning, briefing or handover time built in (Ofsted, 2011: 15). It is suggested that an hour a week is insufficient unless regular practice is built into the week, with some language consolidation incorporated into other subjects and classroom routines. Here are some ideas that, if taken up, will contribute towards regular practice and use of the target language in other subjects and at other times than in the children's formal lesson.

In the classroom   Classroom routines

Basic classroom routines can be reinforced by the use of a foreign language. The use of commands (imperative forms of verbs or what we may choose to call 'bossy verbs' with younger children) can be a simple and effective means of getting children's attention, wrapping up a lesson or getting started.

Gaining children's attention

Use your focus language to attract attention – for example, 'Ecoutez!', 'Attendez!' (accompanied by 's'il vous plaît') – or count down or up in your target language. You could play Simon Says (Jacques a dit) using, for example, 'Asseyez vous!' or 'Levez vous!', with the possible teaching point of the difference between an imperative in the plural and singular (Lève-toi!).

During the lesson

To reinforce learning strategies use the phrases 'Parlez/Discutez avec ton partenaire', 'Ecrivez sur le tableau/dans vos livres', 'Répétez encore une fois!'.

Alternatively, departing from using imperatives, you could make requests or timed expectations or show approval or disapproval by saying, 'Vous avez dix minutes', 'Très bien!', 'Pas mal!'.

Ending the lesson

You can use suitable phrases, miming what must be done, such as 'Ramassez vos papiers!', 'Rangez vos affaires!', 'Montrez moi ...!'.

Integrating languages into other curriculum areas

Language learning lends itself par excellence to integration. Indeed, the approach taken to language teaching in some parts of the world, not least some of our European neighbours, is to teach a subject such as science in secondary schools in the medium of English (or whatever language is being taught). This approach is called immersion or sometimes *content and language integrated learning* (CLIL). While this presupposes a certain level of understanding and experience in the target language, it is not nearly as difficult as may be supposed. Going into CLIL in more detail is beyond the scope of this chapter, but it is worth looking into and there are many other ways, too, that language can be integrated meaningfully into other subjects. The learning objective may well be a geographical or mathematical one, but the medium of communication may be French, German, Spanish or whatever language the children are learning. It is therefore just another way (like using approaches based on different learning styles) for children to reinforce their learning.

In the classroom   A mathematics lesson for six- to seven-year-olds

Times tables, addition and subtraction

The mental/oral starter involved the children chanting in French, counting to and from 50 in tens. Practice in the two times, five times and then three times table followed, first by chanting (deux, quatre, six, huit, dix). Then, each child was given a number (1–30) and held theirs up when it was called out in French. Other activities included children holding odd numbers being sent to the board ('Les impairs allez à côté du tableau') and even numbers to the door ('Les pairs, allez à côté de la porte') and so on.

An extension activity entailed addition for example, 'Cinq plus cinq égalent dix, six plus trois égalent neuf' – then subtraction – 'Vingt moins cinq égalent quinze, douze moins trois égalent neuf' – and, finally, multiplication – 'Cinq par trois égalent quinze, trois par neuf égalent vingt-sept'.

It should be noted, however, that this was only possible because the children had been learning French since the start of the year and were familiar with the vocabulary 'plus', 'par', 'moins' and 'égalent'.

In the classroom   Plan of a mathematics lesson for seven- to eight-year-olds

Describing the properties of shapes

Context

The children are already familiar with numbers and colours in French. They also know that adjectives are usually placed after the noun they agree with.

Starter activity

In pairs, the children are given a variety of shapes of different colours and sizes. As a starter activity, they are asked to sort them. Inevitably the sorting occurs in three ways – by size, colour and shape. The children are then introduced to the new vocabulary – un cercle, un triangle et un carré (square).

(Continued)

(Continued)

Activity 1

The teacher says, 'Montrez-moi un cercle, montrez-moi un carré' and so forth. Then it is the turn of the children in pairs to say this phrase. So, child A would say, 'Montre-moi un triangle', then it would be child B's turn. This activity embeds the understanding of the new vocabulary.

Activity 2

The teacher says, 'Montrez-moi un cercle vert, montrez moi un triangle jaune!' and so on. Then it is the children's turn.

Activity 3

At this stage, a further level of description is added. The teacher says, 'Montrez-moi un grand cercle noir! Montrez-moi un petit triangle vert!' and so on. The children then take up the challenge to use all the new vocabulary.

The three Ps – presentation, practice, production

When planning to teach a language lesson, or sequence of lessons, we need to bear in mind what are known as the three Ps:

- presentation
- practice
- production.

This approach is a useful formula for scaffolding learning and helps to make the move from teacher modelling to pupil autonomy.

It is important for children to see the big picture when learning a new language. If the learning outcome is for children to use a new language structure or a structure they are familiar with but with new vocabulary items, you need to choose a relevant or meaningful situation or context for it. The activities described above, of children sorting shapes according to colour or size, provide a good example of this, of applying a skill already learned (agreement and position of adjectives) in a meaningful learning context. It is an example of moving from practice to production.

Another example might be, when teaching the vocabulary of food and eating, asking the children to describe what they ate for dinner last night and for them to ask a friend what they ate, in a simple role-play situation.

Learning a language in a school situation is an artificial approach to a natural human skill. We must always try to ensure that the language taught has relevance and meaning for the children's everyday lives.

Using the three Ps in your planning

For planning purposes, the following need to be considered.

- How you are going to revisit, consolidate and extend existing vocabulary and language structures? For example, you may want to move children from using the verb j'aime alone followed by a noun to the addition of a phrase with an infinitive verb and a noun, such as, moving from 'J'aime le foot' to 'J'aime manger des frites'.
- Is the language you are using relevant to the children in your class? So, if talking about food, consider what they eat. Is it rice or chappatis, beans or pizza and so forth?
- Does the new structure you are teaching require knowledge of gender or number? In French, if you are teaching quantities, you may also need to introduce the partitive article – du, de la or des – as in the example of a lesson shown below.
- How are you going to move from practice to production? How are children going to use the new phrase in a context that is meaningful to them?

In the classroom   Example of a lesson using the three Ps

The teacher of eight- to nine-year-olds is introducing the phrase 'Combien de?' (How many?), building on their prior knowledge of the phrase 'Il y a' (There is/are).

Introduction and consolidation of prior learning

The teacher and class greet each other, collectively and individually.

Then the teacher and class play 'verbal tennis' with numbers. The teacher mimes batting the number 'quatre' at the class and they mime batting back 'cinq'. The teacher then bats 'quinze', the children return 'seize'. Next the teacher bats 'dix' to an individual child and the child bats 'onze' back. Then children individually bat numbers to each other.

The children next practise the structure 'il y a' using a film clip from the BBC's Learning Zone Broadband, Class Clips – Primary French – video and audio, 'Old

(Continued)

(Continued)

MacDonald had a farm' in French. They are familiar with the song in English and they have sung it in French before – 'Le vieux MacDonald a une ferme'. Singing it again, along with the French children in the video clip, reinforces the children's prior knowledge of this language structure and, as it is sung by French children, this is an opportunity to copy correct pronunciation, too.

Presentation

During the presentation phase, the teacher models the new word or phrase clearly and the children get opportunities to repeat and practise it.

First, the teacher models pronunciation of the new word 'combien'. The teacher says it, the class copies and then the teacher says it again. This is repeated several times, then the teacher writes the word on the board.

To reinforce the children's phonic knowledge and an understanding of how to write the word (graphic representation), their prior knowledge is brought to bear. The children already know the word 'bien' (and 'chien' and maybe 'rien'). Now, with the teacher, they practise segmenting 'bien' into its three component phonemes – b (b), i (j) and en (ε). They practise this several times with reference to the written word, then add the initial part of the word – 'com', practising the phonemes in that part of the word, too. The teacher must emphasise at this point that the 'n' is not sounded out in 'bien' and the 'm' is not sounded out in 'com'. (There are only two phonemes in 'com' – c (k) and om (ɔ)). Practice of the phonics and writing conventions of the target language is vital at this stage, otherwise the children will have great difficulty later on in both pronouncing and writing the language.

The teacher then explains the meaning – that 'combien' means 'how many' – and writes it preceded by the phrase the children already know – 'Il y a combien (de)?' The teacher would then note that 'de' often accompanies the word 'combien'; an explanation of why is not necessary at this stage.

Practice

In this phase, the pupils use the language that has been presented in a controlled context. The teacher can use visual or oral prompts to aid them.

First, the teacher shows pictures of some animals (on cue cards or an interactive whiteboard) and asks, 'Il y a combien de cochons?' The pupils will invariably answer with only one word – 'trois' or whatever the appropriate number is. At this stage, it is necessary to model the whole phrase – 'Il y a trois cochons' – and have the children repeat it. This phase needs plenty of practice.

Next, with the aid of a new visual cue, the teacher asks the children to ask the question, 'Il y a combien de moutons?' Note that it is recommended the more straightforward phrase 'il y a' is used at this stage, rather than the more complicated inversion 'y-a-t-il', placed at the end of the sentence.

The children all repeat the question as a class. Then they all answer the question as a class, 'Il y a cinq moutons'. This phase also needs plenty of practice, until the teacher is sure that the children understand and can use the phrases.

Finally, in pairs, the children take it in turns to ask and answer questions about the animals on Old MacDonald's farm, using visual cues the teacher has prepared (a set of cards for each group or images that change on the interactive whiteboard). You will monitor their correct usage and pronunciation. Some children might like to volunteer to present to the class as a pair, but children should not be forced to do this.

Production

In the production phase, the children are able to take more ownership of the language and use it in a context that is meaningful to them.

First, continuing with the example we have been using here, the children can be encouraged to ask and answer questions in pairs, using everyday items found in the classroom – 'Il y a combien de livres sur la table?', 'Il y a combien d'élèves dans la classe?' and so forth. To vary the groupings, the children can be asked to mix and mingle, choosing another partner to ask questions with.

The activity may be consolidated by some written work, with the children practising writing the question and answer – 'Il y a combien de?' and 'Il y a'. This will both embed the learning and encourage the children to become familiar with using the written French conventions and spellings.

The example of a lesson above, using the 3Ps model, can be applied in many new learning situations and, of course, used for a language other than French. Once a new structure has been learned in this way, it needs to be reinforced with regular practice in subsequent lessons and, if possible, integrated into other lessons, as explained earlier in the chapter.

Intercultural understanding

'A high-quality languages education should foster pupils' curiosity and deepen their understanding of the world.' This statement appears in the 'Purpose of study' section in the proposals for languages in the 2014 National Curriculum (DfE, 2013:

Table 8.3   Intercultural understanding – an overview

Age group	Children should be able to:
7–8	• appreciate the diversity of languages spoken in their school
	• identify the country or countries where the target language is spoken
	• recognise and repeat a children's song or rhyme well-known to native speakers
8–9	• know about celebrations in other cultures
	• compare an aspect of everyday life at home and abroad
	• identify similarities in traditional stories
9–10	• list some similarities and differences between contrasting localities
	• recognise how symbols, products and objects can represent the culture(s) of a country
10–11	• demonstrate understanding of and respect for cultural diversity
	• present information about an aspect of another country

212) and is a critical element in language learning. In many schools, children come from a variety of different heritage backgrounds and there are several (and in some cases many more) languages spoken within the school community. Whether a community language is chosen as the foreign language the school will be teaching or not, valuing children's cultural heritage is very important for their self-esteem and widens all children's knowledge and understanding of the world they live in.

Throughout their language learning experiences, children need the opportunity to ask questions about the cultures of the countries in which the languages are spoken and make comparisons between their lives and those of the children from those cultures. In the case of the two most popular languages taught – French and Spanish – there is, of course, not just one country where the language is spoken. It is important to present examples of Spanish culture alongside that of a South American country or countries and French or Belgian alongside a French-speaking African nation, for example. Likewise, on 'themed days', which are very popular in primary schools, we need to be careful not to encourage a merely 'baguettes and berets' approach to foreign cultures, as that can smack of tokenism, and be clear about encouraging thinking about similarity as well as difference. There are many activities that provide children with opportunities to make comparisons and identify differences and many of these have clear links with other subjects in the curriculum, such as geography, religious education and PSHE.

Table 8.3 gives some targets to aim for derived from the 'Key Stage 2 Framework for Languages' (DfES, 2005), but the lists are by no means exhaustive.

Knowledge about language

Developing a 'metalanguage', that is, the ability to talk about what you are doing, is of importance in any area of study. For children to know and use the word 'multiple' or 'factor' in maths enables them to explain, to themselves and others, concepts that would otherwise take several words, phrases or even sentences to achieve the same thing. The same is true when learning another language. Hopefully, the era of learning to conjugate verbs and decline nouns before ever using them in a meaningful context is long past. However, when, for example, children use the word 'agree' in the following sentence, they are demonstrating a growing knowledge of the French language and, by implication, how it differs from English: 'You need to add an "s" to "rose" to make it agree with "cochons"' (in the sentence, 'Il y a trois cochons roses').

   In the course of learning a foreign language, then, children should develop a vocabulary that helps them explain their understanding in this way. As teachers, we need to foster the use of terminology – not for its own sake, but to enable children to be clear in their understanding of the conventions of another language. These will include using the terms singular and plural, feminine, masculine (and, depending on the language, neuter), gender, noun, verb, adjective, adverb, pronoun, preposition, present tense, past tense, agreement, cognate and more. It is worth noting that all of these terms, with the exception of the gender descriptors, are included in the 2014 National Curriculum for English, so the children will not be encountering them only in their language learning. While some children will struggle to get to terms with some of this terminology, there are many opportunities now for drawing links between English and language learning.

Phonics

Children need to be able to discriminate between sounds in a language to become literate and fluent in it. Activities and exercises to help children enunciate sounds can be a lot of fun. Indeed, some children will be found practising them at other times of the day as they savour the feeling of making a new or different sound!

   Phonics can be taught initially using games, often involving physical actions. An example of such an activity could be getting the children to place both their hands on top of their heads if they hear the [e] sound in the following list: méchant, lion, danser, neuf, bébé, chien, legume. Alternatively, they could clap every time they hear the [ñ] sound in the following Spanish words: señor, mantequilla, cabaña, semana, nada, años, mañana.

   Some sounds are the same, or very similar, to sounds in English, but there are others that have no equivalent – the Spanish j or Greek χ for example. In French, there is a group of nasal sounds that have no English equivalents. Here are some of them:

[ã] dans, sans, méchant, danse, vent
[ɛ] matin, demain, plein
The same is true for the following sound:
[y] tu, super, une, lune.

If you are not confident about pronouncing these yourself, as the teacher, you should use a commercially produced CD or the Internet as a model instead of yourself. Even so, there is really no alternative to not doing them. If children do not learn to hear and mimic sounds correctly in the target language or if they are not taught the spelling conventions and try to read and write using the conventions from English, their opportunity to make progress in this new area of learning will be curtailed.

Other useful ways to display similar sounds are using mobiles in the classroom or having lists on a display. It is often best if the children have a hand in producing these, to help them in understanding the sound patterns and how these are written in a new language. The children could compile a list of homophones for French, such as dans and dents, ton and thon, quand and camp. Whatever method is used, however, pronunciation will need to be constantly reinforced.

The four skills: listening and speaking, reading and writing

Developing literacy in a foreign language should be an holistic process. There is a rather persistent myth in teaching languages to young children that you do not need to bother about reading and writing or else introducing the written form of words can confuse or demotivate. Well, if these are not taught alongside the correct pronunciation, this can happen, but teachers who limit children's access to the written form of the language are actually *more* likely to demotivate their pupils and limit their opportunities to make progress, not less.

Initial listening activities such as choral chanting or drilling can develop into forms of comprehension activities that do not necessarily require the children to speak in the language they are learning. For example, a group of food items could be shown on a whiteboard or the children could have their own food cards. The teacher could then say, 'Montrez moi …', the children holding up the correct card (frites, ananas, oeufs or whatever it is).

This sort of early listening activity reduces the pressure felt to speak when children are being bombarded with a whole new set of sounds and words. They will in time, and some of them will immediately, but, when learning a new language, it is important to respect children who do not want to talk. Krashen (1984) has talked of the 'silent period' – a factor that is recognisable in young children learning to speak their native language, when their understanding far exceeds their ability to express themselves using language. It is also evident in children newly arrived from another country.

Being expected to speak in a foreign language can be scary. It is your skill as a teacher that will help scaffold the activities so the children have just enough support to be able to express concepts simply and use structures, words and phrases they have already learned. To some extent this has already been demonstrated in this chapter, with the example of using the three Ps and in the two maths lessons. Similarly, providing a phrase for children to modify – by changing an adjective or verb or adding an adverb, for example – mimics activities used in English lessons where children are often asked to strengthen the effect of a sentence by supplying a more powerful verb, for example. The same method could be applied to the use of connectives – extending simple sentences to make compound ones. Equally, when introducing phrases that describe the weather, the children could be encouraged to build on the language they have already practised, describing the clothing they wear, as in the example shown in Table 8.4.

In the classroom Examples of ways to extend children's language learning

Table 8.4 Extending sentences

New sentence (given by teacher)	Connective	Example of children's extensions, using prior knowledge
Il fait chaud	alors	je porte mon T-shirt
Il pleut	alors	je porte mon imperméable
Il fait du vent	alors	je porte mon pull

Young children also respond very well to the use of puppets in language lessons. Small glove puppets can enable children to take on different personas, perhaps of a Spanish or French cat or dog, so clearly it cannot speak any other language!

Reading activities in the target language can be as simple as reading target cue cards in a speaking and listening activity or colouring a sheet correctly after reading the descriptions of an animal's clothes. In a more sophisticated version of this reading activity, eight- and nine-year-old children can be asked to draw their own interpretation of what the following text depicts:

Un jour un petit garçon joue dans le jardin de sa maison. La maison est grande avec quatre fenêtres et une jolie porte jaune. Il fait du vent et alors le garçon porte un pull vert. Il y a une rue a côté du jardin et dans la rue il y quatre voitures qui vont vers la ville. Deux sont rouges et les autres deux sont bleues.

Reading and writing in another language provide opportunities for children to consolidate speaking and listening skills. They can build on their phonic understanding and it enables a higher degree of independence in learning. Writing can provide opportunities for differentiation and, although you will know best how to meet the needs of the children in your class, it can be introduced in a simple way right from the very start of language learning. Jones and Coffey (2006: 65) provide the following suggested progression in writing skills:

copying down words and gapfilling letters in known words and phrases; completing known songs with words or phrases blanked out; copying sentences; short dictations; labelling and writing short descriptive phrases; answering questions in a listening activity; describing pictures; gapfilling phrases in a dialogue; finishing off sentences; producing simple sentences; answering questions about something in a text, videoclip or soundfile; writing a fuller description; and finally translating English sentences.

This is a useful list of activities that become progressively harder, but still one of the best ways to encourage children's love of language – as is true of their native language – is to use excellent narrative storybooks that have predictable and repeated text. Writing or filling in words and phrases from something you are familiar with and enjoy is always more fun than doing a worksheet.

Reflective questions

- How can you start to use basic language structures and vocabulary to plan for meaningful interactions?
- How can you ensure correct pronunciation, reading and writing opportunities are incorporated into lessons?
- How can you integrate reinforcement of learned language structures into other lessons?
- How can you ensure that children gain a wider understanding of other cultures?

Conclusion

This chapter has provided an outline of how to approach language teaching to enable children to construct meaning in order to be understood in the new language. It has demonstrated a framework as an example of how to build on existing knowledge.

Children need to be guided through clear stages of progression to maintain enjoyment and motivation in their language learning. This can be achieved by using multisensory activities, such as games, songs and interactive learning using ICT. Much learning, of necessity, will be what might be regarded as rote, copying or mimicry. However, just as it is important for children to be able to have experiences using the four skills of listening, speaking, reading and writing from the beginning of their acquaintance with another language, they must also be enabled to use the words and phrases they have learned in new contexts, to have a go and not be worried about getting it wrong.

Further reading

CILT (National Centre for Languages) (1998) Young Pathfinder Series.
This series of little books offers really useful classroom teaching activities and resources in French, German and Spanish. While the presentation is not eye-catching, the ideas are tried and tested and written by a series of experts in the field. There are various titles, such as 'Let's join in! Rhymes, poems and songs' (C. Cheater and C. Martin), 'Literacy link' (A. Farren and C. Cheater), 'First steps to reading and writing' (C. Skarbek).

Hood, P. and Tobutt, K. (2009) *Modern Languages in the Primary School.* London. Sage.
This book contains a useful consideration of languages in the primary classroom. It shows how languages can be integrated into the wider curriculum and approaches to teaching across the primary phase. It challenges some popular misconceptions and gives some useful practical examples.

Jones, J. and Coffey, S. (2006) *Modern Foreign Languages 5–11: A guide for teachers.* London: David Fulton.
This book provides an excellent overview, of both teaching strategies and how to plan for integration and progression, as well as a section on children's own views. It is essential reading.

References

DfE (2013) 'The National Curriculum in England: Framework document'. Runcorn: DfE. Available online at: www.gov.uk/government/uploads/system/uploads/attachment_data/file/210969/NC_framework_document_-_FINAL.pdf
DfES (2002) 'Languages for all: Languages for life: A strategy for England'. (National Languages Strategy document.) Nottingham: DfES Publications.
DfES (2005) 'Key Stage 2 Framework for Languages' (Parts 1 & 2). Nottingham: DfES Publications.
DfES (2007) 'Letters and sounds'. Nottingham: DfES Publications.

Jones, J. and Coffey, S. (2006) *Modern Foreign Languages 5–11: A guide for teachers*. London: David Fulton.

Krashen, S. (1984) *Principles and Practice in Second Language Acquisition*. Oxford: Pergamon.

Martin Jr, Bill and Carle, E. (1995) *Brown Bear, Brown Bear, What Do You See?* London: Puffin.

Ofsted (2011) 'Modern languages: Achievement and challenge 2007–2010'. Manchester: Ofsted.

QCA (2007) 'Key Stage 2 schemes of work for French, German and Spanish'. London: QCA.

CHAPTER 9

MATHEMATICS

Alice Hansen and Balbir Ahir

Learning objectives

By the end of this chapter you should be able to:

- understand the statutory elements of primary mathematics
- appreciate the key components and concepts of mathematics learning in the primary curriculum
- plan effective mathematics lessons
- use resources creatively and effectively to enhance learning
- promote a practical and inclusive approach to teaching primary mathematics
- recognise the importance of talk in learning and teaching mathematics.

Introduction

In the 'Statutory Framework for the Early Years Foundation Stage' (EYFS, DfE, 2012a), mathematics is a specific area of the seven learning and development requirements. Mathematics in the EYFS involves 'providing children with opportunities to develop and improve their skills in counting, understanding and using numbers, calculating simple addition and subtraction problems; and to describe shapes, spaces, and measures' (DfE, 2012a: 5). All the areas of learning and development are interconnected, however, so we need to consider the individual needs, interests and stage of development of every child, using this information to plan a challenging and enjoyable experience for each of them.

Mathematics is a core subject in primary education. Effective teaching and learning of mathematics means that all children (DfE, 2012b: 1):

- become **fluent** in the fundamentals of mathematics so that they are efficient in using and selecting the appropriate written algorithms and mental methods, underpinned by mathematical concepts

- can **solve problems by** applying their mathematics to a variety of problems with increasing sophistication, including in unfamiliar contexts and to model real-life scenarios

- can **reason mathematically** by following a line of enquiry and develop and present a justification, argument or proof using mathematical language.

Mathematics is usually taught every day during a dedicated mathematics lesson that lasts up to one hour. Often, links can be made to mathematics in other subjects, too, such as constructing graphs in science or writing notation in music.

Mathematics specialist teachers (MaST)

In the 'Independent review of mathematics teaching in Early Years settings and primary schools' report (DCSF, 2008: 23), it was recommended that there 'should be at least one Mathematics Specialist in each primary school, in post within 10 years, with deep mathematical subject and pedagogical knowledge'. It was suggested that these mathematics specialists should be drawn from the existing workforce, trained to champion mathematics in their school or cluster of schools and act as mentors to colleagues.

A few years into the programme, there have been positive evaluations of the impact MaSTs are having on children's learning and the improvement of schools. Several of the eight providers of the programme were intending to continue the programme in some form, despite funding reductions, because of its successful outcomes and schools' desire to train staff to become MaSTs.

Improving mathematical knowledge and making cross-curricular links

There are many books available for primary teachers, as well as online audits (such as the NCETM audits at: www.ncetm.org.uk/self-evaluation), which offer support in mathematical pedagogical subject knowledge for areas in which you may lack confidence.

Seeing and making connections between mathematics and other curriculum subjects also needs to be given consideration in your planning. Children need the chance to make connections across mathematical procedures and concepts in ways that ensure fluency, mathematical reasoning and competence in solving problems. Children can be given opportunities to use their developing mathematical skills in science, geography, history and design and technology. Cross-curricular discussions with other teachers can highlight such valuable opportunities.

Key facts about mathematics

All schools are required to set out their school curriculum for mathematics on a yearly basis and make this available online. Teachers must ensure that they set high expectations for all children, focus on spoken language and use ICT to best support the children's learning.

Approaches to teaching primary mathematics

What knowledge, skills and understanding do children need to develop?

The specific aims of teaching mathematics in the primary years, as stated by the Advisory Committee on Mathematical Education (ACME, 2008), are for children to gain an understanding of the subject that will:

- be beneficial in enabling them to apply mathematical ideas in everyday life to allow them to function independently, such as dealing with money, being numerate, understanding time and so on, 'so that they can recognise and use mathematics in their own lives inside and outside school for a variety of purposes' (ACME, 2008: 3)
- bring an enjoyment of learning and doing mathematics creatively by engaging in and using it to solve problems, puzzles and investigations, which also develop generic thinking skills
- provide a better understanding of the world and its major role in society: 'Mathematics provides a powerful universal language and intellectual toolkit for

abstraction, generalisation and synthesis. It is the language of science and technology. It enables us to probe the natural universe and to develop new technologies that have helped us control and master our environment, and change societal expectations and standards of living' (Smith, 2004: v).

In order to fulfil the above aims, children need to have knowledge of certain facts and information, such as multiplication and division facts, conversion facts and symbols for notations. Mathematical facts are often learned as individual pieces of information, but, collectively, they help to develop a conceptual understanding of mathematics and are essential when learning mathematical skills.

Proficiency in mathematics also involves learning mathematical skills, such as knowing standard written methods for the four number operations (addition, subtraction, multiplication and division). Thus, children practice and consolidate the skill of column addition by having this modelled for them by the teacher and then doing it for themselves.

Children also need to have an understanding of conceptual structures, which are the 'Big Ideas' (ACME, 2008) behind a notion. For example, it is vital within the conceptual understanding of place value, that children understand it refers to the value of a digit within a number, which involves notions of partition, equivalence and conservation – for example, 461 is equal to 400 + 60 + 1 and 400 is also equal to 40 tens. The concepts within mathematics are nurtured by the different connections and relationships the teacher encourages the learners to make. The better children's conceptual understanding of the 'Big Ideas', the better they are able to communicate and see the usefulness of the subject.

Mathematical skills, knowledge and understanding need to be developed via a *relational understanding* of the subject. A relational understanding can be defined as the building up of conceptual structures (schemas) from which the learner can develop new ideas. Skemp (1976: 2) describes relational learning as knowing 'both the "what" and "why" of mathematics'. To cultivate a relational understanding requires opportunities for discussion, appropriate engagement in practical work, direct teaching, the nurturing of independence and exploration of key mathematics skills by means of problem solving and application across the mathematics curriculum. Such understanding allows learners to be confident in their reasoning in mathematics so they can approach problems in a creative, inquisitive and meaningful way.

The key mathematical skills that are applied throughout the mathematics curriculum

Application and problem solving

In order to understand the usefulness and value of mathematics, children need to be given the opportunity to apply different strands of mathematics to different contexts.

This includes making connections within the subject. For example, in a lesson on solving word problems in the context of measurement, children will need to make connections and then apply the following different mathematical skills:

- their knowledge of conversion facts for units of measurement
- being able to choose and use appropriate methods of calculation
- being able to draw on their knowledge of number facts.

The ability to apply mathematical knowledge, skills and concepts in order to solve problems demonstrates the use of mathematics in a meaningful, real-life context.

⌨ **In the classroom   Mathematics across other subjects**

A class of five- and six-year-olds were investigating their local area as part of a geography lesson. They explored the key features of the area, including where children lived in relation to the school. The teacher then focused on how the children travelled to school, which was going to be central to the next lesson.

The children were asked how they travelled to school that day and, as a whole class, they constructed a block graph using big multilink cubes. The teacher consolidated what the features of the block graph were by adding labels for each block and a title. She then helped the children to analyse the graph, emphasising the model and what the results showed.

This illustrates effectively how the teacher incorporated learning about data handling into a geography lesson.

Communicating and representing

Mathematics requires children to understand the language of mathematics, which includes technical terminology and vocabulary, models, images and pictures, symbols and practical equipment. Children are required to develop strategies for communication so that they can read, write, talk and listen, as well as make connections between these components to access and express their understanding of mathematics. For example, during the early stages of counting, it is important that children are given experiences of saying and representing the names of numbers, using familiar practical equipment, and relating these to symbols (whether they are formal or informal).

Part of communicating also involves fostering the importance of mathematical talk and discussions between the teacher and each child but also the children with each other.

 **In the classroom   Fostering mathematics talk during a guided group session**

The children, working in pairs, were given six cubes – two red, two blue and two yellow. The teacher explained that the learning aim of the lesson was to find as many different ways of organising the cubes in a line as they could so that they showed reflective symmetry, and to record the outcomes (see Figure 9.1).

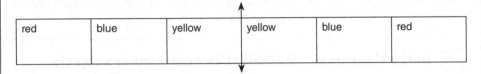

| red | blue | yellow | yellow | blue | red |

Figure 9.1   Colour symmetry

Initially, the children were given time to digest, interpret, interact and have a go at finding solutions to the problem. This encouraged them to become independent problem solvers and support each other. After the initial child-to-child discussion, the teacher intervened to further scaffold their thinking and ideas, building on solutions in a guided discussion.

Reasoning

Reasoning in mathematics contributes to the development of children's thinking strategies. This in turn contributes to problem solving.

 In the classroom   Reasoning in number patterns

A class of seven- and eight-year-olds were asked to investigate the sequence of adding ten to any number. The children explored the pattern by adding 10 to different numbers using the 100 square – 0, 10, 20, 30 ...; 4, 14, 24, 34, 44 ...; 46, 56, 66, 76 ... They then had to explain what happens to the number pattern when you repeatedly add 10 to it. They needed to explain the mathematical reasoning behind their explanation. This was extended to the pattern of adding 5, and looking at the patterns/number sequences in multiplication tables.

Reasoning about mathematics challenges children to explain their mathematical thinking, recognise patterns and relationships, make generalisations and check for the reasonableness of their results.

Developing methods

To carry out tasks efficiently, children need opportunities to develop and use mental, informal and formal methods of calculating across all four number operations. It is not simply about knowing a range of methods and procedures; it is important that they select and use the most appropriate method for the particular situation. For example, when calculating 14×19, it is easier to multiply 14 by 20 [$(14 \times 2) \times 10$ and then subtract one lot of 14 from the answer] than it is to carry out a standard method for this calculation.

Consolidating and recalling

These key skills are those of remembering the terminology, facts, definitions and formulae that need to be known in order to achieve mathematical fluency

Progression in the primary years

A crucial approach to learning mathematics involves children being actively engaged in constructing their own knowledge, with structured and assisted support coming from the teacher. This can only be accomplished if teachers have a deep understanding and are secure in their own subject, pedagogical and curricular knowledge of mathematical concepts and ideas.

Table 9.1   Progression in Early Years settings

Key areas of progression in number	Key areas of progression in geometry and measure
• learning how to count to 20 and beginning to use the vocabulary involved in adding and subtracting • starting to add and subtract two single-digit numbers and count on or back to find the answer	• being able to use everyday language to talk about size, weight, capacity, position, distance, time and money, to compare quantities and objects and solve problems • exploring characteristics of everyday objects and shapes and using mathematical language to describe them

In using and applying, children should develop mathematical ideas to solve practical problems and recognise, create and describe patterns

Table 9.2   Progression in lower primary years–5–7years

Key areas of progression in number	Key areas of progression in geometry and measure	Key areas of progression in data
<ul><li>count up to 100 objects</li><li>place value of partitioning two-digit numbers in different ways</li><li>recall all addition and subtraction facts that total 20 and all pairs of multiples of 10 with totals up to 100</li><li>add and subtract numbers mentally</li><li>use practical and written methods for addition and subtraction of two-digit numbers</li><li>use the symbols +, −, ×, ÷ and = to record and interpret number sentences involving all four operations</li><li>recall 2, 5 and 10 times tables</li><li>recognise simple fractions</li></ul>	<ul><li>visualise common 2D shapes and 3D solids; sort, make and describe shapes, referring to their properties</li><li>estimate, measure, weigh and compare objects, choosing and using suitable standard units and measuring instruments</li><li>use units of time and know the relationships between them</li><li>identify time intervals, including those that cross the hour</li></ul>	<ul><li>practise interpreting data diagrams so they become proficient in extracting information</li><li>apply knowledge of data in science and other subjects as appropriate</li></ul>

In using and applying, follow a line of enquiry and answer questions by choosing and using suitable equipment and selecting, organising and presenting information in lists, tables and simple diagrams
Describe patterns and relationships involving numbers or shapes, make predictions and test these with examples
Present solutions to puzzles and problems in an organised way, explain decisions, methods, organised
Present methods and results in pictorial, spoken or written form, using mathematical language and number sentences

This section of the chapter considers progression during the early and primary years.

In Early Years settings, children should be provided with opportunities to explore mathematics in a personal way, so that they can consider, learn, practice and talk about mathematical concepts and ideas.

Tables 9.1–9.3 detail the progression children make through the curriculum and show how key concepts, such as place value, are reintroduced at different points and developed further each time across the age phases.

This strategy of returning to previously studied areas indicates a *spiral curriculum* approach. Constructing learning using a spiral curriculum was suggested by Bruner (1960: 13): 'A curriculum as it develops should revisit basic ideas repeatedly, building upon them until the student has grasped the full formal apparatus that goes with them'. Such a curriculum involves learners accumulating experience over time and, indeed, through the early and primary years, children are required to revisit ideas and concepts, each time at an increasingly more challenging and intellectual level and degree of difficulty, allowing them to consolidate and extend their knowledge and understanding. In order to do this effectively, children's previous

Table 9.3 Progression in upper primary years – 7–9 and 9–11 years

	Key areas of progression in number	Key areas of progression in geometry and measure	Key areas of progression in handling data
Ages 7–9	• partition four-digit numbers in different ways • use diagrams to identify equivalent fractions • interpret mixed numbers and position them on a number line • derive and recall all multiplication facts and division facts • mentally, add or subtract pairs of whole numbers • develop and use written methods to record, support and explain multiplication and division of two-digit numbers by a one-digit number, including division with remainders	• identify lines of symmetry • describe position and movement on a 2D grid • compare and order angles • read, to the nearest division and half-division, scales that are numbered or partially numbered • choose and use standard metric units and their abbreviations when estimating, measuring and recording length, weight and capacity	• continue to practise interpreting a variety of bar graphs so that they can read, write, analyse and solve problems confidently • continue to apply knowledge in science and other subjects as appropriate

In using and applying, solve one-step and two-step problems
Suggest a line of enquiry and the strategy needed to follow it
Report solutions to puzzles and problems, giving explanations and reasoning orally and in writing, using diagrams and symbols

	Key areas of progression in number	Key areas of progression in geometry and measure	Key areas of progression in handling data
9–11 years	• explain what each digit represents in whole numbers and decimals up to three places and partition, round and order these numbers • find equivalent percentages, decimals and fractions, ratio and proportion • use knowledge of place value and addition and subtraction of two-digit numbers to derive sums and differences of decimals • use knowledge of place value and multiplication facts to derive related multiplication and division facts involving decimals • use efficient written methods to add and subtract integers and decimals and multiply and divide integers and decimals, extending to larger numbers	• read and plot coordinates • visualise and draw on grids of different types where a shape will be after reflection, after translations or after rotation through 90° or 180° about its centre or one of its vertices • measure and calculate the perimeter of regular and irregular polygons • use the formula for the area of a rectangle to calculate the rectangle's area • select and use standard metric units of measure and convert units using decimals to two places	• construct frequency tables, pictograms and bar and line graphs to represent the frequencies of events and changes over time • solve problems by collecting, selecting, processing, presenting and interpreting data, using ICT where appropriate • draw conclusions and identify further questions to ask

In using and applying, solve multistep problems and problems involving fractions, decimals and percentages
Tabulate systematically the information in a problem or puzzle
Suggest, plan and develop lines of enquiry
Represent and interpret sequences, patterns and relationships involving numbers and shapes
Suggest and test hypotheses
Construct and use simple expressions and formulae in words then symbols.

experiences need to be considered and formative assessments carried out so that opportunities can be created for children to make connections between previous and new learning.

Planning for mathematics

Planning for learning in mathematics involves organising a balance between direct teacher exposition, well-planned practical activities and independent learning, presented alongside opportunities for the children to reflect on and apply their developing knowledge (see Figure 9.2). Teachers need to use their professional judgement and skills, making creative use of time, the organisation and overall structure of mathematics lessons so an environment is created in which children are able to learn mathematics effectively.

Most importantly when planning for mathematics, you should ensure that children experience an excitement about learning mathematics in an interactive environment.

Differentiation

The starting point for planning is to consider the children's previous knowledge and understanding and match the learning and teaching activities to their individual needs so all make progress. Planning for inclusion, so that all learners are challenged, can be achieved in a number of ways, including the following.

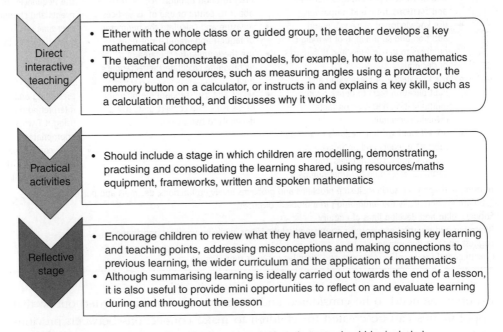

Direct interactive teaching
- Either with the whole class or a guided group, the teacher develops a key mathematical concept
- The teacher demonstrates and models, for example, how to use mathematics equipment and resources, such as measuring angles using a protractor, the memory button on a calculator, or instructs in and explains a key skill, such as a calculation method, and discusses why it works

Practical activities
- Should include a stage in which children are modelling, demonstrating, practising and consolidating the learning shared, using resources/maths equipment, frameworks, written and spoken mathematics

Reflective stage
- Encourage children to review what they have learned, emphasising key learning and teaching points, addressing misconceptions and making connections to previous learning, the wider curriculum and the application of mathematics
- Although summarising learning is ideally carried out towards the end of a lesson, it is also useful to provide mini opportunities to reflect on and evaluate learning during and throughout the lesson

Figure 9.2   The stages of mathematics lessons and what elements should be included

- *Task* Pitch the task so that it is challenging for all learners.
- *Support* This can be provided by peers, teaching and other assistants or the teacher. Arranging for children to work with partners ensuring that there is a mix of abilities allows them to support one another. Also, guided group work with the teacher or teaching assistant allows for focused support.
- *Resources* Allow the same task to be completed by all children, but differentiate it by, for example, allocating specific resources to children who may require a visual representation of mathematical concepts.

In the classroom   Some eight- and nine-year-olds investigate the magic square

Working with the magic square involves the children using all the numbers from 1 to 9 once in a 3 x 3 grid, so that every row and column adds up to 15.

In the mixed-ability class, all the children had the same task, but it was differentiated in terms of resources. The higher-ability children had whiteboards and pens to work out the problem. This allowed them to develop speed in the addition of three single digits and think about patterns and ways to record the mathematics they were doing.

The middle-ability children had number cards, 1–9, which they could move and manipulate. They were also given a starting point, so a number was given to them.

The lower-ability children worked using a spreadsheet that the teacher had set up in the form of a 3 x 3 grid, which automatically showed the totals for each row and column once the numbers had been inserted in the cells. This allowed them to focus on the arrangements of the numbers without worrying about the calculations.

All the children worked in pairs, enabling discussion and collaborative thinking.

The use of models and images

Providing children with a hands-on approach to learning mathematics is essential if they are to understand mathematical concepts. This involves using a range of equipment and appropriate models and images.

Resources should accurately model the mathematics that is being taught and support the children's thinking. Constantly review the impact that a resource has on learning. Most children will need to use a range of resources and models in mathematics before they can use general mathematical ideas and relate to symbols with confidence and understanding. The role of the teacher is to use resources and subject-specific vocabulary to support explanations that will further the children's understanding of mathematics.

In the classroom   Some eight- and nine-year-olds develop knowledge of equivalent fractions

When developing the concept of equivalent fractions, the teacher used a fraction wall image to demonstrate the relationships. This was a tactile resource with which the children could interact.

The idea of equivalence (as meaning same as or equal to) was consolidated and the children were then asked to explore equivalent fractions. They were asked to identify equivalent fractions using the fraction wall, provide reasoning, explain the relationship between a set of equivalent fractions and then generalise by providing other examples. The fraction ½ was their starting point.

The children were soon showing equivalence and making recordings such as 1/4 + 1/4 = 2/4 = 1/2; 1/8 + 1/8 + 1/8 + 1/8 = 4/8 = 1/2.

At first they used the strips from the fraction wall to do this and then they moved on to using the correct numerical symbols. They also started to think about the pattern of all the equivalent fractions that equal ½ and noticed the numerator was always half the denominator. They were also able to give other equivalent fractions, such as 7/14 = ½; 15/30 = ½, and explain why.

This process was repeated with equivalence to ¼. Also, as an extension, the children were asked to think together to predict the rules/pattern for the ¼s.

In the classroom   Some eight- and nine-year olds explore quadrilaterals using geo strips

The teacher asked the children to construct a four-sided shape using geo strips. They then discussed the properties of the shape they had constructed.

The children were then asked to make another four-sided shape, without making any changes or deconstructing the geo strips. This provided opportunities for the children to make connections and find similarities and differences between a square and a rhombus, a kite and an arrowhead and so on.

Mathematics outside the classroom

Providing children with opportunities to learn outside the classroom relates back to the specific aims of teaching and learning mathematics – namely, to contribute to a better understanding of the world, making mathematics meaningful and real. It can also provide challenge and excitement for all learners to be problem solvers.

One way to initiate mathematics learning outside the classroom is to plan a 'mathematics trail'. This is an organised route that explores a specific area of mathematics. It provides opportunities to consolidate, explore, problem solve and make connections and links between the different areas of mathematics.

The flexibility of a mathematics trail means that it can be organised in any environment, around the school building, in the playground, in the local environment and beyond.

In the classroom   Some four- and five-year-olds go on a number recognition trail

The teacher had hidden various laminated numerals ranging from one to ten in the school's outside space. The children had to find the numerals and put them in a line in the right order.

In the classroom   Some six- and seven-year-olds explore shape

A group of children explored examples of symmetry around the school to consolidate the work they had been doing in the classroom. They took photographs of examples of simple symmetrical patterns and then explored them further when back in the classroom.

Children's misconceptions

When trying to make connections between key mathematical skills, children can develop misconceptions. There are many causes of these, such as an over-reliance on rules and procedures with little depth of understanding, problems with the language and vocabulary of mathematics and children developing ideas with their own personal meanings based on previous experiences.

When misconceptions do arise, it is important to explore the thinking behind them in a positive way, so that the process supports learning. For teachers, misconceptions are a valuable insight into children's thinking and can often highlight gaps in their knowledge and understanding.

There are various things you can do to address misconceptions, such as pre-empt as many potential misconceptions as possible during the planning stage to prevent them occurring in the first place. You should also discuss and listen to children's reasoning and then work collaboratively to provide strategies to find and remedy any misconception that still occurs.

It is important that both correct and incorrect responses are valued in a positive manner in order to create an encouraging attitude towards mathematics. Children need to be reassured that misconceptions are an important part of learning and can have positive consequences.

Managing mathematics

How you manage mathematics in your classroom will reflect your understanding of how children learn. Consideration of resources is key and there is a vast selection available. These include mathematical manipulatives (structured or unstructured), such as Cuisenaire rods, Multi-base 10 (Diene's) apparatus and multilink; images, such as an abacus, bead string or number line; ICT such as programmable robots, calculators, the Internet, interactive whiteboards, tablets; games; worksheets and textbooks; and other everyday materials, such as rulers, scales and thermometers, that support mathematical ideas in everyday contexts.

Resources can:

- support teaching by providing a model everyone can share
- provide different forms of representation of mathematical ideas
- develop mental imagery
- act as a bridge between children's own experiences and mathematical ideas
- provide a focal point for learning from peers and communication of ideas (adapted from Drews and Hansen, 2007: ix and 21–5).

Managing resources effectively is important. In addition, teachers need to provide an environment in which children can manage their own learning. Reflecting on the following ideas can help you to consider how resources can be managed appropriately.

Access to resources

What rules about the children's access to resources do you have in your classroom? Are the children allowed to select their own resources and use them to help them with a task or do you provide the resources that they are allowed to use? Giving children access to resources gives them access to enhanced learning. Making their own decisions fosters independence and self-reliance.

Displays

There are many reasons for displays proving worthwhile resources for mathematics. They enable a focus on valuing children's achievements and effort, which engenders a sense of pride, worth and self-esteem. Displays can also be part of a 'mathematics area', where children can explore ideas and games in their own time or as part of the classroom routine. Displays can also share information with children, parents and the wider community, as well as share targets.

Anything related to mathematics can be displayed: it isn't always necessary to undertake work in exercise books. For example, it is possible to display mathematical work by sharing the outcomes of an investigation that has been undertaken, presenting photographs of children in practical activities with captions, displaying key vocabulary, or artefacts, pictures or books related to the current topic to stimulate discussion. Using titles, labels and summaries of the work informs visitors and reminds children of learning and key areas of focus.

Learning walls

Learning walls are a particular type of display where teachers present their modelled work and prompts, such as vocabulary or process questions, related to the focus for the week or unit of work. A learning wall can also show the intended learning outcomes for the lesson or week.

Displaying children's work on the wall can reinforce your expectations and include reminders of what you are looking for in your assessment of the children's attainment. Children can be encouraged to interact with the display during the mathematics lesson or at other times to reinforce or extend their thinking about the topic.

Managing other adults

Teaching assistants and voluntary helpers provide an invaluable resource requiring careful management. Developing an excellent working relationship with classroom support staff is crucial, as is building in enough time to plan with or brief them in advance of the lesson.

Teaching assistants can model ideas for the children, support discussion, promote positive behaviour, observe and assess children and manage resources. Teaching assistants may also have a significant impact on children's achievement as a result of working with them in small-group intervention programmes.

Volunteers often bring a wealth of knowledge and interests to the classroom. It is worth finding out what their expertise and interests are. For example, a parent volunteer might be able to explain how the gears on a bicycle work or how a patchwork quilt uses tessellating shapes.

Guided group work in mathematics

Guided group work is a highly effective way to support children's progress. Choosing which children to include in a guided group session is determined by prior assessment. It needs to be carefully planned so that, in a small group, you can address the needs of each individual child in a focused way, offering appropriate support and scaffolding, targeted questioning linked to prior learning or relevant cross-curricular links.

Guided group work can itself provide assessment information that is more difficult to capture in the whole-class context, allowing you to discuss mathematics in more detail with individuals in the group and therefore use this knowledge to inform future planning.

Collaborative working in guided group work gives children opportunities to:

- engage in exploratory talk, deepening their understanding as a result of the interaction and stimulation from peers and their teacher
- develop problem solving skills
- develop turn-taking skills
- learn to negotiate and see things from someone else's point of view and argue their own point of view
- build relationships with a wider circle of people than their own immediate friendship group
- engage in active learning – this is explicitly about learning skills, processes and strategies.

Assessment and target setting should be integrated into everyday teaching and learning in mathematics. Assessment will include day-to-day assessment, the development of periodic assessment and the use of assessment data and tracking of children's progress to support them towards their targets.

Whole-class teaching

Effective whole-class teaching looks deceptively simple, but needs to be considered when planning so that opportunities for the following can be incorporated:

- modelling
- scaffolding
- questioning
- making connections within and beyond mathematics
- making connections between what the children are learning in this lesson, how it relates to previous learning and where it will lead
- focused assessment.

Talk in mathematics

It is important to plan for and include plenty of open questions as these will encourage children to think and test their ideas. Talk is just as crucial in mathematics as it is in other subjects. It is vital that the teacher and the other adults in the classroom fully understand the vocabulary and concepts they will be discussing with the children. The correct use of mathematical language should be modelled. Skilled use of questioning and management of discussion enables teachers to gain insights into children's mathematical understanding.

Theory tells us that learners construct their mathematical knowledge as a result of their experiences of the world. Vygotsky (1978) noted that when children learn together they are able to then use the newly learned language as a way to organise their own activity. Pimm (1995: 79) noted:

> Children need to learn ... how to use mathematical language to create, control and express their own mathematical meanings as well as to interpret the mathematical language of others.

Research indicates that high-quality, exploratory talk may be difficult to generate between children in class. Mercer and Sams (2006) suggest that this might be because:

- children may not bring a clear understanding of what they are required to do
- even when an explicit instruction of 'talk together' is given, the children may not know how to discuss their ideas effectively.

The Williams review, 'independent review of mathematics teaching in Early Years settings and primary schools' (DCSF, 2008: 4) identified talk as one of the two most important current issues for teachers:

> Two issues only are singled out: the need for an increased focus on the 'use and application' of mathematics and on the vitally important question of the classroom discussion of mathematics. ... It is often suggested that 'mathematics itself is a language'

but it must not be overlooked that only by constructive dialogue in the medium of the English language in the classroom can logic and reasoning be developed – the factors at the very heart of embedded learning in mathematics.

The Thinking Together project

The Thinking Together project, reported on in the Williams review, was based on research into a dialogue-based approach to children's thinking and learning, taught children:

- how to gain relevant knowledge of mathematical operations, procedures, terms and concepts
- how to use language to work effectively together to jointly enquire, reason, and consider information, share and negotiate their ideas and make joint decisions.

Findings from the research supported the notion of a strong relationship between social and psychological development, such as the following:

- *Quality of group work* When taught how to work with others in a group, the children engaged more effectively with tasks for longer periods of time, with all participants being included more in the group's work on the task.
- *Quality of talk* The quality of children's talk changes significantly once they are directly taught how to discuss their ideas. More features of exploratory talk, such as reasoning, sharing a range of points of view and clearer explanation, appear in their problem solving discussions.
- *Individual attainment* Individuals show improvement in maths (and science) attainment and in non-verbal-reasoning.

The teacher's role in talk

The teacher has a crucial role in modelling and organising classroom discussion and dialogue. When planning lessons, you may wish to consider Alexander's (2004: 32) advice for organising classroom interactions:

- structure questions to provoke thoughtful answers
- encourage answers that expect further questions and are seen as the building blocks of dialogue rather than its terminal point
- chain individual teacher–pupil and pupil–pupil exchanges into coherent lines of enquiry rather than allowing disconnected one-word responses.

Reflective questions

- Reflect on your own learning in mathematics as a child and compare it to the guidance given in this chapter. How does it differ and what is the same? What challenges and opportunities present themselves for you?
- Now think about how you use mathematics as an adult. Why do you think the key knowledge, skills and understanding outlined in this chapter are important for primary school children to develop?
- What elements of planning for primary mathematics are most challenging for you and why? How can you develop your confidence and competence in these areas?
- High-quality talk in mathematics is one of the most essential aspects of learning and teaching this subject. How do you intend to develop your own work with children to enhance talk?

Conclusion

Despite being a compulsory subject in education, mathematics can be a particularly difficult subject for some to learn and teach. This chapter has focused on the main aspects of learning and teaching mathematics to support those working with children to improve their understanding of mathematics in primary school and continue their journey to successful mathematics teaching.

The first key aspect to consider is the knowledge, skills and understanding that children need to develop. Crucially, these include being able to apply mathematics and solve problems involving mathematics; communicating and representing; reasoning; developing methods for calculating; and consolidating and recalling facts.

The second key aspect is progression. All children learn at different rates and in different ways, but we have provided a general overview of the typical progression found in the primary school years. Planning is the third key aspect.

In this chapter we have identified the components to consider when you plan a mathematics lesson. These include differentiation, using models and images, children's misconceptions, managing the classroom and people within it, talk in mathematics and the teacher's role in talk. These key aspects introduce to you the complexity of primary mathematics and how to learn and teach it.

Further reading

Barmby, P., Bilsborough, L., Harries, T. and Higgins, S. (2009) *Primary Mathematics: Teaching for understanding*. Maidenhead: Open University Press.
This book identifies the connections, representations, reasoning, communication and misconceptions that you and the children need to understand for effective mathematics teaching and learning.

Hansen, A. (ed.) (2014) *Children's Errors in Mathematics: Understanding common misconceptions in primary schools* (3rd edn). Exeter: Learning Matters.
This book will help you to understand why children make mistakes in mathematics and what the most common errors are.

Haylock, D. (2010) *Mathematics Explained for Primary Teachers* (4th edn). London: Sage.
Consistently the most popular book in England for primary mathematics. Every aspect of the curriculum is explained.

Rowland, T., Turner, F., Thwaites, E. A. and Huckstep, P. (2009) *Developing Primary Mathematics Teaching: Reflecting on practice with the knowledge quartet*. London: Sage.
This book helps you, regardless of what stage you are at in your teaching career, to reflect on your mathematics teaching practice and improve it.

References

ACME (2008) 'Mathematics in primary years: A discussion paper for the Rose Review of the Primary Curriculum'. London: ACME. Available online at: www.acme-uk.org/media/1769/rose%20review%20maths%20paper%20final%20sept%2008.pdf

Alexander, R. (2004) *Towards Dialogic Teaching: Rethinking classroom talk*. Cambridge: Dialogos.

Bruner, J. S. (1960) *The Process of Education*. Cambridge MA: Harvard University Press.

DCSF (2008) 'Independent review of mathematics teaching in Early Years settings and primary schools'. Nottingham: DCSF Publications. Available online at: http://dera.ioe.ac.uk/8365/1/Williams%20Mathematics.pdf

DfE (2012a) 'Statutory Framework for the Early Years Foundation Stage'. Runcorn: DfE. Available online at: http://media.education.gov.uk/assets/files/pdf/e/eyfs%20statutory%20framework%20march%202012.pdf

DfE (2012b) 'National Curriculum for mathematics Key Stages 1 and 2 – Draft: National Curriculum review'. London: DfE. Available online at: http://media.education.gov.uk/assets/files/pdf/d/draft%20national%20curriculum%20for%20mathematics%20key%20stages%201%202.pdf

Drews, D. and Hansen, A. (eds) (2007) *Using Resources to Support Mathematical Thinking: Primary and early years*. Exeter: Learning Matters.

Mercer, N. and Sams, C. (2006) 'Teaching children how to use language to solve maths problems', *Language and Education*, 20 (6): 507–28. Available online at: http://thinkingtogether.educ.cam.ac.uk/publications/journals/MercerandSams 2006.pdf

Pimm, D. (1995) *Symbols and Meanings in School Mathematics*. London: Routledge.

Skemp, R. R. (1976) 'Relational understanding and instrumental understanding', *Mathematics Teaching*, 77: 20–6. Available online at: www.grahamtall.co.uk/skemp/pdfs/instrumental-relational.pdf

Smith, A. (2004) 'Making mathematics count: The report of Professor Adrian Smith's inquiry into post-14 mathematics education'. London: The Stationery Office. Available online at: http://dera.ioe.ac.uk/4873/1/MathsInquiryFinalReport.pdf

Thinking Together project, University of Cambridge. Available online at: http://thinkingtogether.educ.cam.ac.uk/about

Vygotsky, L. S. (1978) *Mind in Society: The development of higher psychological processes*. Cambridge, MA: Harvard University Press.

CHAPTER 10

MUSIC

Carol Wetton

Learning objectives

By the end of this chapter you should be able to:

- understand past and present approaches to music education
- recognise the range of music provision offered outside the curriculum
- understand how music can be embedded with other curriculum subjects
- structure a music lesson in the primary classroom.

Introduction

Since the time of the ancient Greeks, most formal education has included music in some guise. In this chapter, there will be no attempt to justify the place of music in the primary school curriculum; rather, the aim here is to illustrate different ways to teach music successfully, based on research and experience. There is a musician inside each of us and primary school teachers have a vital role to play in children's musical development.

There may be some confusion about what is meant by music education. Mills (2005: 2) describes some activities that are not music education: 'drawing a flute, reading about Mozart's life, making a musical instrument, or learning how to operate a piece of computer software'. These activities may support musical learning but, essentially, it is about performing (singing, playing, movement), composing (inventing with sound) and listening.

The title of Keith Swanwick's book, *Teaching Music Musically* (2012), sums up this concept, which is to teach music by doing it rather than talking about it. An holistic approach is generally agreed to be good practice by most music educators today – that is, combining the three areas of performing, composing and listening, as illustrated in the example described below.

In the classroom   An holistic approach

Some nine- and ten-year-olds are studying gospel and spiritual songs. The teacher has selected three songs to include in a concert for parents and friends. These are 'People get ready', 'Gospel medley' and 'Oh happy day' (all available at www.singup.org).

The children will decide on the arrangements of the songs (a composing activity), such as the movements to enhance the singing. They will then practise and prepare for the concert (a performing activity). The concert will be filmed and then the children will appraise their performance (a listening activity).

As primary school teachers, we have the chance to introduce children to the wonderful world of musicmaking. If they do not get this opportunity, then a door slams shut and may well stay that way for life. As the great music educator Zoltan Kodály maintained, 'Music should be for everyone'. By music he did not mean passive listening but active participation. Peak experiences in life can happen when we take part in musicmaking and it should be every child's right to have an excellent music education.

We should teach music via music, be clear in our musical purpose and plan enjoyable activities that consider carefully the age and stage of learning of the children. The word 'fun' should be avoided, though, when planning music sessions as this can reduce music to a frippery.

There is much research to support the view that music can help children develop attributes such as communication, problem solving and the ability to work with others, to name just three key skills. As all primary school teachers would want to develop such attributes, this chapter focuses on finding practical ways to teach music and develop social skills alongside musical appreciation.

History of music education – how did we get here?

There is documentation regarding music education in Europe before the advent of compulsory schooling. Two examples are song schools in medieval England (44 choir schools remain today) and musical instruction books for the upper classes in nineteenth-century England. We can usefully take a brief look at music education in the United Kingdom from the late nineteenth century to the present day.

The Education Act of 1870 led to compulsory education for 'the masses' and singing became a statutory subject. A standardised singing curriculum, dominated by regimentation and drill was established. Singing was possibly seen as something to be endured rather than enjoyed!

Changes in educational theory in the early twentieth century led to a decline in drill-based music education. The concept of the 'primitive child', influenced by Darwin's theory of evolution, led to a more creative approach, which included movement and dance. The educational work of the Hungarian composer mentioned above, Zoltan Kodály, and the Swiss music educator Emile Jacques-Dalcroze, profoundly influenced the teaching of music worldwide and continues to do so.

Music lessons continued to be compulsory throughout the twentieth century, but consisted mainly of singing, movement and untuned percussion bands, until German composer Carl Orff introduced tuned instruments (xylophones, glockenspiels) to the educational arena in the 1950s. At the same time, the recorder was being mass produced for the first time and was used by many teachers as a first instrument for young children. Advances in technology led to radio broadcasts and television programmes such as *Singing Together*.

⌖   In the classroom   1963

I vividly remember the *Singing Together* radio broadcasts during my time at primary school. At a set time every week, the teacher turned on the radio and we got out our songbooks and, for half an hour, really enjoyed singing songs of the British Isles and around the world. It was a wonderful experience and, on reflection, started a lifelong love of singing as I still sing with a local community choir. The idea of the whole country singing these great songs at the same time really inspired all my classmates and me. We all looked forward to our *Singing Together* lessons. I still remember most of the words today! (Steve, 59)

During the 1960s, the progressive education movement led to the concept of creativity within the arts being central. This was encouraged by John Paynter, who is arguably the founder of modern musical education theory. The National Curriculum was established in 1989 and the notion of an holistic approach to music teaching and learning involving performing, composing and listening, became statutory and remains so throughout England.

There have been many changes in recent years, but one initiative generally known as Wider Opportunities has meant that all children in upper primary classes now have the right to an opportunity to learn an instrument with funding provided by the government. The Sing Up campaign continues to encourage singing for all and provides training for teachers and resources, including a subscription website. 'The importance of music' (DfE, 2011) document outlines plans for the future of music education. Central to the plan is the establishment of local music hubs from September 2012. These hubs are seen as a way of providing 'joined-up' music education, promoting the notion of inclusivity that is at the heart of 'Making every child's music matter: Music manifesto report no. 2' (DfES, 2006).

Music in the curriculum

Music is a compulsory subject for all children from the ages of 5 to 14. In England, the National Curriculum is statutory, which means that all children in England have nine years of music education. This sounds wonderful – so why is it that so few pupils opt to take GCSE music (currently 8 per cent)? Why is 'a good or outstanding music education [only delivered] in 33 of the 90 primary schools ... inspected' (Ofsted, 2012: 5)?

At present, all primary teachers are required to teach the National Curriculum in music. Teacher training courses will usually provide some training in music, but this is often very limited. Indeed, Ofsted (2012: 19) found that, 'nearly all non-specialist teachers demonstrated professional, efficient lesson organisation and effective classroom management strategies. However, the activities themselves were often unmusical – for example, drawing pictures.' Ofsted (2012: 27) also tells us that teachers often taught lessons without 'sufficient musical dimension' and 'the quality of access to and impact of CPD for teachers was inadequate or non-existent in 33 of the 90 schools visited.' Effective training for teachers, then, either during their initial teacher training or as part of their continuing professional development, has therefore been judged as lacking. 'The importance of music' (DfE, 2011) addresses these issues by recommending further training for new teachers.

In many schools, music is taught by a specialist or another member of staff – sometimes a teaching assistant. There is no statutory time allocation for music in primary schools. In the hierarchy of subjects, the place of music is very often near the bottom of the list despite the fact that everyone involved in working with young people tends to see music as a 'good thing'. Also, even though there have been initiatives encouraging inclusivity, 'excellence for everyone' remains a dream rather than a reality.

All this needs to change. According to Paynter (cited in Salaman, 1988): 'All that matters in music education is that what we do is musical … I would applaud whatever was happening in a classroom, provided that it was actually involving pupils in the musical experience.'

Music outside the curriculum

It is not uncommon for some children to receive music tuition outside the usual school day. This can lead to a situation in which some of the children have greater subject knowledge than the teacher.

Parents are often keen for their children to learn to play an instrument and seek out private tuition, but what is available? Anyone can offer lessons outside school without having to have formal qualifications. Many people are surprised to find this but, just as an unqualified plumber can be the cause of household disaster, it is possible for an unqualified music teacher to cause untold misery. Qualifications do not necessarily result in good teaching, however. Also, many instrumentalists resort to teaching as a way of making a living, but may lack the vocational drive of a dedicated teacher.

So, what qualifications are there? There are many accredited bodies offering a graded exam system in performing. These include ABRSM, Trinity Guildhall and Rockschool. These graded exams are not teaching qualifications, but some bodies also offer teaching diplomas.

Children may, then, experience music lessons of varying quality outside the curriculum. These could be on any instrument, voice or musical genre and are often dependent on parents' spending power and interests. Lessons may be in groups or individually. Often, such musically educated pupils are seen in school as 'gifted and talented' when really they were just fortunate enough to have been given an opportunity! A lottery indeed in the quest for 'excellence for everyone'.

Some schools also offer extracurricular music activities. These can be many and varied and often happen as a result of a staff member's interest or skill. Some examples are a lunchtime recorder group, after school choir, school orchestra and dhol drumming group. Such groups are sometimes led by peripatetic teachers. These teachers travel from school to school and are sometimes self-employed and not always qualified. Often provided by local hubs (previously 'music services'), they teach a mix of individual, group and whole-class lessons and sometimes lead ensembles.

Some hubs also offer ensembles for instruments and voices at local centres. Children may progress to national ensembles, such as the National Youth Orchestra. To complete the picture, there are large-scale initiatives, such as Young Voices, which give children the opportunity to sing in large arenas with professional musicians. Community musicians are also sometimes employed by schools to enhance the curriculum. One example might be a samba group, which might come in to school and spend a day with the children working on samba drumming. These kinds of experiences enrich pupils' lives, but it must not be forgotten that the music curriculum is for everyone and to make good progress in music entails regular engagement in musical activities.

Music across the curriculum

You may have musical self-confidence because of past experience. Maybe you had clarinet lessons or sang in a church choir. If you lack musical self-esteem, however, this is usually because of a lack of opportunity or a poor experience. All effective primary school teachers share classroom management expertise, know the children and enjoy listening to music. Being able to read music or play an instrument are not essential skills for the successful teaching and learning of music.

We will now turn our attention to how we can enrich the whole curriculum with musical activities. It is important that the activities are musically valid if we are considering children's musical development.

In the classroom   **Examples of cross-curricular activities**

Literacy

A class of eight- and nine-year-olds are listening to 'Pictures at an Exhibition' by Mussorgsky.

They listen carefully and then discuss how the different pieces of music paint a picture with sound, commenting on the mood created. They use musical vocabulary to describe how the musical dimensions are used within the pieces. As a class, they choose the piece 'The Gnome' and use the music as a stimulus to create their own poem with the same title.

Mathematics

A class of seven- and eight-year-olds are practising their multiplication tables using 'Sing Your Times Tables' (available online at: www.singyourtables.com).

(Continued)

(Continued)

Musical learning would include activities such as listening to rap, pop and rock styles and keeping to a steady beat while using voices.

Science

A class of five- and six-year-olds are investigating life processes. They compose a piece of music using voices and instruments as well as movement to represent a seed growing into a flowering plant. This is rehearsed and performed as part of an assembly presentation.

Design and technology

A class of six- and seven-year-olds are working with materials to make musical instruments – shakers. They experiment with different containers and materials, such as sand, lentils and rice. Once the products have been made and evaluated, the children use them to accompany a song they have been learning, composing their own musical patterns.

Computing

A class of nine- and ten-year-olds are using the software GarageBand to create, test, improve and refine sequences. When the compositions have been completed, they are played at a specially organised playtime disco. Votes are cast for the best composition.

History

A class of eight- and nine-year-olds are finding out about the Tudors. They learn a song recalling the facts: 'Henry the VIII he had six wives. All of them lived in fear of their lives. Two were beheaded and one of them died. Two were divorced and one survived'. The musical learning involves singing in two parts with clear diction and musical expression. The song will be performed at the end of term concert.

Geography

A class of nine- and ten-year-olds are investigating the water cycle. They compose pieces of music in groups to reflect the stages, carefully considering the use of instruments (including voice) and musical elements. Each completed composition is recorded for evaluation and is part of a display where pupils and adults can listen to the compositions while looking at the display.

Art and design

A class of 10- and 11-year-olds are designing a CD cover for a recording of their summer concert in which they all participated. This will be sold to parents and be a tangible reminder of their work in music. As they design their work, they listen to the recording and appraise the performance.

Physical education

The upper primary children are preparing an end of year play (*Jungle Book* from Disney Kids, available online at: www.mtishows.com). They create a dance using a range of movement patterns. This dance is then performed as part of the play.

PSHE and citizenship

The lower primary children are preparing an assembly about recycling. They are learning the performance song 'Do anything but throw it away' (by Durant and Mooney and available online at: www.singup.org). The message of the song is clear from the title. Musical learning includes the blues style and the teacher uses the 'tactics' section of the website for ideas for performance.

Languages

A class of seven- and eight-year-olds are learning the names of body parts in French. The teacher uses the song 'Heads, shoulders, knees and toes', using French words to replace the English ones. For musical learning, the children develop their 'thinking voices' and internalise the pulse.

The examples described show how music can enrich and enhance all areas of the curriculum. It is also crucial that musical learning is always considered as being important in its own right.

In the next section, musical learning is considered in more detail, beginning with listening.

Listening

Listening is the application of the mind to the sounds which the ear, a purely physical organ, may or may not hear. (Buck, 1971)

A young child will be exposed to different sound sources throughout the day, such as toys, computers, radios and televisions. There may be few opportunities for silence and quiet contemplation. The long-term impact of this kind of noise pollution has not yet been fully researched.

How can we teach children to listen rather than simply hear? There are four ways to respond to music that should be considered when planning a listening activity:

- physical
- emotional
- imaginative
- intellectual.

It is possible to combine all four, as in the example below.

 In the classroom   A listening activity

A class of five- and six-year-old pupils are listening to a recording of 'Royal march of the lion' by Saint-Saëns.

They role-play waking up slowly in the introduction and prepare for the march. They move around like proud lions in the 'marching' section, then pause and imitate 'roaring' with their arms during the middle section, then continue to march, ending with a final 'roar'.

During this activity, the children respond physically (moving like lions and 'roaring'). This reflects the structure of the music (intellectual) and calls on them to use their imagination (pretend you are a lion), as well as respond emotionally (feeling strong and proud). Listening with concentration is essential in developing musicianship skills and is central to all musical activities. Developing the physical response to music is vital in the early years and beyond.

Music and movement

A child's first physical experiences are often rhythmic in nature, such as sucking, rocking, crawling and walking, and the heartbeat is our life force. As music educators, we must capture and build on this natural feeling of life's rhythms if we are to achieve a real understanding of music. In many societies there is no single word for music that does not include dance. In modern Britain some communities seem very reluctant to dance and appear to have lost the sheer joy that can be felt through movement to music. Although children have their own internal rhythms, we still need to guide them to respond to an external pulse. 'Feeling the pulse' is one of the most important skills to develop in young children (and one sadly lacking in many adults).

Music educator Emile Jaques-Dalcroze established an approach to learning about music initially by means of movement, now referred to as Dalcroze Eurhythmics. He realised that the first musical instrument to be trained is the body. That was in 1887. Eurhythmics means 'good rhythm' and is based on three underlying propositions:

- all elements of music can be experienced via movement
- all musical sounds begin with motion
- there is a gesture for every sound and a sound for every gesture.

How can primary school teachers apply this philosophy in today's classroom?

In the classroom   Feeling the beat

Using recorded music (for instance, 'Radetsky march' by Strauss), the teacher and a class of six- and seven-year-olds stand in a circle. This is a useful method for turn taking and assessment.

Each child or adult invents an action in response to the beat (sometimes called *the pulse*) of the music. Movements without sound encourage careful listening whereas stamping and clapping make it difficult to hear the music clearly. Movements such as bending and stretching fingers, hands or arms work well. The children are encouraged to bring in their own recordings of favourite music for this activity. The main purpose is to 'feel the beat', so the teacher should encourage the children who find this difficult by demonstrating a movement that has a clearer relation to the pulse.

This activity also encourages improvisation skills. Different genres of music from around the world can be used like this to enrich listening experiences.

The above example would follow lower primary work on 'walking the pulse'. Working in a large space with shoes and socks removed, the children walk the pulse, stopping and starting and moving in different directions as they listen to and respond to the music. The teacher or one of the children with a secure sense of rhythm could tap the pulse on a tambourine. When the music stops, the children freeze, as in the game of musical statues.

Responding to different qualities of movement takes this to a higher musical level (marching, elegant walk, burglar creep and so on). Walking a set number of beats and stopping (for example, walk four beats and stop four beats) gives children an idea of rests in music. With practice, a developing sense of rhythm means that eventually the children should 'internalise the pulse' – that is, walk feeling the pulse inside without anyone playing the tambourine.

For further details of this approach, visit the Dalcroze website (at: www.dalcroze. org.uk).

Singing

> Since singing is so good a thing I wish all men would learn to sing. (William Byrd, 1588)

> Singing can improve pupils' learning, confidence, health and social development. It has the power to change lives and build stronger communities. (DfE, 2011: 34)

Much has recently been said about how singing can help children in many areas of their lives and organisations such as Sing Up and the Voices Foundation have provided training and resources to help teachers deliver singing teaching in an enjoyable and structured way. The music hubs established countrywide in September 2012 have been given a brief to develop singing strategies in schools, and children should also have the opportunity to join choirs and vocal ensembles in wider educational settings.

Put simply by 'Making every child's music matter', 'singing should be at the heart of all music making activities in the primary school' (DfES, 2006: 34). Most primary teachers are enthusiastic advocates of singing, but there are still many schools where little singing takes place. What a sad state of affairs! Many teachers do not feel confident about leading singing and time constraints can lead to music being marginalised.

The important thing to remember is that it is beneficial for children to sing together and simultaneously learn some facts, but, for their musical development, we need to be sure that we focus on musical progression, too.

In the classroom   A song in stages

Here is a guide to teaching a song that is to be performed. This is done in stages, over a period of time or in one lesson. The stages are:

1 choose the song – analyse its usefulness
2 provide motivation and model performance learn the song

---

3 learn the song
4 arrange the song
5 perform the song and appraise the performance.

1. Choose the song – analyse its usefulness

The musical purpose of a song should always be considered. Ask yourself, 'What do I want the children to learn about music from this song?' Music should always be enjoyable, but it is not enough to say, 'I chose this because it's good fun'. Every activity must have a purpose. The song should be analysed to ensure that it offers the skills required and ensures *progression*.

The resources recommended at the end of this section will explain how songs can be analysed in this way and can help to identify musical teaching points. These resources also include high-quality recorded performance and backing tracks that can be used for teaching and performances.

Example model: 'What shall we do with the drunken sailor?', for eight- and nine-year-olds

Style: Folk song
Structure: Verse and chorus
Key: Minor
Range: 9th
Tempo   Fast
Others: This song is a sea shanty, a work song, and so the singing should be vigorous, with plenty of energy. It is important to convey this mood during the performance.

The song in this example has been chosen as part of a group of songs about the sea for an assembly presentation. Two more songs with different learning intentions are also being used: 'Sloop John B' and 'Octopus's garden'. There will also be a performance of the class composition 'Storm at sea'.

2. Provide motivation and model performance

The children need to hear the whole song and understand the mood and feeling they will be trying to convey. Therefore, the model performance (by teacher, pupil or recording) must be excellent or we fail before we start. Teachers should use their skills to motivate the children using stories, pictures, puppets and so forth to engage

(Continued)

(Continued)

them. Consider using 'active listening' at this stage – for example, ask younger pupils to move as they listen or ask older pupils to listen out for instruments they hear.

3. Learn the song

Children in lower primary classes will probably not use written words (as this can lead to it becoming a literacy lesson rather than a music lesson) whereas children in upper primary classes can find it helpful to have words or a score. An interactive whiteboard is usually more successful than sheets of paper for displaying lyrics because its position means that children look ahead rather than down.

Two basic methods for learning a song are:

- *segmentation* learning it bit by bit
- *absorption* learning by means of repeated listening.

A mixture of the two methods can be useful. Continuing with 'Drunken sailor' as a model, the children can learn the chorus and then the song can be performed with the teacher or another child singing the verses and the children singing the chorus. This is known as *partial singing*.

This part of the plan may take a few weeks, during which the teacher should choose a focus to work on and improve. It can sometimes be helpful to slow the tempo while you are working on a particular area. When it has been practised and is improving, try it again at the correct tempo. The teacher should only sing when appropriate and listen and appraise the rest of the time.

4. Arrange the song

The children should be involved in the decision-making about how the song should be performed. They should be enabled to consider when and where it will be performed and who the audience will be.

A performance doesn't always have to be formal – the class could simply ask another teacher to come and listen, for example.

The children should also be involved in deciding who will direct the performance. It may or may not need a conductor, but if it does who will that person be?

Ask the children what they think they should wear and how they should stand. For this performance the children may like to wear pirate style props. They may like to add movement – but they should understand that movement must enhance the singing.

Also talk with them about whether or not there will be any accompaniment. Music could be live if you have access to a musician or musicians or a recorded backing track could be used, with or without added percussion parts. An unaccompanied performance is also an option.

Finally, the children can give some thought to whether or not there will be any solos or part-singing. Will we sing some parts loud/spiky and so on? Consider musical expression and if the audience will be able to hear the words clearly.

5. Perform the song and appraise the performance

A video of the performance will help with evaluation. Think about who will film the performance and leave time for an appraisal of the performance by the children.

One method is to ask each child to offer two stars and a wish (that is, two things they thought were good and one thing the performers could improve on). This feedback can take the form of a discussion or written work for older children. The evaluation, too, could be audio or video recorded for a complete record of the work.

Apart from this process being used for the purposes of evaluation, recording during the learning process can also be a useful tool to help improve the performance.

There follows a short review of the Hungarian composer, ethnomusicologist, pedagogue, linguist, philosopher and educator, Zoltan Kodály, who believed that singing was the best way to approach music education.

The Kodály approach

Zoltan Kodály believed passionately in the concept of teaching musicianship by means of singing. His approach to singing teaching is still applied throughout the world.

The principles of the Kodály approach are:

- teach music by means of singing
- use the voice as the first instrument
- continue to use the voice if you take up an instrument
- use high-quality material – mainly folk-based – which takes into account the mother tongue and cultural background
- progress methodically, going from the simple to the complex by taking tiny steps – if the steps are too big, the learning will not be effective

- teach an element unconsciously at first and bring it to the point of the children being conscious of it once the element is well established – rather like the way in which children acquire language
- use multisensory learning – involve hearing, sight, muscle movement.

To become a qualified Kodály practitioner takes years of training, but this list can be helpful for primary school teachers. The Kodály games and songs for Early Years settings are excellent and encourage good pitch and confidence in singing (further details of courses and resources can be found at www.britishkodalyacademy.org).

Playing instruments

Most primary schools have a range of untuned instruments (instruments of indefinite pitch), such as drums and maracas, and some tuned instruments (instruments of definite pitch). Children are expected to learn how to play tuned and untuned instruments with control and rhythmic accuracy in lower primary years and be able to improvise rhythmic and melodic material in upper primary years.

When considering working with musical instruments, it is important to be aware of the work of Carl Orff. Tuned instruments such as xylophones (wood) and glockenspiels (metal) are commonly used in Orff work. These instruments can be very useful in primary classrooms as they stay in tune, do not require major maintenance, do not require the learning of special techniques initially and can sound wonderful in large ensembles. They enable an inclusive approach to music education, too. Indeed, inclusion is at the heart of the Orff approach, as is the use of ostinato (repeated patterns) to create musical performances. The only drawbacks are that the instruments are relatively expensive and do require some storage space.

The games in the example below can all be played on a mix of tuned and untuned percussion instruments. Further information on the Orff approach can be found online (at: www.orff.org.uk).

Other instruments often used in primary schools are recorders and guitars. There may be a piano available or keyboards and sometimes orchestral instruments such as violins. The scheme generally known as Wider Opportunities or First Access under the national plan for music (DfE, 2011) sets out as a right that all children in primary years have the opportunity of one year of free music tuition. Usually this is achieved via whole-class teaching, with a visiting teacher giving the lessons. For details of how the scheme works in your area, contact your local music hub.

> #### In the classroom   Creative soundscapes with six- and seven-year-olds
>
> The children wanted to compose a piece called 'Winter wonderland' to perform at the school's Christmas concert. They experimented with sounds and instruments and composed the following, including the words.
>
> - 'The snow fell in the night' – repeated descending pattern E B G D A E, played four times.
> - 'In the morning icicles had formed' – very high short, random sounds.
> - 'I got out my sledge and walked down the lane' – quiet, steady, muffled beats played eight times.
> - 'Up the hill and whizz down' – patterns from low to high in steps, then slide from high to low.
> - 'It's still snowing' – repeat first section.
> - 'Here come the carol singers' – sing and play the rhythm of 'Jingle bells'.
> - 'Merry Christmas everybody!' – all shout together.

Such creative soundscapes can be generated with all ages and any variety of instruments, not forgetting that the voice is one of them. Some starting points for creative soundscapes include feelings, movements, locations, weather, animals, machines, book or TV characters, fantasy, and special events. Try also telling a story and adding music (such as *Goldilocks*) or set a poem to music.

A useful structure you can use is 'A – B – A'. This is three sections, the middle section contrasting with the first and last sections, which are the same or similar. So, for example, you would work with the children to compose section A (for example, a hopping rabbit), then a contrasting B section (a resting rabbit), then repeat the A section. This is a structure used extensively in all kinds of music.

If the children are to make progress in their instrumental work, they need some skills-based activities, too. Here are a few you can try.

- Playing along to the beat of recorded music or song.
- 'Musical statues' – as above, but stopping and starting.
- Playing the rhythm of a well-known song, such as 'Baa baa black sheep'.
- 'Plug the gap!' In a circle, the children play four steady beats followed by four silent beats. Each child composes his or her own pattern in the gap.
- Ice-cream flavours. Choose four – for instance, chocolate, peach, strawberry, vanilla. Choose and play the rhythm of the words in the chosen order. By repeating the pattern (ostinato), the children can create a longer composition or accompany a song.

Structuring a music lesson

All schools should have a music policy to set out an overview. The curriculum leader for music should update this as necessary. The document should also give advice on the time allocated for music. It is often left to the class teacher to organise medium- and short-term planning and assessment. So, where do you start?

There are published schemes of work, such as the Music Express series (A&C Black), which include lesson plans and supporting resources. Ofsted (2012) was not impressed with a 'one size fits all' approach, so it is advisable to use the lesson plans as starting points and then adapt them. Without sufficient training or specialist skills it can be an intimidating task to plan successful music lessons from scratch in which the children make progress. Many colleagues have therefore found schemes such as Music Express a very helpful starting point. Below are some pointers to guide you in your planning.

Performing, composing and listening should be well integrated with one another. This goal must be kept in mind when planning. Many teachers use half-termly medium-term plans to set an overview for the sessions and this should fit with the school's policy.

Singing should be included in every music lesson. This could be vocalising as part of a composition, rapping or beatboxing, as well as simply singing songs. One useful strategy is to choose three contrasting performance songs per half-term and work towards a performance (formal or informal). When children perform their own arrangements of songs, they will be including composing, as this is their creative input. Always pay attention to improving some other important aspect such as posture or diction.

One hour a week is recommended as a minimum for music. One option that is good practice in planning is the three-part lesson (although this is not compulsory).

1. *Starter* Engage everyone! Briefly recap on previous learning and share learning intentions (10 minutes).
2. *Main* This should be the longest part of the lesson (40 minutes). Consider whole-class work, group work and individual work. Keep pupils focused, with changes of activity or refreshers (such as a stretching game). Always consider how any additional adults can enhance learning. Importantly, don't talk about it – do it! Learn about music via music.
3. *Recap and review learning* Remind the children of long-term aims, including what they will be doing next and any homework to extend learning (10 minutes).

Here are some other pointers for successful music teaching and learning.

- It is useful to set up the classroom before the lesson begins, if this is possible. Monitors can be useful for this task.
- If working with instruments, it is important that the children obey the rules. When handed an instrument it is only natural that they will want to play it, but

set your rules clearly and stick to them. For example, help the children learn that they do not pick up or touch an instrument until asked to do so. Also, teach them to respond rapidly to a 'Stop' signal.

- The children must learn to respect each other by listening attentively to performances and offering positive feedback.
- Have high expectations and set challenges for the children. Do not overpraise work; save remarks such as 'It's brilliant' for very special occasions.
- All activities should have a clear musical purpose. Differentiated tasks should include something to stretch the more able and strategies to deal with children with special needs.
- Use digital technology to *enhance* teaching and learning rather than *drive* the learning.
- 'Good planning shows ambition to improve the quality of pupils' responses, to improve their musicality' (Ofsted, 2012: 6: 2).

 Reflective questions

- Think back to your own experiences of music at school. What factors either encouraged your progress or inhibited it?
- What experiences in the classroom have you had that demonstrate how music can be effectively integrated with other subjects, what are the key challenges?
- Not all children will have the same level of musical aptitude. How can you ensure all children have been involved in the lesson?

Conclusion

The purpose of a good music education should be to nurture children's musicality – and we are all musicians – by achieving engagement with practical and progressive musical activities. Developing the listener, composer and performer inside every child should be our aim. In the words of Kodály (cited in Bonis, 1974: 124), 'A bad music teacher may kill the love of music for thirty years in thirty classes of pupils.'

The importance of primary school teachers in a child's musical development is invaluable. We pay tribute to all teachers who strive to enrich children's lives by means of active musicmaking, who endeavour to help them 'make friends with music' and provide a strong foundation on which to build a lifelong love of music.

We all need music in our lives to help us through the bad times and enrich the good times. An excellent music education should be a right for everyone, not a privilege for a few.

Further reading

The following resources are recommended for singing:

- publications from www.outoftheark.co.uk
- subscription website www.singup.org
- the Voiceworks series – *Voiceplay* (EYFS), *Young Voiceworks* (KS1) and *Junior Voiceworks 1 and 2* (KS2), Oxford: Oxford University Press.

Find out more about how the work of Kodály, Dalcroze and Orff continues today by visiting their websites at:

- www.britishkodalyacademy.org
- www.dalcroze.org.uk
- www.orff.org.uk

McPherson, G. (2009) *The Child as Musician: A handbook of musical development*. Oxford: Oxford University Press.
This book has 24 chapters written by eminent music educators and explores all aspects of musical development.

References

Bonis, A. (ed.) (1964) *The Selected Writings of Zoltan Kodály*. London: Boosey & Hawkes.
Buck, P. (1971) *Psychology for Musicians*. Oxford: Oxford University Press.
Byrd, W. (1588) 'Psalms, sonnets and songs of sadness and pietie', in S. Gillingham (2012) *Psalms Through the Centuries*. Oxford: Wiley-Blackwell.
DfE (2011) 'The importance of music: A national plan for music education'. Runcorn: DfE. Available online at: https://www.gov.uk/government/uploads/system/uploads/attachment_data/file/180973/DFE-00086-2011.pdf
DfES (2006) 'Making every child's music matter: Music manifesto report no. 2: A consultation for action'. Nottingham: DfES Publications. Available online at: http://webarchive.nationalarchives.gov.uk/20130401151715/https://www.education.gov.uk/publications/eOrderingDownload/Music_Manifesto_Report2.pdf
Mills, J. (2005) *Music in the School*. Oxford: Oxford University Press.
Ofsted (2012) 'Music in schools: Wider still, and wider'. Manchester: Ofsted.
Paynter, J. (1970) *Sound and Silence*. Cambridge: Cambridge University Press.
Salaman, W. (1988) 'Personalities in World Music Education No. 7: John Paynter', *International Journal of Music Education*, 12 (1): 28–32.
Swanwick, K. (2012) *Teaching Music Musically*. Abingdon: Routledge.

CHAPTER 11

PHYSICAL EDUCATION

Emma Whewell, Karen Woolley and Robert Kellam

Learning objectives

By the end of this chapter you should be able to:

- promote an understanding of the aims and purposes of physical education in primary school
- provide support and guidance in planning and delivering the primary curriculum for physical education
- give examples of good practice that will enable you to deliver outstanding lessons via a child-centred approach.

Introduction

This chapter aims to challenge the notion of traditional primary school physical education being a mirror of the multi-activity secondary school model and show its fundamental importance in developing motor skills and movement in young children. That is because children's experiences of physical education in the primary years form the basis of a foundation of movement skills and a lifelong love of physical activity, movement confidence and creativity.

It is important to clarify at this point that, for the purpose of this chapter, by physical education is meant the physical education taught in curriculum time. When referring to sport, activities outside curriculum time are meant, such as after school and junior clubs.

The Glasgow Commonwealth Games 2014 and London 2012 Olympics and Paralympics have meant that, in some areas, there has been a rise in access to and the status and awareness of sport, physical activity and physical education in schools. They have allowed a celebration of endeavour and skill that, it is hoped, will filter into physical education via legacy funding and activities.

Prior to these events, physical education had for some years struggled in terms of its status in primary schools. Its exact purpose had been elusive and interpreted differently. Limited initial teacher training experiences and low-quality personal experiences of physical education had led to a large number of primary school teachers being without the desire, confidence or support to teach physical education.

Although the benefits and outcomes of physical education are wide-ranging, it would be foolhardy to assume that they will occur automatically. Teachers thus have an important role to play in developing knowledge and understanding of fitness and health and a lifelong love of activity.

Physical education in the primary years is largely taught by generalist primary school teachers. Griggs (2012: 14) suggests that high-quality physical education provides an inimitable and valuable contribution to children's learning, noting, 'the time is now here for the state and status of the subject in primary schools to be protected, enhanced, celebrated and more clearly articulated.'

Physical education in the Primary National Curriculum offers the chance to develop social, cognitive and emotional capacities in every child, contributing to their health and well-being. Capel (2007: 494) argues that one of the most important reasons for physical education is:

> its unique contribution to the development of motor skills (particularly gross motor skills) [and that] recently the government has identified an important role for physical education in raising pupils' attainment and as a tool for whole school improvement.

Children have different experiences of physical activity and a range of attitudes and expectations of what physical education can offer them, but physical education in primary schools has this vital role to play in developing all children's movement skills. We believe that it should focus on the fundamental movement skills that underpin all games, sports and activities.

The development of children's physical abilities has been identified as a prime area in education that is of equal importance to number and language for children from birth to the age of five. Work in this field has shown that well-taught physical development activities allow children to develop a love of movement and interact with their peers, in addition to fostering creativity. To achieve this, primary physical education should provide a bridge between 'structured and unstructured play' (Griggs, 2012: 16). When children move into lower primary classes, their experience of physical education should be of individual and group activities designed to allow them to experience a variety of movements and mini/modified versions of the full-sided games we see in secondary physical education.

Table 11.1 indicates the range of fundamental movement skills (FMS) that children need to master. Skilfully planning for them to master individual skills and then combine them in context allows children to become effective movers. FMS are rarely performed individually; instead a combination of all three tends to be seen. So, for example, the movements run, catch and stop would allow a child to demonstrate awareness of the footwork demands of a sport such as netball.

FMS form the basis of all physical activity and are a vital factor in developing *physical literacy*. Physical literacy is defined as (Whitehead, 2010) a disposition in which individuals have:

the motivation, confidence, physical competence, knowledge and understanding to value and take responsibility for maintaining purposeful physical pursuits/activities throughout the lifecourse.

Table 11.1 Examples of fundamental movement skills (FMS) (adapted from Griggs, 2012)

Locomotion (travelling)	Non-locomotor (object control and manipulation)	Stability (balance)
Walk	Throw (sending)	Landing
Run	Catch (receiving)	Stopping
Gallop	Kick (sending)	Twist/turn
Side step	Ball roll (sending)	Spinning
Skip	Dribble (travelling with)	Stretching
Jump	Strike (receiving and sending)	Dodging
Climb	Trap/stop (receiving)	Ready position
Swing	Volley (receiving and sending)	Cross-lateral work

By using and understanding how to combine FMSs, children can perform these skills in new contexts, grow in confidence at using and applying appropriate physical skills and talk purposefully and critically about the choices they have made. The primary school years are critical to developing and mastering these skills and it is recommended that, rather than concentrating on 'isolated skill development' (for example, throwing), these various skills should be applied in enjoyable, meaningful and relevant ways in the form of a wide range of physical activities (Murphy and Chronin, 2011).

In the classroom   The animals came in two by two

A class of five- and six-year-olds had been looking at the story of Noah and the building of his ark. This led to a combined drama and dance lesson in which the focus was on developing and describing the movements of different animals as they made their way into the ark.

The children worked in pairs. From a box, each pair selected a card that showed an animal. They then had to write down two words that described the animal's movements (a word bank was provided to support the children). After a period of thinking time, the children had to then travel across the hall, mimicking the actions of the animal.

Each pair was encouraged to exaggerate the way they travelled as an animal and use as many movement points as possible in their whole body. As each pair became secure with the movements of one animal, they would then select a different card and repeat the process. The next step was for the children to join up with another pair and then perform their method of travelling. This led to the children trying to guess what animal was being mimicked.

The session finished with them selecting their best animal moves and then, two by two, they travelled across the hall to a coned area that represented the ark. Photographs were taken of this and added to the classroom display.

This activity links to work done in literacy, storytime and drama.

Physical education in the curriculum

Physical education in primary schools currently sits within the wider curriculum, but remains statutory in England from the ages of 5 to 16. The new National Curriculum (DfE, 2013) is much slimmer in terms of content and structure than previous curriculums. The subsequent guidance for the foundation subjects simply provides for core knowledge and teachers can use this as the foundation for their curriculum to develop children's knowledge, skills and understanding. The key aims of the physical education curriculum continue to include a focus on active and healthy lifestyles, developing competence across a number of physical activity areas and for children to be active for sustained periods of time. Children are now encouraged to engage in competitive sports and activities.

Until 2010, schools in England were required to report the amount of curricular and extracurricular physical education and school sport they were providing by completing the National School Sports Survey. As schools are no longer required to report their provision, it is difficult to ascertain if they are indeed fulfilling the recommended two hours. Subjects competing for curriculum time and the rigours of standard testing have been cited as reasons for physical education provision perhaps not meeting the recommendations. The changes to schools games organisers' and school sports coordinators' roles have adversely impacted primary school physical education and sport. Also, reduced time to work with cluster primary schools has diminished the support and guidance given to primary school teachers by their secondary colleagues.

In primary classrooms, physical education is usually taught by the class teacher. Teachers may have had only a limited amount of time devoted to physical education in their teacher training and may not have had the opportunity to deliver physical education in their school placements. Some schools will employ specialist physical education teachers who lead the curriculum area, supporting other teachers in their delivery of the subject. Increasingly, schools are turning to private companies who provide sports coaches to deliver curriculum physical education. This development may bring with it specialist teaching in limited activities and little understanding of the pedagogical and assessment requirements. One might also argue that it is further deskilling the generalist teacher.

Alongside the acquisition and application of skills, physical education can provide children with opportunities to experience important but more generic areas of learning and development. For example:

- an understanding of why following rules is important and demonstrating the ability to do so in activities
- successfully completing challenges in problem solving and scenario-based learning
- improving on a personal or team best in athletic and aquatic activities
- working together in a team in cooperative and competitive activities
- experiencing both winning and losing, which allows children to learn to manage their feelings and to respond appropriately
- exploring leadership opportunities, which allows children to become independent learners and self-assured individuals
- opportunities to represent the class or school in school competitions, outside school tournaments or races, which can develop pride, self-confidence and a collegiate attitude.

Throughout the primary phase, progression should take the form of gradually increasing the complexity of movement sequences, quality of performance, independence in learning and understanding and effective use of higher-order thinking skills. To reinforce children's knowledge and understanding, there should also be further opportunities for them to use their developing physical skills in after-school activities. These provide a context for further learning, enhance the children's skills and knowledge and allow them to explore more sport-specific skills. For children showing further interest in specific activities, it is important to have positive links with outside clubs.

In essence, good teaching in physical education focuses on:

- developing existing skills and acquiring new ones
- selecting the appropriate skills and applying them in context
- evaluating the effectiveness of the decision and looking to change or improve
- understanding the fitness and health demands of physical activity.

Table 11.2 summarises the key ideas relating to physical education in the primary curriculum. It draws together the traditional areas of study in the National Curriculum in England, ideas in Margaret Whitehead's movement forms (2010, 2011) and work by the Youth Sports Trust (YST, 2012), all of which identify the content and range for physical education. What is apparent from all three models is the variety of learning opportunities and contexts that exist. This is encouraging for teachers, in that it means it is possible to exercise autonomy in planning and implementing the curriculum.

Table 11.2 also demonstrates that you can offer the children various learning experiences in the lessons and the richness and variety offered in the physical education

Table 11.2   Physical education in the curriculum (adapted from Whitehead, 2010, 2011; YST, 2012 and the National Curriculum)

Whitehead, movement forms (2010, 2011)	Competitive activities	Aesthetic and expressive activities	Adventure activities	Athletic activities	Fitness and health activities	Interactional/ relational activities
Youth Sports Trust (2012)	Physical me Thinking me Social me	Physical me Thinking me Social me	Thinking me Social me Physical me	Physical me Healthy me Thinking me	Healthy me Physical me	Social me
National Curriculum	Swimming, games and athletics	Gymnastics and dance	Outdoor and adventurous activities	Athletics, swimming and games	Knowledge and understanding of fitness and health	Activities with a requirement to work with others in a cooperative or competitive situation

curriculum links both across subjects and within subjects. Underpinning all curriculum design are the knowledge and skills that can be fostered by effective teaching, such as thinking skills, social skills and the recognition of what it is to be healthy.

Approaches to primary physical education

It is important to be able to provide opportunities for children to practise how movements are developed and how movement patterns are combined and created in the context of an activity. Whitehead (2010, 2011) suggests that grouping the movements into 'movement forms' will allow teachers to plan a wide variety of activities. This structure allows the fundamental movement skills to be developed in a number of contexts, giving teachers the autonomy to use a range of games, dance and activity sessions in lessons. This diversity can encourage thinking and the application of skills, tactics and composition. An essential element for every child is promotion of the confidence to experiment with movement and decisions, looking at the most effective way of solving a problem or applying a skill or skills.

In lower primary classes, physical education should be largely skill-specific, focusing on FMS and children's acquisition and development of compositional awareness. These should be applied in the context of individual, paired and small group activities. In upper primary classes, these skills can be applied in more complex contexts, such as small-sided games and small group compositions in gymnastics and dance. Once children are aged 9 to 11, however, they are able to take part in modified versions of games with full numbers in each side, such as High 5 netball, Tag rugby, and larger group compositions with more complex choreographic demands in dance and gymnastics.

At each stage, the activities should be appropriate to the children's stage of development, not necessarily to their chronological age. A strong grounding in the FMS is necessary in all lessons to enable the children to acquire and develop motor skills, tactics and compositional skills.

Competitive and athletic activities

Games in physical education should be enjoyable and sociable experiences when they are delivered in a manner that is well-planned, differentiated and focused on the application of skills and developing these. They may become an arena for physical dominance by those children who have mastered the skills of sending, receiving and travelling at the expense of those who have not. Avoiding social exclusion while at the same time fostering a fun and enjoyable learning experience remains one of the biggest challenges when planning for games. Collaborative games can present a wonderful opportunity to explore competitiveness and cooperation and allow children to experience sportsmanship, fair play, problem solving and leadership. Allow opportunities, too, to reflect in teams or individually.

Athletic activities at their most basic include running, jumping and throwing. They demand that the FMSs are made use of early in primary school in order to allow for later athletic development. There is also an opportunity to explore using numbers and measurement, making concrete links with the core curriculum.

Swimming is normally delivered in the upper primary years (unless the school has the means to do so earlier), due to the cost and logistical challenges this presents. It is largely taught by class teachers, supported by local authority swimming teachers or specialist physical education teachers. Either way, it is important that the life-saving potential of learning to swim is not ignored or marginalised.

Aquatic activities also have the potential to incorporate other areas of the physical education curriculum and movement challenges. You can teach aesthetic and creative elements through synchronised swimming and jumping activities, adventure activities via personal survival and lifesaving activities, and competitive and athletic activities by incorporating into your planning games such as water polo and timed challenges. Not only will they allow the children to make connections between the various activities but they will also provide varied and exciting elements in the lessons.

Aesthetic and expressive activities

Dance and music have long been a part of almost all cultures and can promote a shared understanding of each other and of emotions. They offer a form of expression and communication. Using movement to tell stories provides an opportunity to explore history and for children to learn about other cultures. This opens up an exciting array of opportunities to 'go back in time' and look at medieval dance, traditional dances such as Scottish country dancing or travel continents to explore dance from around the globe, such as bhangra and the world of Bollywood or line dancing and Latin dancing.

Inviting dancers or storytellers from the local community to perform different dances or use their stories as a stimulus for dance (such as Gypsy storytellers or myths and legends associated with African dance) can promote understanding of different cultures and help break down barriers. Using a wide range of stimuli that reflect cultural diversity, such as video, sculpture, art, clothing, poems and musical instruments, can provide a 'hook' to inspire and stimulate children's interest.

> ### 🖋️ In the classroom   Dance and movement activity
>
> Some children aged 9 to 11 had been reading *Journey to Jo'Burg* by Beverly Naidoo (2008) as part of their literacy lessons and learning about South Africa in their topic-based learning.
>
> Using this as a stimulus for their dance lessons, the children explored a number of key issues from the book. They were asked to describe how they might feel if they were separated from their parents for a length of time. They recounted feelings of loneliness, isolation, fear and sadness. They then translated these into dance movements, demonstrating exaggerated emotions by their posture, speed and the types of movements they made.
>
> The children also explored some of the adventures and challenges experienced by the children in the book along their journey and chose one to translate into a dance phrase. This challenged the children to use their choreography skills in groups to create movements that demonstrated the space, actions and dynamics of the adventure without 'acting it out'.
>
> The final part of their dance concentrated on the abolition of apartheid and on the celebrations that happened when the children were reunited with friends and family. This was a whole-class dance phrase, using traditional celebration dances from South Africa, led by an African dance teacher.
>
> This activity has links to literacy, geography, history and PSHE.

Gymnastic movements demand that children are aware of key words, such as 'tension', 'extension' and 'fluidity', and are able to show practical examples of high-quality movements. Linking gymnastic skills and balances to form routines requires children to discuss and recognise good examples of such movements. These skills should all be applied on the floor and when using apparatus to further challenge their routine development. Key words associated with apparatus such as 'over', 'under', 'around', 'through' and 'across' encourage children to plan their use of the equipment in a creative way.

Adventure activities

Traditionally, outdoor and adventurous activities (OAA) have been delivered in the later primary school years and partially been fulfilled by a trip to an activity centre. OAA provide many opportunities for creative and purposeful school-centred or locally based activities, as well as interactional and relational challenges and 'thinking' – problem solving encourages creative thinking and purposeful discussion.

> ### In the classroom   An outdoor and adventurous activity
>
> #### Dinosaur orienteering project
>
> A group of 10- and 11-year-olds had been away on a residential visit to Wales and one of the activities that they were keen to repeat was orienteering.
>
> Because of this interest, it was decided to create a photograph orienteering course in the grounds of the school that connected with the current dinosaur topic. The children were sent out with digital cameras to take photographs of different locations in and around the playground and these then became the control points. As a group, they decided on 20 locations and at each of these control points, the children left a dinosaur fact.
>
> The children then ran an orienteering session for the rest of the school. They ensured everyone had photographs of the control points. At each point, they recorded the dinosaur fact before moving on to the next location.
>
> The children who created and ran this orienteering project were full of enthusiasm and excitement. Their positive attitude rubbed off on the other year groups who followed the course, and the high levels of learning and teamwork that arose from this activity were apparent at every stage.
>
> This activity has links to geography, digital literacy and PSHE.

There is much that a school-based adventure curriculum can offer to children's learning and development. To set these up in lower primary classes, challenges can be incorporated into other activity areas, such as designing paired balances. In upper primary classes, adventure activities can make a significant contribution to the whole curriculum, with specific skills, such as with maps and a compass (orientation) work, linking directly with the geography and mathematics curriculum. Also, skills developed in problem solving and problemsetting can promote social development (communication) and engage higher-order thinking skills.

Fitness and health activities

The health of our primary-aged children is coming under increasing scrutiny, with concerns being expressed about links between childhood obesity and activity patterns. Physical education has a large part to play in educating children about their bodies, reinforcing the benefits of and providing information about living a healthy and active lifestyle. Incorporating this ethos into a whole-school approach could include such initiatives as Healthy Schools and Active Schools Awards, as well as the schools travel arrangements, with walking buses, cycle routes to schools and so on.

Children need to be exploring health-related activities during warm-ups, cool-downs and main activities. Learning about how the body works can empower children to make healthier choices. For example, teachers can offer chances to investigate changes in heart and breathing rates during different intensity or types of activities and what these mean and children can learn muscle names and their locations and functions.

Relational and interactional activities

Many of the areas above offer rich opportunities for children to work with others in a variety of contexts and challenges. The ability to interact and achieve together fosters skills that develop the whole child. Planning opportunities for children to communicate, empathise, demonstrate tolerance and so on will allow learners to develop as responsible citizens and effective individuals.

Lessons should include chances for children to demonstrate listening, problem solving and thinking skills. The children should be made aware that you expect to hear language of enquiry, language of question and language of cooperation.

Planning for physical education

Planning involves considering the following points:

- *Clear learning objectives* When the children and teachers are clear about their collective learning goal, then learning is focused and specific. This will also form the basis of your assessment for learning (AfL) activities.
- *Learning by doing* Learning is reinforced if the learner is actively engaged in the learning. Plan activities that encourage the children to be active, involved and take ownership and leadership in their activities.
- *Repetition* Young children learn best when they are given repeated opportunities to practise a skill in numerous contexts, such as sending skills using different balls or limbs. Sufficient time should always be given to allow real progression – lots of brief activities do little for confidence, mastery of a skill or motivation.
- *Reinforcement* Positive reinforcements, such as praise and rewards, embed learning. Look for opportunities to build in positive reinforcement, such as peer tutoring, leadership and assessment.
- *Include thinking activities* How can we get from A to B … (without touching the floor, in a gymnastic manner, before the ball, before the opponent)? This will encourage the children to look at what and how they are learning. Thinking activities are an effective way of incorporating cooperative problem solving skills.
- *Show me* Use demonstrations, peer tutoring, images and video to help the children see what you or they are describing.

The children in your class will arrive with a wide array of movement experiences. They will need you to teach them how to progress from the simple activities of early childhood to the more complex demands of activities in later childhood. Child-centred teaching should take into account the growth rates, previous experiences and learning of every child. What is important is the need to plan for them to have a chance to interact with other children, their environment and the task.

When planning to promote the acquisition and application of and progression in skills and tactics, it is important to remember to differentiate activities. This is simple to achieve and can be delivered via the task set, the approach to teaching or the outcome expected. A class-wide learning objective will not be appropriate for all learners, so thought should be given to the various ways in which the children can achieve, so all are appropriately challenged.

Managing the learning of children identified as gifted and talented in physical education can be daunting. Gifted and talented pupils are recognised as having a talent or gift that sets them apart from their peers. A 'gifted' child is generally accepted to have academic ability at a higher level than that of his or her peers, while a child identified as 'talented' will show an above average ability in a particular sport or creative activity.

Fortunately, you can choose from a number of areas to develop their physical skills and tactical awareness or develop individual characteristics, such as 'thinking me' and 'social me' (see Table 11.2), to provide alternative learning challenges. For example, when teaching games to five- and six-year-olds, a learning objective such as, 'I can send and receive an object in a number of different ways' allows scope for extremely simple activities, such as rolling a large ball to a partner. Alternatively, the activity can be made much more complex, such as using a Unihoc stick and puck to perform a push pass and stop to a partner in a defined area. Developing good links with local junior teams and clubs will allow such talented children to progress.

Table 11.3 shows how to utilise the STEP framework to plan for an inclusive approach, to help all learners achieve. By offering an activity that is flexible in its use of equipment, groupings of children and time of completion or teaching approach, you allow for the possibility of the lesson being tailored to suit individuals within it.

Use of ICT

Physical education offers children the chance to use ICT in, for example, evaluating and improving, communication development, knowledge and understanding of how, why and what needs to be put in place to see progression of an activity or isolated skill.

Table 11.3   Using the STEP framework to ensure effective inclusion

Space	*Increasing the space* in which children are working affords more time to perform the skill/make decisions. For example, a take-off zone in athletics jumping
	Decreasing the space challenges children to perform/make decisions more quickly. For example, varying the playing area for 3v1
	Personal/communal space – decide whether pupils work independently or with others. For example, dancing independently/interacting with others
Task	Take into account the pace needed and the physical effort/concentration required
	Use *open-ended tasks* that have a number of successful outcomes – for example, in gymnastics, design a routine that includes the actions balance, travel, jump, roll
	Use a *circuit-based idea*, providing a number of opportunities to demonstrate success throughout the lesson.
	Incorporate an *interactional/relational* element into the lesson
Time	Be *flexible with timings* – do all groups need to do the same thing at the same time?
	As with other subjects, would the children benefit from *revisiting skills/tactics* next time?
Equipment	Use *modified or alternative equipment* – for example, changing the size, texture or bounce of a ball
	Modifying/conditioning games to use a variety of balls/bats/size of goal
	Use *inclusive games*, such as Boccia or Stoolball
	Use *inclusive reciprocal cards*, which offer a picture, translation or a more challenging version of the activity
People	Use a *buddy* system and *peer tutoring*
	Look at *methods of grouping* – gender/friendship/random/ability
	Use *support assistants/assistants/adults other than teachers (AOTTs)/sports coaches*
	Offer activities with *leadership* opportunities
Pedagogy	Use *clear and achievable success criteria* that are displayed throughout the lesson
	Feedback on success criteria should be individualised and achievable to develop listening and communication skills
	Have a *flexible approach to your curriculum content*, equipment and organisation
	Be *realistic and clear on demands* and essential safety rules and challenge unacceptable behaviour
	Keep *instructions* short and to the point, accompany them with a visual demonstration, cue card or sign and break a skill down in to its basic movements
	Place emphasis on *effort, fun, participation and achievement*
	Establishing a routine for the start and end of an activity/lesson will help children to recognise patterns

To watch their own performances and those of others provides children with immediate visual feedback and can scaffold discussions around improving technique, quality or composition. For instance, having demonstrated and taught an isolated skill in gymnastics, a tablet can be used with the children in pairs. The children can record the isolated skill and then watch their performances of it. The children can then assess their performances against your criteria and communicate their own thoughts about the positive elements and how improvements could be made.

This technique can be further developed over a scheme of work to include group choreography. The children can design their own sequence to your criteria (for example, a start position, two travels, two rolls, two pair balances and a finish position). They can record and replay their sequence. They can evaluate not only how they can improve and progress but also whether or not they have included all the criteria for the routine. When working over a number of sessions, the recordings can be available for them to use to help them remember the routines and the areas of improvement from previous weeks' learning.

In these and other ways, technology offers excellent opportunities for discussion, teamwork and progression. As a teacher, planning these opportunities into your lessons will also help you to assess the children's work and plan for progression. Tablet technology also, usefully, provides teachers with a visual copy of performance and play.

Assessment in physical education

Assessing physical education is a significant challenge, even for experienced teachers. Physical education lessons should be busy and active, but finding opportunities to regularly observe the children is a crucial part of planning.

Such regular observation in line with the learning objectives you have set will allow you to give feedback that is tailored to individual children's needs. Ensuring that the planned tasks present sufficient challenge and are at an appropriate level for the individuals in your class, means the children will not all complete the same task at the same time at the same level, but then we would not expect this in any other lesson. With careful formative assessment, you will be able to plan effective activities that allow individuals to be challenged and supported in improving their skills while understanding and considering the different levels of ability in your class.

Assessment for learning (AfL) involves being able to recognise and record success, effort and progress. A focus on assessment means that, over a number of weeks, you will be able to move the children towards their next target and involve them in discussions about how this can be achieved. It is important to communicate success criteria to pupils and when reporting to parents and carers.

Lesson aims, objectives and success criteria should be clearly set out. Videos may be used to show and explain the process or reinforce a visual demonstration. Provide assessment opportunities over a range of contexts and time and make assessment a two-way process to ensure the children understand what is required of them.

> ### In the classroom   Formative assessment in gymnastics using tablet technology
>
> Some seven- and eight-year-olds in a gymnastics class were placed in small groups and then given the task of selecting six different balances and rolls that they then needed to connect by using controlled movements. As a class, we created a series of 'steps to success' (child-friendly learning objectives) that highlighted the need for smooth and balanced transitions.
>
> The children were given rehearsal time and, at the end of this time, they reviewed their routine by putting smiley faces against the objectives of quality of balances, rolls and transitions.
>
> The next step was to place two groups together. They took it in turns to film each other's performance using the tablets. This allowed the performers to review their routines while having the support of the members of the other group as they offered constructive advice. This helped the children identify two aspects they could improve on for their final performances.
>
> During the final performances, the children were filmed a second time and this was played back in the classroom, allowing them to reflect on all the improvements they had made. This use of technology allowed the children to see their own routines clearly and led to not only improved technique but also developed their self-assessment skills.
>
> This activity has links to digital literacy.

Organising learning

Lessons should have a consistent structure (see the example of a lesson plan in Table 11.4) and will usually involve the following steps:

1. a warm-up activity so the children have opportunities to prepare their bodies for the lesson ahead but also to focus on learning about the human body
2. a focus on teaching the children a new skill or consolidating a skill they already possess
3. children applying their learning in the context of a game, activity, event or movement phase
4. a plenary to consolidate learning
5. a suitable cool-down phase.

Throughout the lesson, there should be opportunities for questions, demonstrations, discussion and exploration. These activities need to link directly to your assessment criteria and learning outcomes.

Think carefully about how you group the children. Try to group them on the basis of their stages of development, abilities and confidence. The combinations will be different for different activities, as they would be in class. Ensure that you plan to use other adults effectively and that they are aware of the learning outcomes, needs and assessment activities.

Organising resources

The organisation of resources is paramount. Equipment should be stored in an accessible but safe way that the children can manage themselves. One recommendation would be to colour code the equipment to allow working groups to easily identify which equipment they will be using. When planning lessons, make use of diagrams and plans to help organise the space and resources. This is particularly helpful when planning gymnastic apparatus lessons.

ICT resources such as interactive whiteboard technology and hand-held devices are extremely effective in modelling techniques and reflecting on work done, providing accurate demonstrations and explanations that allow children to see effective models of skills. Having a screen in the hall will allow for whole-class discussions, assessment and viewing.

In the classroom   A teacher talks about summative assessment

Summative assessment of physical education in our school had never been an easy task, so we decided to create a system that could be managed not only by the class teachers but also by the children themselves. The school organised a decathlon day for upper primary children.

On one day of the summer term we would organise the school field so that all the decathlon events would be set up. Class by class the children would come out and each child would take part in each activity. The children would record their own results and this would be supported by a group of older children who would work as 'games makers'. Using a spreadsheet we would then input the results and, just like a real decathlon, the children would each be given an overall score as well as a breakdown showing their results for each event.

This score was then recorded and the event repeated, so this allowed us to check year-on-year progress in athletics. This data also informed the children so they could discuss which areas and skills they could work on in the future.
(This has links to digital literacy and mathematics.)

Organising space

The teacher has a responsibility to ensure the space used is adequate and fit for purpose. Before and throughout the lesson, the environment should be checked for obstructions, hazards and so forth, which should be removed. If using a swimming pool, you should ensure that the water clarity meets the standards set out in the normal operating procedure, which, in real terms means you should be able to see the bottom of the pool at all times. Ensure that your lesson is suitable for the weather or terrain and always have a contingency plan in case the weather should deteriorate.

Staying safe

Safety is paramount for both the children and the adults working with them. The children should learn about applying safe practices and being responsible participants in an activity.

Position yourself so you can scan the group and assess any potential hazards. Have an effective stopping signal that you have rehearsed with the children, so you can quickly stop the children should you need to. The teacher has a responsibility to the children in the lesson and as such should be mindful of some basic principles:

- be competent to teach the activity safely (in terms of knowledge, expertise, qualifications)

- be proactive in planning lessons (ask, 'Is what I want to do safe?')

- have good behaviour management and group management skills

- know the children's individual needs

- model the wearing of clothing and footwear appropriate to the activity

- ensure the children adhere to general safety guidelines – jewellery removed, hair tied back; refer to your school policy. (Whitlam, 2012)

Talk in physical education

Talk in physical education plays an important role in developing not only children's subject awareness but also their affective skills, which are 'the ability of the child to relate to others and to take personal and social responsibility' (Azzarito, 2008 in Armour, 2011: 146).

Learning is a social activity and, as such, involves purposeful discussion and learning with others. Activities that develop children's cognitive skills include decision-making and discussing their own and others' performances, tactics, strategies and compositional ideas. Talking will help develop children's ability to justify, critique, evaluate and analyse their work. Structuring lessons to incorporate discussion time, mini-plenaries, keywords, questions and evaluative activities will promote purposeful talk.

Children need to be given opportunities to develop their subject-specific vocabulary as well as their social vocabulary. *Subject-specific vocabulary* is the keywords in that subject, such as forward roll, cannon and unison, tactic. Vocabulary can be promoted by having words displayed on a working wall and asking the children to ask and answer questions using the words for that lesson. Using task cards for older readers, which have the keywords for skills and tactics with pictures, will allow the children to make the connection between the activity and the vocabulary. Indeed, when children have English as an additional language (EAL), their language learning can be accelerated by the notion that each action or skill they perform has a word associated with it (Kirk, 2005). This can be valuable, allowing contact and communication with their peers.

Social vocabulary is the words and sentences that children can use when applying their thinking. For instance, when evaluating their own and others' work, you may provide them with sentence starters such as:

- 'If I were to suggest any changes, they would be ...'
- 'In my opinion the ... that worked the best was ...'
- 'My favourite part of the routine was ...'

These will allow simple thinking to be described. To encourage more analytical thinking and discussion, you may look to more complex sentences, such as:

- 'Our most effective idea was ... This was because ...'
- 'When we tried ... it was difficult/easy/faster/more effective to ...'
- 'One way we could change our tactic/composition to make it more effective/ desirable would be ...'

Use question starters with group evaluative tasks, such as:

- 'What might happen if … ?'
- 'If we remove … what do you think will happen?'
- 'If you had one more … what might you be able to achieve?'

Such starters help children to bring structure to their discussions. With practice, their responses will be more specific. Children are more likely to remain on task if they are taught how to provide effective feedback.

In the classroom   Key elements of a lesson

Analyse the example of a lesson plan given in Table 11.4. Can you identify opportunities for the children to be 'interactional' with each other or the teacher?

Discuss with a partner the opportunities for inclusion and challenge provided throughout. Can you identify any other ways to support or challenge the children?

Can you identify clear opportunities to meet the assessment for learning requirements?

Table 11.4 Lesson Plan

Date	Time	Class	PE	Risk assessment/health and safety issues
	45 mins	Year 3	Gymnastics	Hair should be tied back
				Jewellery removed
				Bare feet
				T-shirts tucked in
				Floor area should be clear and clean
				Children with inhalers/medication should have it with them
				Surfaces of mats should not be damaged or torn

Learning objectives

Healthy me To recognise and describe the short-term effects of exercise on the body during different activities and know the importance of suppleness and strength

Physical me To explore combinations of floor, mats and apparatus, and find different ways to use a shape, balance or travel

Thinking me To improve their ability to select appropriate actions and use simple compositional ideas

Social me To describe and evaluate the effectiveness and quality of a performance and recognise how their own performance has improved. Use technology to help development and progression individually and as a pair by means of evaluation

Description of main activity focus

To perform a routine of movements showing different body shapes with control and body tension

(Continued)

Table 11.4   *(Continued)*

Action points from previous lesson(s)
It is helpful if children have made short sequences of 'unlike' actions, such as jump–roll–balance, remembered and repeated sequences accurately, linked actions on the floor with actions on the apparatus, copied a partner's actions and modified their basic actions, such as different levels, shapes, speeds, pathways, body parts

Resources
One mat between two. One TA and a whiteboard

Differentiation
Joe is hard of hearing and needs to be close to staff to hear instructions, so needs to be at the front facing the teacher. He also requires sounding out of key vocabulary and a visual cue
Josephine is gifted and talented, a club gymnast, so requires additional tasks. Very good for demonstrations. Her targets are to improve her compositional skills

Assessment opportunities
The children will have viewed other children's performances on the tablet and will be able to answer question(s) on how well the shapes were linked and whether or not the individuals/group have an element of control
Children can remember and repeat their composition
Children can include elements that improve/vary their composition

Success criteria
On completion of this lesson:

- the children will have had an opportunity to perform a range of different body shapes and linked them into a small routine
- the children can ask and answer questions about improving quality
- the children can design and modify their composition

Curriculum links
Literacy Key vocabulary, speaking and listening, describing and using instructional speech
Numeracy Counting out, estimating
Digital literacy Using technology to enhance the success criteria
Science Parts and functions of the body, heart function, types of fitness
PSHE Working together, giving constructive feedback, listening and sharing

Timing	Organisation of teaching space, equipment and children	Teaching points to develop skills and key questions	Differentiation and use of other adults
Changing	**8 mins**		TA to assist Joe and help with hair and jewellery issues
Healthy me Starter and warm-up	Discuss the area available and what space the children will be moving around in	• What happens to your body when you warm up?	Check pupils with poor hearing are close by you or your TA
10 mins	Tell the children about the importance of listening to instructions. Create different shapes on command. Play fun game 'Simon says' – stand tall, crouch down, curl into a ball, be twisted and stretch out wide	• What is a pulse? • Why is exercise important? • What is your/personal space?	If pupils can't balance to stretch, show a similar stretch that reaches the same muscle on the floor Ask the children to demonstrate a stretch for key muscles

Physical me What skill will they be learning or consolidating? **10 mins**	Ask the children to explore a variety of shapes their bodies can make, adding different levels – high, middle and low. Then ask them to start adding two shapes and two heights together Ask them to get into pairs and share their two shapes and heights (giving them four) Ask them to face each other and practise their routine of four shapes with height change	• Use talk partners to discuss ways, moves or shapes to add to their routines • Look at body control (tension) in movements and focus on holding each shape still for three seconds	Teacher to work with groups, advising and assisting with skills and composition, responding when children raise their hands for help. TA to support Joe and his group, offering him assistance with discussions Gifted and talented pupils have the opportunity to add more shapes and some aspects of travelling
Thinking me How will the children demonstrate they can apply their skills? **8 mins**	Ask the children to refine basic skills, illustrating specific body shapes. Look further into presentation, pointed toes. Ask the children to add a starting and finishing position and complete the design of their routine. Then, they are to present their routine to the two children on a mat next to them. They are to demonstrate their skills carefully and with gymnastic quality	• Show two examples of good strong body shapes, pointed toes • Explain how to hold posture to be strong, discussing which example was the best • Show the children what a good starting and finishing position looks like and how long to hold that position	Give positive feedback throughout the lesson to all pupils – focus on the learning outcomes Give developmental feedback – how can the child progress? Encourage the children to use keywords when discussing work
Thinking me and social me An activity that requires evaluation of their own or others' work **8 mins**	After refining their routines and further practice, they are going to become professional judges and also be judged. They will be evaluating their own and their partners' work by recording it on the tablet and playing it back to them, discussing together the good parts of the routine and the areas that require improvement	• All comments should be worded positively and constructively • Tell them the part of their routine that impressed you the most and why • Discuss the footage with good vocabulary – tension, posture, pointed toes, timing, sequence, fluency and presentation	TA to be with Joe, assisting with discussion – provide keyword cards Teacher to ask questions and support the children in evaluating the routines Use the children to show examples of good tension and extension
Healthy me Plenary and cool-down **5 mins**	Keep the recordings for next week's lesson and add to them Clear away the equipment with the children Cool down, lowering the heart rate Walk round the room, incorporating key stretches from the beginning – can they remember them, can they show them?	• Why is it important to cool down? What does it do to your heart rate, body temperature? • Talk to the children about the after school gym club	Check all the area is clear and praise the children on their achievements Send Joe out to start getting changed
Changing	**6 mins**	Use of rewards for being fast, efficient, tidy and getting changed	

Reflective questions

- How can you effectively challenge the high-ability children in your class while meeting the needs of the others? Take some time to model this approach in your lesson planning.
- Consider how you may now modify your physical education plans in the light of reading through this chapter. What would be your immediate priorities?

Conclusion

This chapter has offered a summary of the aims and purposes of physical education. The guidance on lesson content and lesson planning should enable you to teach outstanding lessons.

Physical education, when taught well, can develop children's social, physical and intellectual skills. It can be a vehicle for learning in other curriculum areas. We trust that you will enjoy teaching physical education to your children and they will enjoy learning by taking part in the many physical activities you will provide for them. Maybe you could enable them to reach the very highest level of performance as future Olympic champions, but you will have also succeeded if every child gains an insight into the crucial importance of physical activity throughout life.

Further reading

Lavin, J. (ed.) (2009) *Creative Approaches to Physical Education: Helping children to achieve their true potential*. Abingdon: Routledge.
This is an excellent book, full of ideas for creative teaching in physical education. It links well to the matters discussed in this chapter.

Lawrence, J. (2012) *Teaching Primary Physical Education*. London: Sage.
This is a user-friendly book that tackles many of the issues raised in this chapter, as well as subject leadership, inclusion and cross-curricular approaches.

Pickup, I. and Price, L. (2007) *Teaching Physical Education in the Primary School: A developmental approach*. London: Continuum.
This book proves a unique perspective on physical education in primary schools. Rather than adopting a curriculum-led approach, it views PE through the lens of a focus on children's physical development requirements.

References

Armour, K. (ed.) (2011) *Sport Pedagogy: An introduction for teaching and coaching.* Harlow: Pearson.

Capel, S. (2007) 'Moving beyond physical education subject knowledge to develop knowledgeable teachers of the subject', *Curriculum Journal*, 18 (4): 493–507.

DfE (2013) 'The National Curriculum in England: Framework document'. Runcorn: DfE. Available online at: www.gov.uk/government/uploads/system/uploads/attachment_data/file/210969/NC_framework_document_-_FINAL.pdf

Griggs, G. (ed.) (2012) *An Introduction to Primary Physical Education.* Abingdon: Routledge.

Kirk, D. (2005) 'Physical education, youth sport and lifelong participation: The importance of early learning experiences', *European Physical Education Review*, 11 (3): 239–55.

Murphy, F. and Chronin, D. (2011) 'Playtime: the needs of very young learners in physical education and sport', in K. Armour (ed.) *Sport pedagogy: An Introduction for Teaching and Coaching.* Harlow: Pearson. pp. 140–152.

Naidoo, B. (2008) *Journey to Jo'burg.* London: HarperCollins.

Whitehead, M. E. (ed.) (2010) *Physical Literacy: Throughout the Lifecourse.* Abingdon: Routledge. Available online at: www.physical-literacy.org.uk/definitions.php

Whitehead, M. (2011) 'Key features of a curriculum to promote physical literacy'. Paper presented at the University of Bedfordshire, June 2011. Available online at: www.physical-literacy.org.uk/keynote-mw-pl2011.pdf

Whitlam, P. (2012) *Safe Practice in Physical Education and School Sport.* Leeds: Coachwise.

Youth Sport Trust (2012) For courses and more details visit: www.youthsporttrust.org/how-we-can-help/programmes/matalan-top-sport.aspx

CHAPTER 12

RELIGIOUS EDUCATION

Ellie Hill

Learning objectives

By the end of this chapter you should be able to:

- understand how religious education is taught in primary schools
- explore some activities to use in class
- know the breadth of learning opportunities in religious education to enhance the classroom and wider school.

Introduction

Religious education involves children reflecting on and considering their own beliefs and values in relation to others. It is an opportunity for them to learn about things that have a direct effect on their lives now and will have an impact on their future. They will not necessarily learn about this anywhere else. Children need to acquire knowledge of global events in order to be more tolerant. They may come from homes where religious practice and belief is central to their family and community or have entirely secular backgrounds. Religious education allows children to ask the questions they want to ask, creating their agenda for learning.

In the classroom   Christingle with seven- and eight-year-olds

Christingle is a popular event for families and communities in the Church calendar. The candlelit celebration can include songs, prayers, performances and a collection in aid of the Children's Society. The main part of the celebration is the lighting of Christingle candles.

A class of seven- and eight-year-olds discussed symbolism relating to Christingle:

- the orange represents the world
- the red ribbon indicates the life and blood of Christ, that he has given his life for the world
- the dried fruits and sweets are symbols of God's creation
- the lit candle symbolises Jesus, the light of the world.

To make the Christingle candles, the children attached a ribbon around an orange and made a small cross in the top of the orange and placed a square of silver foil over it. They firmly pressed the foil with a candle into the orange. They also threaded a selection of dried fruit and sweets on to four cocktail sticks and inserted them into the orange around the candle.

The class discussed the importance of Christingle to Christians – that it is a way of sharing the key messages of the faith and helping to raise money for vulnerable children. They also listened to the story of the first Christingle, in which three poor children wanted to give a gift to Jesus. They used an orange, the girl's hair ribbon and some dried fruit. The top was going green so the eldest placed a candle there. They took it to the church for Christmas mass where the priest showed it as an example of true understanding of the meaning of Christmas.

This story can lead on to an exploration of the importance of light in other religions.

A range of faiths

Religious education remains a statutory subject in British schools. The 1988 Education Reform Act said that religious education in schools should recognise the importance of the place of Christianity in Great Britain but that consideration should be given to the other principal religions represented in Great Britain. The implication is that learning about faiths other than Christianity gives an insight into what other people believe. Learning about other cultures and religious practices enables children to understand themselves and others and be more respectful and tolerant of all.

In the classroom   Two examples of children's incomplete understanding of others' religious beliefs and practices

Sikh turban discussed with six- and seven-year-olds

A child asked, 'Why is the boy wearing fancy dress?'
The teacher explained that the boy belongs to the Sikh faith. The turban is important to the identity of Sikhs and they believe it is a spiritual crown. There is no other religion that wears the turban on a daily basis. It is a statement of belonging to the Guru and shows commitment to the faith. Turbans cover the top of the head to protect the hair as Sikhs never cut their hair as a show of respect to God as creator. It is an important part of the dress of a Sikh.

Diwali discussed with eight- and nine-year-olds

The children's view was that 'Diwali is like bonfire night.'
The teacher explained that the festival of Diwali celebrates the victory of good over evil. It usually falls in October or November. Diwali is known as 'the festival of lights'. It is held in memory of the story of Rama and Sita coming home and being welcomed by diva lamps and lights to mark their way. Fireworks are also used to mark this celebration.

Religious education develops children's frames of reference to a higher level and helps them to understand their own lives in relation to those around them. This deeper understanding of themselves and others is crucial in the diverse, global society in which we live. Religious education teaching can also help to combat prejudice as the children learn from the 'voice of experience'. Visits from people with a range of religious beliefs can have a powerful impact. The learning experience is enhanced by a stimulating encounter with a person of faith, sharing their experiences, insight, beliefs and practices.

In the classroom   A visitor to the classroom –
'a Jewish view'

A class of six- and seven-year-olds prepared for a visit from a Jewish visitor. The children had been learning about the life of a Jewish boy and noting similarities with their own family practices.

The class had been thinking of the things they would like to ask the visitor. They had either written or had their questions scribed for them on to speech bubbles and they were very excited that they could ask someone about the things they were really inquisitive about.

The visitor has been into school beforehand to meet the teacher and discuss objectives, timing and approaches to take to ensure the children would be engaged throughout. On the day, she arrived early to set up while the children were in the playground.

At the start of the session, the visitor told the children about her life and her family. She talked about all the artefacts she had brought along, revealing them to 'Ahs' and 'Oohs'!

The children then used the following prepared questions to engage with the visitor.

- 'Why do you like being Jewish?'
- 'What is your favourite Shabbat food?'
- 'What is Yom Kippur?'
- 'Why do only boys wear the kippah?'

The questions encouraged the visitor to talk with passion about her beliefs, practices and values. The children were given challah bread to taste and chatted about the things they had learned.

As a follow-up to the visit, the children wrote thank you notes, highlighting a point they had found interesting. They also made their own scrolls, very carefully, without mistakes, following the visitor's explanation of this. They demonstrated that their careful and tidy work was very important because this was a very important item to Jewish people.

So, religious education, by engaging and interacting with the community and faith visitors, can broaden the perspectives of children. Hearing the Jewish visitor expressing her passion for her lifestyle and religious practices is the first-hand experience children need to reflect on their own ideas in comparison to another point of view. The use of effective resources enhanced this experience further.

It is crucial when planning a visit that the teacher meets with the visitor beforehand to discuss the objectives for the session. A clear, joint understanding of the purpose of the visit is important. The school's ethos and curriculum will underpin the goals of the visit and must be shared with the visitor at the planning stage. The style of presentation must communicate an open and respectful approach. An interactive style is important, to engage the children and involve them in the learning. The authentic voice of faith is valuable.

Visiting a sacred space

An important part of teaching and learning in religious education is visiting sacred spaces. Here, children can engage with living religions and meet faith leaders and members of faith communities. Places of worship for different Christian denominations, mandirs (Hindu), mosques (Islam) and gurdwaras (Sikh) and synagogues (Jewish) are all fascinating and valuable for children to visit. Many cathedrals and exhibitions of religious paintings and sacred texts (such as the Islamic Middle East Gallery at the Victoria and Albert Museum) are also superb examples of learning outside the classroom to embed effective religious education. Peace gardens such as the Beth Shalom Holocaust Centre in Nottinghamshire are also suitable for developing an understanding of the importance of sacred spaces. The opportunities for learning during such visits are multifaceted. Sacred spaces can provide a stimulating and sensory experience. Each locally agreed syllabus will suggest which religions are to be taught at each age phase and each will support planning curriculum opportunities to visit places of worship. The emphasis will be on learning about and from religion and belief.

Visiting a sacred space will develop knowledge and understanding about beliefs, teachings, worship, religion in the family and community and beliefs in action. The cross-curricular skills of enquiry, investigation, collecting and recording evidence, interpretation and communication are all developed during and after such visits.

🖎 In the classroom   Planning a visit to the gurdwara

Prior to the trip, the teacher contacted the gurdwara and arranged to discuss her goals for the visit. A useful discussion and tour took place. The teacher then felt suitably prepared to supervise her class on the visit. She also had the opportunity to speak with the education officer and share the objectives for the visit. They discussed the length of the talk at the gurdwara.

The teacher informed parents that the children needed head covering for the visit. She took a donation and instructed the children to remove their shoes. The children knew they would be visiting the langar (kitchen) for some food and were prepared to try the food offered to them.

The preparation enabled the class to have a wonderful visit, about which they created a display when back at school.

There is no valid reason to prevent children from any faith taking part in educational visits to other places of worship. Some parents may be sensitive about their children visiting a sacred space that is not the same as their own faith background. It is important to reassure parents of the values and purposes of such visits, which enable children to experience the wider world.

The opportunity to promote spirituality through that 'good to be alive' feeling is there for us as teachers in the natural world. Encourage children to explore some of the mysteries of the world by choosing a feather, leaf or blade of grass and considering what a human would have to do to make this. These special, reflective and thoughtful moments support the holistic development of the children in our care.

Religious education in the curriculum

Religious education provokes challenging questions about the ultimate meaning and purpose of life, beliefs about God, the self and the nature of reality, issues of right and wrong and what it means to be human. It can develop pupils' knowledge and understanding of Christianity, other principal religions, other religious traditions and worldviews that offer answers to questions such as these.

(DCSF, 2010: 7)

Religious education is not part of the National Curriculum, but is a statutory entitlement for all children of legal school age. As mentioned above the legal requirements governing religious education were set out in the Education Reform Act of 1988 and confirmed by the Education Acts of 1996 and 1998. Religious education is statutory for all pupils on the school roll.

Religious education differs from other subjects in the curriculum because it is organised on a local basis to reflect the communities of the area each school serves. The non-statutory national framework for religious education provides a basis for local authorities and their Standing Advisory Council for Religious

Education (SACRE) to develop local statutory syllabi. These are reviewed and revised every five years.

Schools designated as having a religious character are free to construct their own syllabus, ensuring it reflects the religious traditions of Great Britain. The agreed syllabus provides a clear structure for religious education teaching and learning, with appropriate levels and assessment arrangements. Because of the nature of the subject, parents are given the right to withdraw their child from the lessons if they so wish.

While English and mathematics take up a large proportion of a child's time in a primary classroom, there must be time and space for religious education, too, which has so many contributions to make to the holistic education of a child. Religious education can be taught in regular weekly slots or in blocks of time throughout the year. Alternatively, it can be taught thematically throughout the curriculum with cross-curricular links.

In the Early Years Foundation Stage (EYFS), there is no statutory requirement for, or entitlement to, religious education. The EYFS Framework, however, does have many links with personal, community, religious and cultural identity and promotes the exploration and celebration of religious diversity, as well as associated skills and attitudes. The religious education topics featured in agreed syllabuses for Reception year (four- and five-year-olds) are selected for their ability to be explored within an holistic curriculum and a locality, local community and parent-linked context. Emphasis is always placed on experiences and opportunities for first-hand and active learning.

In the classroom   Journeys

Using *Mr Gumpy's Outing* by John Burningham (2001) as a starting story, the teacher encouraged the children to talk about journeys they had undertaken. They were encouraged to remember the names of places and special things they saw or people they met.

The teacher then talked about a special journey in Christianity – the Nativity story. Using puppets and props, the story was told, helped by the children, and a sense of awe and enchantment filled the circle.

The attainment targets

The teacher has a statutory role to plan, teach and assess religious education using two attainment targets: learning about religion and belief (AT1), and learning from religion and belief (AT2). The first involves enquiry into and investigation of the nature of religion, its beliefs, teachings and ways of life, sources, practices and forms of expression. The second target is about developing pupils' reflections on and response to their own and others' experiences in the light of their learning about religious education. Their own ideas and questions of identity and belonging are to be explored. The following example illustrates how these can be applied in a classroom activity.

In the classroom   The Five Pillars of Islam

The children had been learning about the Five Pillars of Islam. They listened to interviews online with Muslims who are living their faith according to the Five Pillars.

The children were then encouraged to make links between their own experience and the experience of many Muslims. They rehearsed their responses to questions such as, 'All the time, Muslims believe ...' and began their sentence, 'All the time, I believe ... '. They filmed themselves giving their answers and produced their own short video. In this way, they learned from religion and belief and reflected on questions about their own lives and beliefs.

The religious education classroom environment

A successful teacher will foster a learning environment that takes into account the spiritual, moral, social and cultural elements of the curriculum. The learners' interests should be at the heart of the classroom, with an ethos of question and answer that opens the minds of both the children and the teacher. Images and music from different cultures and faith groups, including models and interactive toys in the role-play areas of lower primary classrooms, help children understand their lives in relation to those around them.

In the classroom   Using resources for four- and five-year-olds in the role-play area

In the role-play area the structure had been draped with glorious fabrics. Within the 'den' there were a model Hindu temple, some costumes to dress up in and several

(Continued)

(Continued)

books depicting the stories from the Hindu religion. Artefacts and resources, signs and images adorned the walls and shelves. Music was playing gently with options for the children to select different pieces. The children had free access to the area and were encouraged to take photographs of each other in their play. A display of the photos with recordable speech bubbles of their talk was displayed in the area outside the classroom, where the parents and carers collect their children.

Skilful recording of the play by the teacher and assistant gave value to the area and the important, yet non-explicit, differences between the cultures were explored in a child-led play area.

Approaches to religious education

The most effective religious education uses active learning at its core. Dance, drama, poetry, rap, art, music, cooking, drama and role-play and ICT all enrich and develop learning opportunities. Children need to explore the big ideas that faiths tackle and be supported to be sensitively reflective. The use of imagery and music together can be very effective to promote expression of meaning, purpose and truth and is a way of exploring the values and commitments of believers and the children's own identities.

 In the classroom   The storyteller approach

A candle is lit to denote that a special story is to be told. The children sit in a circle near the teacher, who becomes the storyteller.

The Hindu god Ganesha is introduced via a storytelling activity, revealed slowly from under a beautiful, coloured cloth. The children are drawn to the intriguing characteristics of the statue as they move away from the story area to their activities.

The teacher initiates discussion with one group and asks for their responses to the story. She scribes their thoughts and captures some of their commentary on tablets. Two pairs listen intently to the story again on headphones, drawing on paper as they listen. A table is adorned with sequins and mosaic pieces for an artistic response to the stimulus. Beautiful music at a gentle volume is piped throughout the classroom. A buzz of involvement is entwined with the serene and peaceful atmosphere.

Table 12.1 provides examples of stimulating activities to use alongside stories in religious education.

Table 12.1   Suggested ways to use stories in religious education

Story maps	Retelling a story
Story sacks/story boxes	DVD, paused at important part
Story circles	Representing a story in art, dance or music
Artefacts/through the keyhole boxes	Developing an accompanying soundtrack or sound effects
Pictures and photographs	Retelling for a younger audience
Puppets, shadow puppets, finger puppets	Retelling as a diary or poem
Questioning and 'I wonder' statements	Animations
Role-play, drama, mime	Scriptwriting a story

Key vocabulary should be shared and displayed and the children should be invited to think about the story and the points that are most important to them. Going beneath the surface of the story and telling it, rather than reading it aloud, develops the opportunities for learning from religion and belief. This will be enhanced if the children are helped to develop key enquiry skills (Ofsted, 2010: 5):

> Where religious education was most effective, it used a range of enquiry skills such as investigation, interpretation, analysis, evaluation and reflection.

Active learning

There are many approaches to teaching religious education that will engage your learners and enable them to enjoy religious education and remain motivated and curious while developing their thinking:

- debate
- dance
- display work
- making models
- cooking
- concept mapping
- research
- meditation
- handling artefacts
- puppets
- poetry/rap
- using photographs

- ICT
- discussion
- hot seating
- thought tapping
- teacher in role
- diaries.

Using ICT

Using an interactive whiteboard to project virtual tours on the Internet, for example, allows both preparation for a visit and consolidation and reflection after a visit. If a physical visit to a sacred space is not viable, Internet video tours provide a useful alternative resource that allows the children to 'see' what it would be like inside a special place of worship they have not visited. A useful source for such activities is the RE:Online website (www.reonline.org.uk).

Via the Internet, children can also listen to the views of those from other faiths and cultures as they talk about their beliefs. Equally, images of religious artwork or depictions of the face of Christ, for example, can be projected and discussed with the class or printed out to use as a stimulus for the children's own artwork. Tablets can be used to create artwork using apps.

The Religion & Ethics section of the BBC's website (www.bbc.co.uk/religion) is a good starting point for developing subject knowledge. Teachers may feel that their own subject knowledge is not extensive when teaching religious education, but it must be seen as being of equal importance to any other area of the curriculum. The information available on the Internet is comprehensive and can be used by both teachers and children. It is the teacher's organisation of how such information is accessed, discussed and considered that makes it useful. Caution is required, however, to ensure a website is authentic and suitable. Be aware of websites that may have a bias and explore them thoroughly before using them with the children.

Teachers plan religious education activities to allow children time to explore, but also to offer opportunities for discussion and clarification. It is their own confidence in their subject knowledge, along with an understanding of how religious education understanding develops in young children, that enables teachers to question incomplete understanding. Teachers can also move children towards recognising their own uniqueness and view of their world, feeling confident about their own beliefs and identity and being willing to go beyond first impressions, recognising diversity. In order to do this, children need to develop skills to enhance their exploration, sensitivity, imagination, curiosity, respect and self-confidence. These skills are the foundations for lifelong learning and being a fair citizen and member of a community (DCSF, 2010: 15):

> Effective religious education can play a key part in promoting inter-faith understanding and dialogue and can address the prejudice brought about by a shallow knowledge of world religions and provides pupils with a safe forum for the discussion of controversial issues.

Planning for religious education

A key feature of planning for all subjects is the depth of the teacher's subject knowledge. An additional layer within religious education planning is the need for sensitivity and building one's own confidence. You can use the local agreed syllabus as a basis for quality planning, which, combined with an understanding of the context of your classroom and locality, will provide meaningful and relevant opportunities for the children to learn about and from religion and belief.

Learning objectives need to focus on the skills and attitudes that are being developed and refer to the pedagogical approaches for the best religious education teaching and learning. Learning objectives need to be in child-friendly language and shared with the children. Success criteria must be explicit and visible to the children, too, so they can use them to achieve the learning intentions. Teachers and other adults should give formative feedback to the children in line with the learning intention and success criteria so they know how to improve their outcomes in religious education.

Some concerns of student teachers are:

- 'I'm an atheist; how can I teach religious education?'
- 'I'm not a Sikh so how can I teach about it?'
- 'I can't teach religion because there are so many different religions in my class, I would offend somebody.'

As a student teacher, you will come to your initial post with a collection of experiences from your own schooling and family backgrounds. This needs to be explored before teaching religious education to children in your care.

All the belief systems that teachers have experienced are valid and do not undermine their ability to teach religious education effectively. That is because religious education is not about 'teaching a religion'; it is about developing open-mindedness, appreciation and knowledge about others so that children can grow up as harmonious and broad-minded citizens.

Like every subject in the primary curriculum, there is a need to immerse oneself in subject knowledge when preparing to teach it. There is a wealth of resources both online and off that will support teachers planning a unit of work on an unknown aspect of religious education. It is essential that the pedagogy is strong so the subject knowledge researched can be taught in an interesting and memorable way.

How do children learn best in religious education?

- When they are given opportunities to express their learning in different ways, such as in music, poetry, drama, dance.
- When there are stimulating displays showcasing their work and imagery from different cultures.

- When background music and/or a candle is used to denote RE learning and set the tone for the learning.
- When they feel safe and valued and can speak up and be listened to.
- When they are praised and encouraged and their involvement is noted and supported.
- When the activities are varied and appropriately challenging.
- When effective questioning is used by the teacher and other adults to stretch their answers and re-engage their thinking.
- When their contributions are taken seriously and respected.

The following example illustrates how these features can be incorporated into lessons and how key skills can be developed in a safe environment.

In the classroom   Using artefacts

A class of seven- and eight-year-old children were investigating artefacts. They were recording their responses to the following questions.

- What interests you about this artefact?
- Does anything puzzle you?
- What do you think it is?
- Who uses it?
- What do they use it for?
- Why do you think it is special?
- When might it be used?

The small groups wrote some of their ideas on cards and also recorded some on recordable speech bubbles. They discussed their ideas together and sensitively listened to the contributions. The teacher modelled being the 'questioner' and probing further. For example, when a child answered with an initial, 'It is interesting because of the colours', the teacher asked, 'What is it about the colours that interests you?' 'I haven't seen anything that is so brightly coloured in my church.' This interaction encouraged contributions from other group members about their experiences and artefacts they had seen in homes and places of worship that were brightly coloured. After some discussion, the children decided to photograph the artefact and draw it so they had a record of their discussion.

The contribution of religious education to the wider curriculum

The ethos and values of a school are felt as soon as one enters the building. Religious education makes an important contribution to this and across the curriculum. Social, moral, spiritual and cultural (SMSC) development is essential in a school. High-quality pictures, artefacts, music and books displayed around the school create an inclusive environment that is broad-minded and encourages understanding and an appreciation of different faiths and cultures.

The personal development and well-being of children is the foundation of their capacity to learn. Effective teachers of religious education use many strategies to promote well-being among their pupils. The open and safe environment of the religious education classroom establishes a positive learning culture where children's behaviour for learning is fostered.

Provoking challenging questions and building a sense of one's own identity is a core purpose of primary education. Religious education is an ideal forum for the teaching of these elements. Many key thinking skills are practised in religious education classes. This grounding in effective learning approaches establishes an excellent pattern for growth, both academically and socially. Positive relationships within the classroom, both between teacher and child and within the class as a whole, are the key to successful outcomes and engaged learners. Religious education provides the opportunity to develop these relationships.

Citizenship

Citizenship is a non-statutory aspect of the primary curriculum. Guidance is given by the Department for Education to support schools planning their whole curriculum. Values education is another term some schools use. Educational opportunities should be given so that active qualities of empowerment, empathy, identity, diversity, ethics, action and vision are explored and developed (see Table 12.2).

Table 12.2   A summary of active citizenship

Empowerment	Having the confidence and personal ability to take an active participant role – having a 'voice' and being heard
Empathy	Being able to understand one's own and other people's feelings, empathise when necessary and see other people's points of view
Identity	Seeing where you fit in personally, having and gaining a sense of your identity as a member of a local, national and international community, and a strong sense that your own issues can be, and are, addressed
Diversity	Knowing about the wide variety of issues that affect citizens, from the very local to the global, even if these issues are not personal to you
Ethics	Having an ethical framework for deciding between conflicting interests, in order to make sound, just judgements
Action	Having the opportunity to learn about citizenship and democracy by 'doing it' in real-life projects
Vision	Having a sense of what a better community or world would look like and having the opportunity to debate this and try to implement change in appropriate settings

In the classroom   'Operation amphibian'

Using the British Red Cross online teaching resources, a group of 9- to 11-year-olds explored how to role-play assessing people's needs, keeping themselves safe from landmines, planning a camp and learning some first aid to treat the injured.

The key skills of teamwork, critical thinking, planning and prioritising, and empathy with those affected by disaster were put into action. A scenario was presented of a disaster area, where the key needs were shelter and clean running water. They also needed to reunite separated families.

The children 'became' Red Cross workers. They learned about the disaster and what to do. They applied first aid and used maps to consider the local area. Collaboratively, they built a bridge, a safe camp and access to clean water. They endeavoured to locate loved ones who may have been lost.

Through such an activity, children learn about themselves as developing individuals and members of their community. They learn to be healthy and safe and behave well. They learn social skills and to be responsible. As they enter the upper primary years, they grow and change and become more mature and independent. They develop a sense of social justice and may encounter and resist bullying.

Reflective questions

- How would you ensure that your lessons were active and engaging at all times?
- Why is it important to plan for both attainment targets?
- Consider your response to a child or parent who spoke inappropriately about another religion. How would you handle such a situation?
- Think about your own beliefs and identity. How can you present all features of religious education without bias or personal viewpoints? Should you share your beliefs with your class? You may want to discuss this and the previous question with your mentor or team leader as part of a professional dialogue.

Conclusion

Teachers are expected to respect the social, cultural, linguistic, religious and ethnic backgrounds of children. They must treat the children consistently, with respect and consideration. They should demonstrate and promote the positive values, attitudes and behaviour that they expect from the children.

Good practice in religious education is seen when teachers have high expectations and a determination to organise an active approach to learning. Teachers should draw from the experiences in the classroom and the locality. Work needs to be appropriately challenging with a focus on questioning and personal reflection. Children and teachers need to enjoy the learning and learn from each other.

If you ask a class of children, 'Can each of you tell me five things you wouldn't have known if it had not been for religious education?', the list will be endless. Religious education is an intrinsic part of high-quality primary education and it allows children to make sense of the world around them.

Further reading

The following are some useful websites for classroom resources and curriculum information.

www.northamptonshire.gov.uk/en/councilservices/EducationandLearning/services/sacre/
   Documents/PDF%20Documents/Websites%20for%20RE.pdf
Useful list of RE websites.

www.flickr.com/groups/900167@N25
Around the World in 80 Faiths flickr page – has some fabulous photos.

http://subknow.reonline.org.uk
Catalogue of information for subject knowledge in RE.

www.retoday.org.uk
An online magazine that will take you to further resources and publications.

www.re-handbook.org.uk
An easily navigable site giving clear explanations of various aspects of continuing professional development for teachers, including information on different religions.

www.bbc.co.uk/religion
The Religion & Ethics page on the BBC's website – has useful links to a variety of videos, images and facts.

www.religiouseducationcouncil.org
A wealth of information and links to support planning and subject knowledge.

References

Burningham, J. (2001) *Mr Gumpy's Outing*. London: Red Fox.
DCSF (2010) 'Religious education in English schools: Non-statutory guidance 2010'. Nottingham: DCSF. Available online at: www.gov.uk/government/uploads/system/uploads/attachment_data/file/190260/DCSF-00114-2010.pdf
Ofsted (2010) 'Transforming religious education'. Manchester: Ofsted.

CHAPTER 13

SCIENCE

Babs Dore and Lyn Dawes

Learning objectives

At the end of this chapter you should be able to:

- talk to children about their understanding of the natural world and help them to achieve a more scientific point of view
- plan and teach effective practical science lessons
- evaluate the quality of your own lessons and assess the children's learning in science.

Introduction

The aim of this chapter is to explain the nature of teaching and learning science in primary schools, in which it is a practical and inclusive subject, offering the opportunity for children to learn a particular way of thinking – to use evidence for reasoning.

Science encourages children to look again at their familiar world. Children watching a snail crawl up a perspex sheet, playing with cornflour and water paste or observing the phases of the Moon are engaged in a process that can challenge their existing ideas and prompt them to seek deeper understanding. Via scientific enquiry, children can explore their environment more closely. They can develop ways of working that not only offer answers to their questions but also, in the process, encourage them to query the validity and reliability of their evidence and the scientific process itself. The knowledge, skills and attitudes that young children develop as they study science contribute to their learning across the curriculum and beyond.

In the classroom   Developing ideas via practical work – the orange

A group of nine- and ten-year-old children were asked to discuss whether they thought an orange would float or sink if placed in a tank of water. They shared a range of everyday ideas – 'the orange will float better if the water is deeper', 'it will not float because it's heavy', 'it will float till it soaks up water, then it will sink'.

A floating orange can be thought of as being prevented from falling any further by the water. The downward-acting force of gravity on the mass of the orange (its weight) is balanced by the water's upthrust. The orange displaces less than its own weight of water.

Once the group had discussed the floating orange in terms of balanced forces, they were asked then to predict what would happen if the orange peel was removed. Again there was a range of ideas – 'the air in the orange will escape, so it will sink', 'it will become waterlogged and sink', 'it will be even lighter without the peel so it will float'.

An orange is full of sugar solution, which is denser than water. The layer of orange peel acts to make the orange light for its size – less dense than water – so, without the peel, the orange sinks.

To help the children develop their ideas, they were asked to try and explain their observations to one another, draw annotated diagrams of the orange in the tank, before and after removing the peel, and try some extension activities – weighing the orange and peel; stirring salt into the water in the tank; seeing if the results were the same for other fruits; and making boats out of orange peel, to see how much weight they would hold before sinking.

Discussion, focused on the inclusion of structured scientific learning in primary classrooms, began well before the introduction of the National Curriculum in 1988. In the late 1980s and early 1990s, the Science Processes and Concept Exploration (SPACE) Project (1999) revealed that young children develop everyday ideas about science related to their limited experience of the world and they may generate non-scientific explanations of what they observe. These ideas, some of which may be misconceptions, can prove useful starting points for more structured learning. This research emphasised the need for effective science teaching at primary level to enable children to develop their understanding along more scientific lines.

In the classroom   Examples of children's incomplete understanding of science concepts – misconceptions

Light and dark: child aged 7 years

'Dark comes in when the light is turned out'

Why do trees have leaves?: child aged 6 years

'Trees have leaves so we know when it's Autumn'

Day and night: children aged 8 years

Teacher (holding a beach ball to represent the earth by a lamp, and rotating it): So the Earth goes round – this is us – and the sun keeps still

Child: But if it did that it would go dark, light, dark, light, all the time, pretty fast –

Teacher: That's a good way to put it. Night, day, night, day. Once a day

Child: Oh! Yes!

Electricity and magnetism: child aged 10 years

Child: If you put a metal object near a power line, the electricity would pull – because electricity and magnetism are the same force, the power line would conduct the piece of metal and bring it towards it

---

Light and shadow: child aged 5 years

Teacher: Look, your shadow's following you now. It's walking behind you (*Christy tries walking backwards*)

Child: It's going the other way

Teacher: Why is that, what do you think?

Child: It's got slow. (*To the shadow*) Come on, hurry up! (*Runs towards the sun*)

The variety of life: children aged 6 and 8 years

Teacher to child 1: Can you name three birds?

Child 1: Sparrow. Blackbird. (*Pause*) Vulture

Teacher to child 2: Now, can you name three birds?

Child 2: Peter and Paul

Learning about science in primary classrooms contributes to children's developing knowledge and understanding of the world around them, but, crucially, it also enables them to begin to recognise the importance of reasoning about evidence. Taking part in orderly observation and enquiry activities, reflecting on findings and evaluating the process of scientific enquiry all help children towards thinking in scientific ways. In addition, collaboration with classmates provides opportunities for using and applying technical vocabulary and testing out their growing skills in reasoning and interrogating evidence.

Science, then, is a complex subject, even at primary level. Rather than simply a collection of facts, it is also a way of working. In addition, the attitudes carefully fostered in scientific study – that is, independence, perseverance, cooperation, respect for evidence, creativity and inventiveness, open-mindedness and respect for living things (de Boo, 2006) – provide children with a toolbox of skills and approaches to take into other areas of learning.

Science in the curriculum

A robust science curriculum specifies a clear introduction to all areas of science in the primary phase. In addition, it is essential to emphasise the process of science and the need for children to engage in relevant, genuine enquiry to further their understanding. Children need time to explore not only the practical aspects of science but also discuss their experiences and build these into a developing understanding.

Many primary schools do not teach science on a weekly basis; instead it is taught in alternate half-terms or within dedicated science weeks. Such an approach can create an unhelpful lack of continuity. Teachers may find it difficult to relate isolated science lessons to children's experiences, while the children themselves may not have the consistent exposure to enquiry and reasoning that is needed to develop a scientific way of thinking. However, individual schools may design their own approach to ensure coherence in their science teaching.

The 2014 National Curriculum in England (DfE, 2013) provides a basic framework that can help to structure and organise science teaching and learning. Progression is especially important, as is a breadth of knowledge and an understanding of the nature of science as enquiry.

It is a child's entitlement to have access to all areas of science knowledge and be familiar with the skills needed to question, investigate, conclude and communicate. The new curriculum acknowledges the importance of oral language in eliciting and developing primary children's thinking in science. The convention of asking a question to which you already know the answer and choosing a child with their hand up who will provide a one-word child response will not be appropriate for teaching primary science. What is needed is dialogue. Children can be taught how to talk to you and one another productively in science.

Approaches to primary science

Learning science in primary school involves engaging with a scientific point of view, which may differ sharply from a child's intuitive, everyday view of how the world works. Rather than the simple acquisition of science facts, emphasis within the curriculum is on approaching science knowledge and understanding by means of exploration and investigation. Science is a practical subject and children need time to explore their world, observe and question what they see, rehearse their own explanations and share that possibly incomplete understanding with their teacher.

Teachers plan science activities to allow children time to explore, but also to offer opportunities for discussion and clarification. It is your own confidence in your subject knowledge, along with the understanding of how science knowledge develops in young children, that enables you to question incomplete understanding and move children towards a more complete, scientific view of their world.

In order to do this, children need to develop skills in exploration and investigation. These skills – known as *process skills* – arise from and build on children's natural curiosity. Developing process skills in science enables them to begin to look for answers to questions in a more systematic and reliable fashion. Many of these skills are not exclusive to science but all would be recognised by practising scientists as the way in which they approach their work.

The basic process skills used in science can be identified as:

- observing
- sorting and classifying
- questioning
- inferring
- predicting
- measuring
- communicating.

These are common human activities and, in their simplest forms, attributes we would hope to see in young children as they start school. Much early work in science concentrates on encouraging children to refine these skills. However, more complex skills are also needed to foster and develop scientific thinking. These can be identified as:

- identifying and controlling variables
- making models
- collecting and interpreting data
- hypothesising
- investigating.

Such skills evolve slowly as children are offered further opportunities for practical exploration and reflection.

 In the classroom   Progression in science skills – sorting

Provide objects such as toys or classroom equipment, made from a range of materials (paper, metal, cork, plastic, wood, oil, water, fabrics of various kinds, card, sand). Ask the children to sort the objects into groups.

Younger children will use immediately observable features, such as colour or size, or put things together that match (such as sand and a bucket). That is, they may sort the objects rather than the materials. This is a good chance to discuss what things are made of, how we can tell and the properties of a range of materials. The

(Continued)

(Continued)

progression with experience, therefore, is towards sorting objects by material, so that a plastic dinosaur would be grouped with a plastic spoon rather than with a wooden dinosaur.

Ask the children to specify the criteria that inform their sort. Encourage them to think of sorting as a chance to ask questions that have a 'yes' or 'no' answer. For example, 'Does it float?', 'Is it a manufactured material?', 'Is it brittle/flexible/liquid/rigid?' They can consider which are the most productive questions. Children adept at asking such questions can be given ten objects and asked to construct a dichotomous (branching) key, which classmates can then test using different objects made of the same materials.

Next, we shall look in further detail and clarify the all-important process skills.

- *Observing* Children need to be given the opportunities and encouragement to observe using all their senses. This might include carefully drawing leaves, feeling and smelling the changes that take place to chocolate as it is gently warmed, listening to instruments as the pitch is changed or watching the transformation in a playground tree across the year. Observation may be qualitative and use adjectives to describe objects, such as, 'All these fabrics are smooth', or may be qualitative and involve measurement of what is observed, such as, 'This creature has seven pairs of legs'.
- *Sorting and classifying* Opportunities to sort collections of objects or materials encourage observational skills and help develop appropriate scientific vocabulary. Grouping objects together in, for example, a Venn or Carroll diagram, involves children in making decisions about what is similar and what is different about objects. Sorting a collection of plastic animals, for example, can develop understanding of basic biological classifications. More complex sorting may involve looking at which materials might be attracted to a magnet, for example, and may lead on to investigation.
- *Questioning* Questions form the basis of investigation. Children need much experience and practice in order to express questions in a form that naturally leads on to investigation.
- *Inferring* Science proceeds in logical steps – bigger ideas grow from smaller, simpler ideas. It is important, then, that children are helped to make appropriate inferences following their observations. To do this they must learn to reflect on relevant experiences, draw on what they already know or have found out and build understanding of more complex ideas. Inferences may well change as more observations are made and more data are collected.

- *Predicting* When children predict before investigating, they make an educated guess about the outcomes. Prediction is based on observation and inferences drawn from those observations. If the prediction turns out to be correct, then they can have confidence in their inferences.

- *Measuring* Increasing skill in making measurements brings increasing confidence in results. Young children may well measure using non-standard units, such as hand spans or counting blocks. Older children will need help to measure accurately and understand ways in which to add reliability and accuracy to results, such as averaging over a number of repeated readings.

- *Communicating* Whatever we do in science, we need to communicate our findings to share them with others and build new understanding. Children can simply write up their investigations, but, with a little thought and creativity, they might act out their findings or present them as a newspaper report or TV interview. New types of media give children opportunities to communicate their findings in a range of exciting and engaging ways, from multimedia presentations to videos.

- *Identifying and controlling variables* In order to work reliably, children will need to work with only one variable in their investigation. All other variables need to be identified and then controlled so that they are not also changing and introducing error to the activity. For example, if children are investigating what affects how quickly sugar dissolves in the teacher's tea at breaktime, they will need to identify all the things that might change – the temperature of the water, the type of sugar, the amount of water and sugar, if the teacher stirs it – and then decide which aspect they want to investigate more. If they decide to see how the type of sugar affects how quickly it dissolves, then they will need to use the same amount of water and sugar, keep the temperature of the water constant and not stir (or always stir five times, say). They can then measure the time taken for the sugar to dissolve as a direct consequence of the type of sugar used rather than anything else.

- *Making models* In order to explain science concepts, children can express their understanding by using models, either mental or physical. For example, when Jack drew a hamster in a wheel when asked to suggest what was inside a battery, he was using a sophisticated analogy. On questioning, it emerged that he understood a battery could not store electricity but somehow a chemical process resulted in electrical energy being made available by the battery. His analogy grew from having visited a power station and having observed a model of the generators. Similarly, a group of eight- and nine-year-olds watched a video of Emperor penguins huddling together in large groups to withstand the freezing Antarctic conditions. They then devised a model using test tubes bound together and filled with warm water to allow them to investigate how temperature dropped across the huddle.

- *Collecting and interpreting data* In order to produce reliable results, children will need to collect their data in a systematic way. They will need to devise a table of results that might well reveal patterns in their data and help in displaying their findings graphically to aid interpretation. Graphs need to be fit for purpose. For example, block graphs will show how far individual cars travelled across different surfaces to investigate friction, but a line graph is needed to indicate how a continuous value is changing across time, such as how the temperature of water in a cup falls as it is wrapped in different materials to investigate thermal insulation. Carefully interpreting data leads to more accurate inference.

- *Hypothesising* A hypothesis is a tentative explanation for an observation or scientific happening that can be tested by further investigation. Hypotheses are usually stated in the form, 'if … then … because …'.
- *Investigating* This is when children carry out the whole process, from formulating a question to be investigated, such as, 'How does the slope of a ramp affect how fast a car travels down it?', to designing the investigation and recording and interpreting the results.

Planning science activities

Learning in science requires a balance of well-planned and supported practical activities presented alongside opportunities for children to reflect on these experiences. In addition, children need the chance to ask their own questions and devise appropriate investigations; such freedom requires thoughtful planning.

A narrative approach to the teaching and learning of science can promote curiosity and engagement and enable children to ask their own questions about the world around them. Planning can usefully start with considering what the children already know in an exploratory stage, where ideas are elicited, considered and discussed. Following this, they can be offered new experiences and information; they can be supported in redescribing concepts in a more scientific way. Ultimately, children can apply their new learning (a more scientific point of view) to further puzzles and problems. A three-stage approach involving exploration, redescribing and application (Loxley et al., 2010), in which children are in an extended, ongoing dialogue with one another, their teachers and the science experiences they encounter, requires careful planning, but is richly rewarding.

Children will have existing ideas that are grounded in their own experiences and it may well be that some of these ideas are scientifically inaccurate or only partially understood. These misconceptions may interfere with learning a more scientific point of view. For this reason, it is crucial to encourage children to talk about their ideas before providing activities and information to help develop new thinking. Across the different areas of science there are many commonly held misconceptions – for example, 'there is no gravity on the Moon' or 'a seed needs light to germinate'. The SPACE Project (1999) identified many commonly held misconceptions among primary school children.

It is always important to find out what the individual children in your class think, know and understand before beginning a new science topic. There are a number of ways to do this. A closed question, such as, 'Who can tell me what a force is?', is likely to reveal only superficial knowledge of vocabulary (such as push, pull), rather than a deeper understanding of the concepts involved. Stimulating starter activities can help children to articulate their current understanding. A trip to a playground, for instance, offers opportunities to describe forces in action and provides shared experiences that can be discussed back in the classroom. Table 13.1 and Figure 13.1 provide examples of such stimulating starter activities to encourage children to discuss their everyday ideas about science topics.

Understanding children's current ideas enables the teacher to devise practical activities that will provide carefully structured experiences of scientific phenomena. For example, young children may have had only limited experience of objects that float. This experience can lead them to think that all small, light objects will float. Dropping a needle into a tank of water will challenge this assumption and provide a context for a more searching discussion of what makes things float.

It is important to approach children's misconceptions sensitively at all times. Their own ideas may be deeply held and they may need gentle persuasion and lots of practical examples to encourage them to restructure their thinking in the light of new evidence.

Table 13.1   Suggested activities to stimulate interest and reveal children's existing understanding

Well-known stories and poems	*The Three Bears* – hot and cold, keeping things warm *The Three Little Pigs* – strong structures *The Snowman* – insulation *The Gruffalo* – food chains, habitats
Images and videos	Emperor penguins – keeping warm, thermal insulation *Titanic* – floating and sinking
Drawing	Draw what they think is inside an egg or a battery or how a light bulb works Observational drawing of natural materials and creatures Drawing a cartoon to depict uses of energy in the home
Unusual objects	Ice balloons, bubbles, Cartesian divers, mobiles, magnets, friction and other wheeled toys, construction kits, fruits and seeds
Visits	Science Museum, Natural History Museum, local museums, playground, supermarket, bakers, recycling plant
Activities	Soap making, paper making, recycling, baking and cooking, using kitchen chemicals, using battery operated circuits, ramps, levers, springs, investigating soil, water, paper
Concept mapping	A way of organising information that shows how ideas or concepts are linked (see Figure 13.1)
Concept cartoons	A concept cartoon presents alternative viewpoints using minimal text. It can be used to elicit children's existing understanding of concepts or provoke discussion (Naylor and Keogh, 2000)

Figure 13.1   An eight-year-old's concept map for electricity

---

🖾   **In the classroom   A strongly held misconception – Sarah and the red car**

A small group of four- and five-year-old children were investigating what happened when cars were rolled down ramps. They were interested in how far each car would go if it rolled on to the carpet, the lino, the playground.

Before the activity, the children had agreed that they would let the cars go rather than push them – to push would be unfair as some children might push harder than others. Throughout the activity, however, one child, Sarah, pushed her red car every time. Eventually the other children complained and the teacher asked Sarah to talk about what she had been doing.

With some reluctance, Sarah admitted that she had pushed the car each time. With a wonderful twist of logic she explained, 'Red cars always go fast. My Daddy has a red car and it goes fast.'

Scientific exploration as a starting point for science activities

To help children develop their scientific understanding, we need to give them comprehensive opportunities to explore the natural world, objects and materials. We must support children as they build up shared experiences and develop a shared vocabulary for describing what they experience. We need to provide constant chances for exploration, as encouraging children to ask questions and try out ideas is a starting point for more formal investigation. For example, a group of eight- and nine-year-olds were about to look in more detail at reflections. A week beforehand, the teacher provided an exploratory table with plane, concave and convex mirrors, holographic wrapping paper, CDs and kaleidoscopes, which the children were invited to play with. Over the course of the week, they left their comments and questions on sticky notes alongside the display. These ideas formed the basis of a discussion about what the children already knew and what they would like to find out. Collections of similar objects, such as simple musical instruments, seeds, rocks, toys, fruits, and so on, can all be used to stimulate discussion and elicit existing knowledge and understanding.

Figure 13.2 shows a chart illustrating the process of enquiry, summarising the links that enable children to think through an investigation in a logical and productive way.

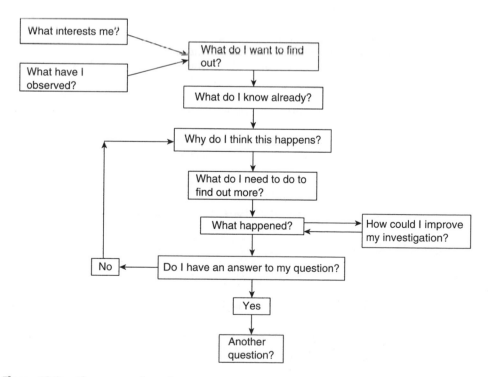

Figure 13.2   The process of enquiry

Methods of enquiry in primary science

Not all primary science investigations are undertaken in the same way. The AKSIS project, developed at King's College, London, in the late 1990s, demonstrated that there are several forms of investigation that children can use in the classroom to find answers to their questions. It is important, therefore, that children are aware of these different investigation techniques and encouraged to choose a method of investigation that is appropriate to the question being asked. Table 13.2 shows examples of the sorts of enquiries regularly carried out in primary settings.

Undertaking a complete science investigation gives children opportunities to investigate real questions that have relevance to them. In carrying out such an enquiry, they will be able to demonstrate the science process skills, from defining the question to designing the investigation and then presenting and discussing the results.

Table 13.2   Forms of investigation children can use to answer their questions

Fair testing	Observing and exploring relationships between variables by changing one variable and measuring the effect this has on another	Which kitchen towel soaks up the most water? Which fabric is best to make Teddy a winter coat? Does the height of the ramp affect the distance a car travels?
Seeking patterns	Making observations and measurements and looking for patterns – larger sample sizes lead to greater reliability in results	Do people with the longest legs jump the furthest? Where in the school grounds are we mostly likely to find snails?
Classifying and identifying	Carefully and systematically collecting and grouping things based on observational data	Can we identify these mystery substances? How many types of wildflowers can we identify in the hedgerow?
Exploring/ investigating over time	Collecting data that builds up to give a picture of an environment over time	What happens to food if we leave it out of the fridge? How does the shape of the Moon vary over time? What foods do the birds most like on the bird table?
Making models	Applying scientific ideas and skills to solve problems	How can we make a snail habitat? Can I make something to measure forces? Can I design a circuit to turn a light on and off?

In the classroom   A winter coat for teddy

A class of six- and seven-year-olds were investigating which fabrics would be best to use to make Teddy a winter coat. They discussed all the things the coat would need to do.

Which is the fabric that would keep Teddy warmest?

Which fabric is waterproof, to keep Teddy dry?

Which fabric is nice and stretchy so Teddy will be comfortable?

They decided that as they had these three different questions to investigate, they should set up three different investigations. For each one they had to decide what they would change and what they would keep the same. For example, the children investigating how warm the fabrics were (thermal insulation) decided to wrap a number of small yogurt pots in the different fabrics and then fill them with warm water, making sure the water was the same temperature in each. They looked at the thickness of each fabric and tried to make sure that each pot was wrapped the same way. They also discussed if they should cover the top of the pot. With help from the teacher they then used a thermometer to read the initial temperature and the temperature after 30 minutes. They were able to produce a simple bar chart to show their results.

When all the groups had finished investigating, they discovered that some fabrics were better for one thing and some for another. After some discussion, the children decided to give each fabric a mark out of ten for each investigation – adding these numbers up gave them the 'best' fabric. Finally, Teddy sat in the corner of the classroom proudly wearing his new winter coat!

Managing practical science

In the classroom   Practical session – a circus of activities

In order to give her class opportunities to share experiences of a wide range of forces in action, a teacher of nine- and ten-year-olds set up a circus of activities. These included:

- using a Newton meter to drag objects across the floor
- dropping film canisters containing different weights into a sand tray
- lowering a stone, a wooden block and a polystyrene block into a tank of water
- exploring how shoes with different soles slide down a wooden ramp.

(Continued)

(Continued)

The children had ten minutes to explore each activity and were encouraged to record however they wanted. At the end of the time they moved on to the next activity.

Finally, the teacher gathered the children together to share their experiences, develop a common vocabulary and discuss how they might investigate certain aspects in more detail.

Planning is the key to effective work in science. Well-planned and well-supported practical activities give children opportunities to begin to reinterpret events in the light of new experience. If children are engaged in a practical way with a topic, they are highly likely to also be engaged intellectually. For example, if children are baking dough to explore the nature of chemical change, the experience of mixing individual ingredients and then waiting for their cooked loaf to cool so they can taste it offers so many more opportunities for learning than watching a television programme of a baker at work.

Practical activities do need to be carefully assessed for risk and very closely supervised.

Talk in science

The links between talk, thinking and learning – not just in science but also across the curriculum – are clear. In science, children need to be taught how to talk productively with one another if they are to gain all that they should from practical activity.

Effective talk for science learning involves enabling all children to share their ideas. They should respect and value the ideas of others, offer reasons for their contributions and understand that learning proceeds from negotiation. They have to know that 'changing your mind' when presented with good evidence is not just possible but essential – it is a way of learning. They must feel that they can question one another, make suggestions and disagree in ways that support their own thinking and that of their group. The effective science teacher establishes groups of children who know that their discussion with one another must focus on the topic in hand and must be completely inclusive of all group members.

You can teach all of these talk skills directly by making them evident in shared learning intentions, expecting children to use the language of equitable discussion in their work together and bringing out good practice in closing plenary discussions. In addition, you can offer your classes a sensible model for exploratory talk – that is, we can talk to children in ways that show them how we want them to talk to each other. For example, asking children authentic questions is key to helping them see how to phrase their own questions. Asking for reasons helps them to see how to do so themselves and note the benefits. Asking a child to say a little more – to elaborate or explain – values their ideas and shows the class that this is a useful talk skill if you want to find out things from other people.

Talk between children in science helps them to put new words to use in a sensible context or practise new uses of familiar words. Finally, children's talk can generate enthusiasm and motivation and help children build up their understanding of science concepts over time.

Reflective questions

- How will you promote an ongoing, interesting dialogue about science between yourself and the class and between children?
- What current issues in science are relevant to the children in your classroom and how can you make these ideas accessible?
- How can you help every child to see what scientists actually do, so that they can begin to consider themselves as potential scientists of the future?

Conclusion

Taking part in science-based activities offers a model of a special way of thinking. Evidence is carefully collected and evaluated, comparisons are made and discussion goes on as long as new questions arise – and there is never an end to questions. Collaborating in classroom science involves every child in reasoning – an invaluable opportunity to practise a key thinking skill. In addition, the world around us is important and interesting. Insights gained in childhood lead to lifelong enthusiasm for aspects of the natural world.

A three-stage approach – in which ideas are shared and discussed, tested and considered – promotes steady learning, with the chance to apply new ideas enabling consolidation. Talk with others in science is also important as it shows how, by understanding one another's ideas, we hear different points of view and negotiating with others, using evidence and reasoning, can enable children to develop a scientific view of the world.

Science is not a standalone subject but a way of thinking about some aspects of things. Its links with language, mathematics, art, music, geography, religious education – indeed any other subject – are clear and important. Children learning

science with their classmates are finding out how the world works and understanding that all knowledge is provisional, while at the same time gaining a way
of thinking that will stand them in good stead in any context.

Further reading

Brunton, P. and Thornton, L. (2009) *Science in the Early Years: Building firm foundations
from 0 to 5*. London: Sage.
This book looks at the effective support of scientific exploration and investigation
within the context of the Early Years classroom.

Dunne, M. and Peacock, A. (2011) *Primary Science: A guide to teaching practice*. London:
Sage.
Written for teacher training students, this book discusses in greater depth many of
the issues introduced in this chapter.

Farrow, S. (2006) *The Really Useful Science Book: A framework of knowledge for primary
teachers*. Abingdon: Routledge.
A clearly written and easily accessible discussion of the science knowledge and
understanding that primary school teachers and trainees require to deliver the primary science curriculum with confidence.

References

de Boo, M. (2006) 'Science in the early years', in W. Harlen (ed.), *ASE Guide to Primary
Science Education*. Hatfield: ASE.
DfE (2013) 'The National Curriculum in England: Framework document'. Runcorn: DfE.
Available online at: www.gov.uk/government/uploads/system/uploads/attachment_data/
file/210969/NC_framework_document_-_FINAL.pdf
Loxley, P., Dawes, L., Nicholls, L. and Dore, B. (2010) *Teaching Primary Science: Promoting
enjoyment and developing understanding*. Harlow: Pearson.
Naylor, S. and Keogh, B. (2000) *Concept Cartoons in Science Education*. Sandbach: Millgate
Publishing.
SPACE Project (1999) For information about the project and its findings, visit: www.nuffield-
foundation.org/primary-science-and-space

INDEX